Delivering Impact with Digital Resources

Planning strategy in the attention economy

Delivering Impact with Digital Resources

Planning strategy in the attention economy

Simon Tanner

facet publishing

Published by Facet Publishing
7 Ridgmount Street, London WC1E 7AE
www.facetpublishing.co.uk

Facet Publishing is wholly owned by CILIP: the Library and Information Association.

British Library Cataloguing in Publication Data
A catalogue record for this book is available from the British Library.

ISBN 978-1-85604-932-0 (paperback)
ISBN 978-1-78330-251-2 (hardback)
ISBN 978-1-78330-252-9 (e-book)

First published 2020

Text printed on FSC accredited material.

FSC www.fsc.org MIX Paper from responsible sources FSC® C013604

Typeset from author's files in 10/14 Palatino and Myriad Pro by Flagholme Publishing Services
Printed and made in Great Britain by CPI Group (UK) Ltd, Croydon, CR0 4YY.

Contents

List of figures and tables

Figures

Tables

List of case studies

About the author

Simon Tanner is Professor of Digital Cultural Heritage in the Department of Digital Humanities at King's College London. He is a digital humanities scholar with a wide-ranging interest in cross-disciplinary thinking and collaborative approaches that reflect a fascination with interactions between memory institution collections (libraries, museum, archives, media and publishing) and the digital domain.

As an information professional, consultant, digitisation expert and academic he works with major cultural institutions across the world to assist them in transforming their impact, collections and online presence. He has consulted for or managed over 500 digital projects, including digitisation of the Dead Sea Scrolls (Tanner and Bearman, 2009), and has built strategy with a wide range of organisations. These include many national libraries, museums and government agencies in Europe, Africa, America and the Middle East. Tanner has had work commissioned by UNESCO, the Arcadia Fund and the Andrew W. Mellon Foundation. He founded the capacity-building Digital Futures Academy that has run in the UK, Australia, South Africa and Ghana with participants from over 40 countries.

Research into image use and sales in American art museums by Simon Tanner has had a significant effect on opening up collections access and OpenGLAM in the museum sector (Tanner, 2004, 2016b). Tanner is a strong advocate for open access, open research and the digital humanities. He was chair of the Web Archiving sub-committee as an independent member of the UK government-appointed Legal Deposit Advisory Panel. He is a member of the Europeana Impact Taskforce that developed the *Impact Playbook* based on his Balanced Value Impact Model. He was part of the Arts and Humanities

Research Council funded Academic Book of the Future research team.

Tanner teaches on the Masters in Digital Asset and Media Management and the BA in Digital Culture at King's College London. He is also Pro Vice Dean for Research Impact and Innovation in the Faculty of Arts and Humanities. He tweets as @SimonTanner and blogs at http://simon-tanner.blogspot.co.uk/. He owns and runs the BVI Model website at www.BVIModel.org.

Acknowledgements

One of the joyful benefits of working within a digital humanities praxis is the acceptance of co-research and collaboration as a regular part of the process. Working together with practitioners has enhanced the Balanced Value Impact (BVI) Model, and at times challenged it. The process of moving from theoretical ideas to implementation is necessarily messy, iterative and recursive. I wish to applaud and give thanks to everyone who came along for this carnival ride.

In the building of the BVI Model 2.0 the earliest champions for it were Harry Verwayen, Jill Cousins and Julia Fallon at Europeana. I have benefited hugely from Harry's breadth of vision and unwavering support. Julia's work to deliver the *Impact Playbook* and our working together, with the rest of the Impact Taskforce, is a constant inspiration. I am delighted to see the *Impact Playbook* flourish and expand into the community as the practical toolset for everyday impact assessment. Thank you to all the members of the Europeana Impact Taskforce and Network Association who have helped me develop my ideas over the years.

Paul Conway has been my peer reviewer. His guidance, experience and wisdom have been utterly invaluable to the completion of this book. My work was also significantly improved by the sage advice, discussion and reading of drafts provided by Karen Colbron, Julia Fallon, Shalen Fu and Andrew Prescott. A particular word of thanks for Helen Carley, who, as Publishing Director for Facet Publishing, commissioned this book: thank you for your patience and knowledge throughout the writing. Merete Sanderhoff and the whole team at the Statens Museum for Kunst in Copenhagen, Denmark, have been generous in allowing me access to compile a case study for this book.

I would like to thank colleagues in the Department of Digital Humanities and at King's College London. My great friends and colleagues, past and present, have profoundly influenced my thinking over the years and made the everyday work of being an academic fun and enjoyable. Thank you all.

Thanks are also due to: Marco deNiet, Laura Gibson, Christy Henshaw, Stephan Hügel, Mandy Kritzeck, Doug McCarthy, Luke McKernan, Alan Newman, Nils Pokel, Melissa Terras, Kim Thompson, Andrea Wallace, Peter Whitehouse and Jeroen Wilms.

My family have been a constant distraction during the writing of this book; always giving me other things to do that are far more important and fun than writing. I am grateful to my siblings Brenda, Linda and Paul for grounding my life in the real world. Alex, Joseph and Toby – you are the best, funniest and cleverest distractions known to humankind; I am so proud of each of you.

This book is dedicated to Clare Page. Clare has been with me throughout the writing of this book as a sounding board, grammar guru, light in the darkness and reason to keep going.

Thank you all. This book is tailored from whole cloth because you are each in the warp and weft of every word and page. Any moth holes found in the fabric are of my own making.

Illustrations acknowledgement

The front cover illustration and Figure 6.2 are illustrations by Alice Maggs of my research ideas, and are reproduced here under licence from Alice Maggs. For more information on this talented artist, see http://alicemaggs.co.uk/.

List of abbreviations

AHRC	Arts and Humanities Research Council
API	application programming interface
BBC	British Broadcasting Corporation
BL	British Library
BVI	Balanced Value Impact
DPSIR	drivers, pressures, state, impact and responses
EC	European Commission
EIA	environmental impact assessment
GDP	Gross Domestic Product
GLAM	galleries, libraries, archives and museums
IA	impact assessment
IIIF	International Image Interoperability Framework
JISC	Joint Information Systems Committee
KPI	key performance indicator
MOOC	Massive Open Online Course
OpenGLAM	Open Galleries, Libraries, Archives and Museums
ROI	return on investment
SIA	social impact assessment
SMART	specific, measurable, achievable, realistic, timely
SMK	Statens Museum for Kunst (National Gallery of Denmark)
SROI	social return on investment
SWOT	strengths, weaknesses, opportunities, threats

Introduction

Life writes its own stories

Impact, values, wisdom and wit are all found in newspaper straplines. The strap 'If You Don't Want It Printed, Don't Let It Happen' in the *Aspen Daily Times* speaks simultaneously to avoiding unwarranted attention and maybe also to cheekily planning ways to garner attention. The *Toronto Star*'s 'It's Where You Live' strapline speaks to a sense of close community engagement, much as does the 'As Waikato as It Gets' of New Zealand's *Waikato Times*. The news is about change, about how things are different, for good or ill, than they were before.

Many newspapers claim a mix of social, economic and intrinsic values:

- 'Life Writes Its Own Stories', or 'As Life Writes' ('Wie das Leben so schreibt') in the *Kleine Zeitung*, Graz, Austria;
- 'All the News That's Fit to Print' in the *New York Times*;
- 'The daily diary of the American dream' in the *Wall Street Journal*;
- *The Sowetan*, South Africa's daily newspaper, with slogans such as 'Power your Future' or 'Sowetan. Building the Nation';
- 'Right is of no sex, truth is of no color. God is the father of us all and all we are brethren', the *North Star Newspaper* strapline reflecting the values of founder Frederick Douglass, who escaped slavery in 1838.

Others speak to measures of size, scale or importance. Britain is pretty boastful:

- the 'Biggest daily sale on Earth', in the *Daily Mail*;

- 'When The Times speaks, the World listens', in *The Times;*
- 'Daily Telegraph. Britain's Best Selling Daily Broadsheet'.

Some newspapers speak to education or knowledge. Such as:

- 'There's nothing more valuable than knowledge', in the *Cape Times;*
- 'Your right to know. A new voice for a new Pakistan', in the *Daily Times* newspaper, Lahore, Pakistan;
- '*The Guardian*. Think ...'.

All these newspapers want our attention; they are all seeking to make an impact on our day and to affect our thinking and behaviour.

Newspapers have fascinated me ever since the first permanent professional role I started in 1989. Daily I had to scour all the broadsheets and produce a current-awareness bulletin from clippings for my company by 9 o'clock every morning. Newspapers are not just for the here and now, though; as the saying goes, newspapers may be considered a first rough draft of history (Shafer, 2010). Memory institutions have thus collected newspapers as slices of *zeitgeist* over the centuries, preserving them for future generations. I have been fortunate to be intimately involved with four significant newspaper digitisation projects: the initial 2 million-page British Library (BL) newspaper project (Quint, 2002); the Digidaily newspaper project at the Swedish National Archives (Ahlberg and Rosen, 2019); the Nineteenth Century Serial Edition AHRC project (https://ncse.ac.uk); and the Welsh Newspapers Online from the National Library of Wales (https://newspapers.library.wales). These are all popular and impactful digitisation projects. They each reach out to refresh the audience for these materials, delivering community and social benefits. These online newspapers are used in schools and by local and family historians. For academics, they 'fill a gap for content that is not found elsewhere' (Gooding, 2017). In the Theatre of Memory consultancy for the National Library of Wales, I identified a huge number and range of special-interest communities that are served by these kinds of collections – drama, music, poetry, sport, religion, science, engineering, food, diaspora and language perspectives to name but a few. There are opportunities to solidify a sense of place and time, a personalised narrative and history, to see it reflected in the national and local stories contained in newspapers.

The Library of Congress Historic American Newspapers site shows 155,290 titles available and 14.8 million pages of searchable newspaper digitised

(Library of Congress, n.d.). The British Newspaper Archive is showing almost 31 million pages as I write (www.britishnewspaperarchive.co.uk). Trove in Australia provides access to over 20 million pages from over 1,000 Australian newspapers (National Library of Australia, n.d.). Yet these digitised collections are only a fragment of the newspaper resources that are available to be digitised. The European Newspaper Survey Report states:

> Over half of the libraries have a cutoff date beyond which they will not publish digitised newspapers on the web. Most frequently, this is based on a 70 year sliding scale … Only 12 (26%) of the libraries had digitised more than 10% of their collection (either in terms of titles or page numbers), and only two of those had done more than 50% – the consortium of libraries represented by the Biblioteca Virtual de Prensa Histórica (58% of their pages were digitised) and the National Library of Turkey, unique for having digitised its entire collection of 800,000 pages and 845 titles.
>
> (Dunning, 2012)

These statistics reflect the challenges of building a digitised corpus where there is so much printed material and so few resources for digitisation. In the BL alone there are approximately 450 million pages of printed material, with roughly 18.9 million pages digitised (McKernan, 2017). Newspapers are multi-faceted content with the potential to deliver an impactful experience to audiences worldwide. This simultaneously large volume of page images and relatively small ratio of collection digitisation should make us reflect on the attention focused online and the potential knowledge gap inevitably created. It ignites the desire to understand better the potential impact of digitisation projects and the effects they may have on our audiences and communities. Nineteenth-century media expert Jim Mussell thinks of 'the aura of old newspapers in hard copy and what happens when this is remediated digitally… Digitisation returns newspapers to us, but differently' (Mussell, 2013).

There thus remain questions of what to select, how to decide if this content is worthy of attention and, when content is made available, whether it has succeeded in satisfying information needs and made a difference to the community of users.

The premise of this book

The digital presence of memory institutions has the power to change lives and life opportunities. It is essential to understand the different modes of digital values to consider how organisational presence within digital cultures can create change. Impact assessment is the tool to foster understanding of how strategic decisions about digital resources may be changing behaviour within our communities. This book will introduce and define digital values within an attention economy, with a clear argument that revealing and understanding these values and their strategic perspectives is a crucial means to develop digital content successfully.

The GLAM (galleries, libraries, archives and museums) sector strategises to gain the attention of those senior decision makers who act as gatekeepers to the limited funds that exist to support the cultural, educative, creative and heritage sectors as a whole. Digital resources are often built within a mostly unfunded mandate (Tanner, 2006). This unfunded mandate includes such desirable features as:

- providing enhanced access to collections and their information content;
- long-term retention of sustainable digital resources; and
- increased engagement with the public record and memory institutions by their communities.

Whatever the type of memory institution, and wherever funding comes from, there is an imperative to demonstrate that digital content is delivered by ever-increasingly efficient means and within a reduced budget.

Those delivering digital resources thus find themselves in a difficult economic position. As intermediaries to collections and enablers of content use from both non-chargeable and bought content, they experience both the upside and the downside of the internet. The upside is the ability to deliver a much wider aggregation of reliable information at a generally smaller unit price than before. The downside is that, whatever the source and the price of the units being delivered, the infrastructure costs continue to rise and the spectre of a rising total cost of ownership and digital preservation costs is clearly apparent. It has been correctly argued that maintaining digital access and addressing preservation is not necessarily a costly enterprise as compared with the analogue world (Rusbridge, 2006). However, digital costs are not replacing analogue costs but offering additional requirements often not fully financed. This forms a growing unfunded mandate that will provide the biggest single threat to future digital economic sustainability. Many years ago, a few staff from the National Library of New Zealand had T-shirts privately made which commented on the new legislative mandate to maintain in perpetuity all digital content deposited with the Library, when the Library itself lived on a three-year funding cycle. The T-shirts stated simply, 'Perpetuity is a Very Long Time'.

Politicians demand evidence of the impact of our sectors. Even though most governmental decision making remains wedded to such measures, alongside those of economy come pressures to demonstrate the social value and worth of memory institutions and their digital activities. The value of institutions like museums is associated with a broader set of values than merely fiscal ones. As Plaza puts it:

> It is obvious that the non-market value of museums (meaning, for instance, their artistic, cultural, educational, architectural and prestige value to society) cannot be calculated by means of financial transactions.
> (Plaza, 2010)

Even when analysts focus on high-performing, exceptional museums set apart from their contemporaries, they visualise a wide set of values. For instance, Frey characterises these 'Superstar Museums' by five aspects:

- a 'must for tourists'
- large numbers of visitors
- world-famous painters and famous paintings
- architecture
- commercialization (Frey, 2003).

This reductive positioning of value as being about large numbers of users, commercialisation in the form of shops and cafés and the fame of the collection seems designed to focus on easily visible comparators. A focus on elite comparison factors also exposes the temptation to focus on ephemeral goals. Museums (or the rest of GLAM) are not so easily categorised and are so 'extraordinarily varied in their origins ... that meaningful comparisons between one and another are rarely possible' (Weil, 2002). The goal of superficial comparison is to show that institutions have expended energies and resources to the benefit of designated communities, and that such investments have beneficial returns to those people.

> Measuring and articulating the value and impact of the sector is more than an academic exercise: given the policy, financial and business structures in which most cultural organisations operate in England, rightly selecting, rigorously measuring and powerfully articulating the value and impact of the sector is one of the key pre-requisites for its sustainability.
>
> (Stanziola, 2008)

An example from the digital domain is the way that the GLAM sector, in particular, has created, purchased or otherwise obtained a mass of digital resources and delivered these online to a range of users worldwide. In the UK alone, over £100 million can be identified as spent on digitisation in museums, libraries, archives and universities between 1997 and 2010 (Tanner and Deegan 2010). The usage statistics of that time inform us that uptake was considerable, and research discovered and identified a considerable range of benefits and value in digital resources and collections (Tanner, 2011). However, many of these resources have subsequently died in 'the "fast fires" of digital obsolescence' as predicted by Anne Kenney (Kenney, 1997). In the UK, research at University College London into the £50 million New Opportunities Fund digitisation programme showed that ~43% (63) of the 147 original web projects reviewed had died, disappeared or gone dark from public access. Another ~27% (40) were only just 'usable and not being maintained or value added' (Hügel, 2012; Mao, 2016).

Thus, there remain questions that we may well not yet accurately know the answers to.

- How do their stakeholders receive and respond to these resources?
- Who exactly are the recipients of the resources?
- What do they do with them?
- Moreover, what impact have they had on their lives?

Moving beyond traditional measures is desirable to address the challenges now facing the creative, cultural and academic sectors. Primary measures of digital have focused on web statistics, anecdotal information or evaluations of outputs (how much digitised) rather than outcomes (value gained). In short, introducing impact assessment responds to the demand for a strategic mechanism demonstrating that digital resources and service ecosystems are delivering a beneficial change to communities, expressed in economic and social terms.

This book seeks to provide both a mechanism and a way of thinking about strategies and evidence of benefits that extend to impact, such that the existence of a digital resource shows measurable outcomes that demonstrate a change in the life or life opportunities of the community. The book proposes an updated Balanced Value Impact Model (BVI Model) to enable each memory organisation to argue convincingly that they are an efficient and effective operation, working in innovative modes with digital resources for the positive social and economic benefit of their communities. The BVI Model is intended to support memory institutions to become more innovative, learning organisations.

The audiences for this book

This book is for practitioners, decision makers and scholars working with digital content and culture in relation to memory institutions. Impact is a worldwide phenomenon. This book will seek to be inclusive of examples and practices from everywhere.

In using the phrase 'memory institution', this book assumes a common aspiration across multiple sectors in preserving, organising and making available the cultural and intellectual records of their societies. This book uses the phrase as a convenience to refer collectively to archives, museums, libraries and cultural heritage but does not assume primacy in their role as 'memory institutions'. As Robinson states, 'a wider variety of organisations, such as schools, universities, media corporations, government or religious bodies could also legitimately be ascribed this title' (Robinson, 2012), and they are referenced and included within this book's conception of memory institution.

The expected reader may well work in, with or around memory institutions and be looking to make the most significant impact with their digital resources and content. They may also be a decision maker, holder of funding, policy maker, development agency or government body that wishes to promote evidence-based impact assessment of activities and programmes that they support or encourage. In response, managers, project managers and fundraisers who are seeking to justify further investment in digital resources should become aware of the importance of the impact agenda and its value to their objectives. There are also practitioners of evaluation and impact assessment looking for a framework to assist in assessing the impact of a digital resource. The BVI Model satisfies these needs and provides a staged approach to ease the management of the process.

Academics looking to establish digital projects and digital scholarship collaborations with collection owners will find this book useful to help define common goals and benefits. Academics in countries where impact measurement is a part of academic evaluation (such as the UK's Research Excellence Framework) will also find the principles described in this book applicable to their research environments. Students and other scholars engaged with librarianship, museum studies, information science, archival studies, digital humanities, digital cultures, internet studies, anthropology, social studies, cultural and media studies and cultural economics will find this book useful and informative to their scholarship.

The guidance offered in this book will be especially useful for managing digital presences as diverse as those in memory institutions; creative and cultural industries (e.g. publishing, media and e-commerce); and web-based activities (e.g. social media, crowdsourcing or user-generated content). Publishing, media and business sectors that may be looking for the best means to measure the impact of their digital offerings or are looking to collaborate and align with collection owners, with academia or with memory institutions will find useful content here as well, particularly in relation to strategy and the attention economy.

This book seeks to have resonance with many sectors, including libraries, archives, museums, media, publishing, cultural and creative industries, higher education, digital asset management, project management, marketing, impact assessment and evaluation consultancies. This inclusive scope reflects the author's wide-ranging fascination in cross-disciplinary and inter-disciplinary thinking and collaborative approaches to interactions between memory organisation collections and the digital domain.

Structure of the book

Chapter 1: the context of measuring impact to deliver strategic value

This chapter articulates the demand for impact assessment, its history and context. The term 'impact' is defined and mapped to the roots of impact assessment in other fields of investigation. There follows an exploration of the early impact evaluations and methods focused on memory institutions or digital content. The intellectual and administrative journey to deliver the BVI Model 2.0 is sketched out.

Chapter 2: The Balanced Value Impact Model

The BVI Model is applied in five core functional stages:

Stage 1: Set the context
Stage 2: Design the framework
Stage 3: Implement the framework
Stage 4: Narrate the outcomes and results
Stage 5: Review and respond.

The chapter describes the core underlying assumptions that drive the adoption of the BVI Model as a model with a nested BVI Framework within for measuring impact. These enable the reader to: make the most effective use of the model; allow for partial or adapted implementation of the Framework; or allow for the concepts embedded to be used independently of the Framework.

The prerequisites for applying the BVI Model are explained.

Chapter 3: Impact in libraries, archives, museums and other memory institutions

This chapter expands on the definition of impact through specific exemplars and case studies of impact assessment in memory institutions such as libraries, museums and archives. The Wellcome Library, first implementers of the BVI Model for their digitisation programme, is an extended case study.

Chapter 4: Finding value and impact in an attention economy

This chapter focuses on how the attention economy influences digital culture. In a response to understanding the influences and motivators in an attention economy, the chapter then considers how the selection and creation of digital content lead towards impactful resources.

Chapter 5: Strategic Perspectives and Value Lenses

Strategic Perspectives and Value Lenses are foundation stones underpinning the BVI Model. The chapter addresses the theoretical background and analytical reasoning for adopting these concepts in an impact assessment. The core of this chapter explains the way strategy interacts with values. It ends with a focal case study from the Statens Museum for Kunst (SMK, National Gallery of Denmark) to illuminate these strategic issues.

Chapter 6: Planning to plan with the BVI Model

Set the context, stage 1 of the BVI Model, is shown in detail. The importance of context, ground truths and baselines to the success of impact measurement is emphasised. Methods of investigating the digital ecosystem, stakeholders and situation analysis using SWOT (strengths, weaknesses, opportunities, threats) are described. Guidance on pairing Strategic Perspectives with Value Lenses is provided. Further advice on how to use stage 1 for strategic goals not associated with impact assessment is also provided.

Chapter 7: Implementing the BVI Framework

Design the BVI Framework (stage 2) is the focus of this chapter. The reader will learn how to set objectives, decided on good indicators of impact and about assigning them to stakeholder groups. The guidance on completing the BVI Framework includes a critical analysis of useful data-gathering techniques and tools.

Stage 3 is introduced and the practicalities of this stage are detailed.

Chapter 8: Europeana case study implementing the BVI Model

This chapter presents a user's perspective on implementing the BVI Model through a case study provided by Julia Fallon of the Europeana Foundation.

The issues focused on in this case study are:

- a reflection on Europeana's implementation of impact assessment, with a focus on one complete cycle;
- the ideas driving how Europeana developed the *Impact Playbook*;
- how these integrate with the BVI Model.

Chapter 9: Using the outcomes of the BVI Model

This chapter explains stage 4 of the BVI Model and how to narrate the outcomes and results of implementing the Model. The chapter focuses on the means of transferring the outputs of data gathering into outcomes that are meaningful demonstrators of impact, to be used effectively by decision makers. Outputs are evaluated and outcomes prioritised. Communicating the results involves storytelling, visualisation, marketing and public relations methods. The next section considers engagement with communities. The National Library of Australia's Trove is critiqued as a case study. The chapter ends with advice on engaging with decision and policy makers.

4.10 Chapter 10: Impact as a call to action

A case having been made for the digital resource through the presentation and communication of the outcomes and results of the impact assessment, review and respond (stage 5) is the moment to follow through and ensure that the purpose of the impact assessment reaps its fullest benefits. It is important to reflect continually on what will be measured, why this is worthwhile measuring and the purposes that measurement serves.

The book ends with a conclusion that brings the threads together and provides a definite call to action. Embedding impact into evidence-based management thinking and culture, avoiding comfortable metrics and celebrating success are all linked to this author's belief that memory institutions can play a pivotal role in the digital future of society.

How to use this book

This book is both a scholarly analysis of the subject of impact assessment and an attempt to fuse deep theory, experience and practice in the presentation of the BVI Model.

For scholars and practitioners, the author desires to ensure that the theoretical background and more profound understanding are accessible through the examples used and sources cited in the earlier chapters (1–4). Context drives the application of impact assessment, so the earlier chapters introduce the subject area, allowing practice to be informed by an understanding of how impact relates to strategy and how impact sits within organisational contexts. There is a greater vastness below the surface of this book's analysis and synthesis of ideas, concepts and theories than can be easily encompassed in a book of this nature.

If the reader is primarily interested in the practical application of the BVI Model, then chapters 5–10 provide a guide to the five stages. Wherever possible, examples, case studies, tools and checklists are provided or linked so as to guide the reader to achievable goals. Chapter 8 discusses the Europeana implementation of the BVI Model and its product to support this, called the *Impact Playbook*. The *Playbook* is highly recommended as a starting point for those wanting to jump into the deep end (Verwayen et al., 2017).

Chapters 5 and 10 provide a good executive summary introducing the broader change management, strategy and policy issues raised by the book for those in senior management or other decision- and policy-making roles.

Links to additional resources

An online resource at www.BVIModel.org supports this book. At this web page may be found:

- BVI Model resources, including:
  - Framework templates
  - an electronic version of this book's bibliography
  - all BVI Model graphics and diagrams;
- a detailed glossary of impact terms and impact data-gathering methods that could be used with the BVI Model;
- the BVI Model wiki community, including key contacts in the world of BVI Model impact assessment plus community-provided papers, case studies and exemplars of BVI Model implementations.

Key definitions and concepts

This book uses a wide range of terms that may be unusual to the reader or which, paradoxically because they are so widely used, may be misleading in their definitions. For clarity, these terms are defined here so that the reader may understand their meaning within the context of this book and the BVI Model.

These definitions and terms are unambiguous, tightly defined and consistently used in this book. However, practice shows that adopting local vocabulary can be essential for the successful implementation of a new idea. A term like 'stakeholders', for instance, is used in this book because it has an exact meaning that is not adequately covered by 'visitor', 'patron', 'user' or 'community'. However, it may be better to accept some looser definitions and less precise terminology if this will prevent people from becoming alienated from the process. Certainly, narrating impact benefits to the public must avoid using these academic terms.

Impact assessment

The International Association for Impact Assessment defines impact assessment as:

> the process of identifying the future consequences of a current or proposed action. Impact assessment is a generic term that can mean either an integrated approach or the composite/totality of all forms of impact assessment such as environmental impact assessment (EIA), social impact assessment (SIA), health impact assessment (HIA), etc.
>
> (International Association for Impact Assessment, 2009)

Impact is a broadly used term with multiple different contexts. These are described in Chapter 1.

Impact as defined in the BVI Model

The BVI Model defines impact as the measurable outcomes arising from the existence of a digital resource that demonstrate a change in the life or life opportunities of the community.

The BVI Model

The BVI Model is a cohesive model that will provide a definition and model of impact for any memory institution, with a pragmatic implementable framework for delivery (BVI Framework). It is specially designed for digital resources and memory institutions. The BVI Model is a measurement model focused on identifying a change in a community arising from the existence of digital resources that are of proven value to the community.

The conceptual model underlying the BVI Model follows a process that stresses the importance of distinguishing between inputs, actions, the output and the outcomes. The BVI Model encourages a continuous assessment to look beyond the immediately measurable 'output' towards the demonstrable outcome, which leads to defining the real impact on people.

The BVI Model is a five-stage iterative process:

Stage 1: Set the context
Stage 2: Design the framework
Stage 3: Implement the framework
Stage 4: Narrate the outcomes and results
Stage 5: Review and respond.

See Chapter 2 for an introduction and Chapters 5–10 for full implementation.

BVI Framework

Use of the BVI Model produces an impact framework as an immediate output, known as the BVI Framework. This Framework structures and guides the process to manage the gathering of impact evidence and control a process that usually has many moving parts occurring over differing timescales, with possibly different teams, resources or points of focus. The Framework itself will mainly be of use to those co-ordinating the activity to track activity and measures against impact indicators and objectives.

The advantage of a framework nested within an overarching model is that it allows flexibility for those tasked with its practical implementation. As long as the conceptual model is recognised, then actual delivery of any one aspect is not prescribed or required. Anyone using the BVI Model should feel free to rename or revise the functional parts in the Framework to suit local needs or to aid cognition or acceptance in their organisation or community.

The model-to-framework approach also accounts for the range of fuzzy elements within an assessment of impact. A high-level conceptual model allows for the thinking, context and perception to be represented, while the Framework allows the products of this thinking to be controlled, contained and then utilised.

See Chapter 2 for an introduction and Chapters 6–7 for full implementation.

Memory institutions and GLAM

The use of 'memory institutions' as a collective phrase for libraries, museums and archives dates back at least to 1994, with the first usage attributed to Swedish information scientist Roland Hjerppe (Hjørland, 2000). In using the phrase 'memory institution', this book assumes a common aspiration across multiple sectors in preserving, organising and making available the cultural and intellectual records of their societies. It also reflects the confluence with the growth in digital. Its usage thus also assumes, as Dempsey avers, to be 'driven by the desire to release the value of their collections into this [digital] space in ways that support creative use by as many users as possible. They recognise their users' desire to refer to intellectual and cultural materials flexibly and transparently, without concern for institutional or national boundaries' (Dempsey, 2000).

This book uses the phrase as a convenience to refer collectively to archives, museums and libraries but does not assume primacy in their role as 'memory institutions'. As Robinson states, 'a wider variety of organisations, such as schools, universities, media corporations, government or religious bodies could also legitimately be ascribed this title' (Robinson, 2012). This book's conception of memory institutions references and includes this wider definition. For instance, these organisations could be included: the BBC (British Broadcasting Corporation); US Public Broadcasting, as epitomised by companies like WGBH in Boston; a university press; or the Wayback Machine and the Internet Archive.

GLAM is an acronym referring to galleries, libraries, archives and museums. Memory institutions are the broad umbrella term within which GLAM exists. When this book uses GLAM, it is specific to that sector.

Digital resources

A digital resource is a resource delivered digitally, with a defined scope and coverage made up of a describable, cohesive set of primary and secondary materials, services, products and activities.

Digital ecosystem

A digital ecosystem is the set of interdependent relationships among the resources, technologies, organisation hosting, creators and consumers, mapped and described to enunciate the ecosystem of a digital resource clearly. Without understanding the digital ecosystem, it is hard to contemplate the full capabilities of the digital resource and its relationship to stakeholders (see Chapter 6).

The attention economy

In an information-rich world, the wealth of information means a dearth of something else – the attention of its recipients to attend to and engage with the information. What we take notice of, and the regarding of something or someone as interesting or important, delineates what we consider worthy of attending to, and thus defines our economics of attention (see Chapter 4).

Strategy

Strategy has many definitions but usually relates to providing purpose, direction and meaning to managerial activities, especially when there is conflict involved – usually illustrated through scarce resources, competition or power structures. At its most reductive, a strategy is about 'maintaining a balance between ends, ways and means; about identifying objectives; and about the resources and methods available for meeting such objectives' (Freedman, 2013).

Strategic Perspectives

In the BVI Model, Strategic Perspectives provide for a holistic application of four perspectives to contextualise organisational strategy. The Perspectives are:

- Economic
- Social
- Innovation
- Operational.

See Chapters 2 and 5 onwards for more information on the formulation and use of the Strategic Perspectives.

Value Lenses

In the BVI Model, there are five Value Lenses that focus attention on specific assessment activities reflecting core values measured for their impact. The five Value Lenses are:

- Utility
- Education
- Community
- Existence/Prestige, and
- Inheritance/Legacy.

See Chapters 2 and 5 onwards for more information on the formulation and use of the Value Lenses.

Stakeholders

Stakeholders are defined as a person, group, community or organisation that affects or can be affected by the ecosystem of the digital resource assessed. See Chapters 5 and 6.

Innovation

The concept of innovation indicates doing something new or different (from the Latin *innovare*, 'to change'). Historically, the term 'innovation' tends to refer to business processes and is tightly linked to improvements in efficiency, productivity, creativity, quality and value in products, processes or methods of research and development.

This book defines innovation as a process through which value (intellectual, cultural, social or economic) is extracted from knowledge via the generation, development and implementation of ideas. The intended result of innovation is to produce new or improved ways of thinking, capabilities, services/products, strategies or processes.

Evidence-based decision making

Evidence-based approaches set out to optimise the organisation's decision-making processes. Leaders improve performance by applying the best evidence to support decision making. They set aside conventional wisdom in favour of a relentless commitment to gather the most useful and actionable facts and data to make more informed decisions. The use of evidence-based decision making as a phrase was popularised by Pfeffer and Sutton (Pfeffer and Sutton, 2006, 2008).

Measuring impact fits into this evidence-based management approach by being a frequent source of actionable evidence and a continuous challenge to revisit and review the strategic status quo. If the organisation is not willing to adopt an overall evidence-based approach, then it will probably struggle with impact measurement.

Digitisation vs digitalisation

This book refers to 'digitisation' and rarely to its counterpart 'digitalisation'. While closely associated, they are distinct terms that should not be used interchangeably. This definition most clearly describes the distinctions:

> We define digitization as the material process of converting individual analogue streams of information into digital bits. In contrast, we refer to digitalization as the way in which many domains of social life are restructured around digital communication and media infrastructures.
>
> (Brennan and Kreiss, 2014)

Sustainability

Sustainability is a product, service or process that can be maintained and developed over an extended period, especially after external grant monies disappear, and that is beneficial to stakeholders and the host institution.

Digital culture

Digital culture reflects on the way humans change the digital domain and in return are changed by it. It relates to the social, economic, political, legal and contextual relationships that occur in the realm of new media like the internet, video games, social media and high-tech tools and where cultures act as distinct ways of digital 'world making'.

Chapter 1

The context of measuring impact to deliver strategic value

The demand for evidence-based strategies in the digital domain

The cultural society we live in has speedily traversed from, historically, primarily live experiences to engaging with recorded ones, and now back to a hybrid of live, social experiences and the digitally recorded. For instance, performance dominated our experience of music before the 1900s; even if one had the sheet music, performance of it defined the common experience. Since then, as the composer Stravinsky noted, recorded music has changed our experience, such that most music is now proportionally experienced in the recorded format:

> When I think that a disc or magnetic tape of a piece of music can be several thousand times as powerful (influential) as a live performance, that disc or tape becomes an awesome object indeed.
>
> (Stravinsky and Craft, 1959)

With the growth of digital media, digitalisation and the transition from the 1990s web initiation, through Web 2.0 and linked data, to our current social media and big data-driven digital culture, almost all interactions with digital content are now mediated such that it is again more of a live experience, with the option to comment, tag or share ever present. For instance, in the UK the average number of connected devices per person is now greater than 3.5 (*Consumer Barometer – Trending Data*, 2017), while 62% go online via another device (e.g. computer, smartphone, tablet) while watching TV (*Consumer Barometer – Second Screens*, 2017). For comparison, these statistics for the USA are 4.1 and 50%, respectively. This 'second screen' use may be enhancing the experience as is often seen in reality TV shows, or it may be distracting, placing the TV as mere background noise.

It is relatively easy to count the people coming to a live performance venue or to observe and even survey people entering a building like a library or a museum. In a digital environment the number of visitors may often be comparatively bigger, but they remain more diffuse and harder to understand. It is not just about knowing the number of people who accessed a resource; it is about understanding the value and worth they place on that visit, which is ever more difficult without additional evidence. In a world where people have multiple devices, and many a second screen, it is harder to assume that a digital click or a visit equals attention or a sense of value.

Ever-present economic pressures lead to a culture of evaluating value, nested in the relationship between the amount paid and the goods or services received. Managers continuously consider how to deliver better services to their community, including extending digital resources, in circumstances of constant or, more often, dwindling finances. This evaluation debate predates the digital revolution, with the literature of the 1950s replete with attempts to cost information services, which evolved into cost-benefit analysis and performance measurement techniques and the 'fee or free' debate of the 1980s (Badenoch et al., 1994). As digital has grown, the point of emphasis shifts from the cost of something to its worth to the consumer. In the digital domain cost of production is so obscure to the consumer that they discount cost in favour of apparent worth (Poundstone, 2011). The result is the temptation or tendency to measure value in terms of 'what is it worth?' as reflected by what is gained or the value derived from the item consumed or purchased. Thus, while a glass of tap water may have a meagre fiscal value, it may have a high worth to the drinker. In the same way, it is inadequate to measure the economic value of a memory-institution visit in terms of the net value of the single trip, the art viewed or the book borrowed. The same need for more evidence also holds for evaluating digital resources.

Socio-cultural benefits and value can be both shifting and persistent over time. When shifting, they exhibit the features of fashion or designed obsolescence (e.g. new smartphone models), where the apparent value shifts regularly, and as dramatically often as those who profit from such changes can get away with. In the case of a maturely emerged and persistently conceived value, then change is slow. It may emerge over long periods, but with matching persistence over extended timeframes (e.g. belief in the value of democracy). Thus, time is a factor in the evaluation. With the growth of digital culture comes a concomitant reduction in the time to respond to shifting socio-cultural changes. Memory institutions, built to last for generations, are finding their collections and services judged not necessarily by persistence but by comparison with social-media digital products reflecting a very different ephemeral context and value.

Another driver towards evidence-based management is the desire to reduce uncertainty and mitigate risk. If the digital domain feels like it is continuously shifting, then the primary benefits of having evidence to guide decision making are that such information reduces uncertainty. Uncertainty increases risks, so having more knowledge about the possible outcomes of a specific course of action allows for planned risk reduction. Thus, if outcomes are predicted, then the investment is more secure; a costed benefit can be attached to the specific objectives and plans. Almost every funding organisation works on the model of expecting a clear statement of the outcomes promised, the anticipated benefits of achieving them and an assessment of the likelihood of the applicant's achieving the stated outcomes within the resources requested. The more information and evidence the applicant can present, the more likely the funds will be released, should the outcomes be deemed worthwhile.

As will be shown in the remainder of this chapter, accountability and the impact agenda are closely linked. Politicians, funding bodies, governmental agencies and non-governmental organisations (for instance, research councils or the National Endowment for the Humanities) are all advocating greater accountability of those organisations that they fund, or are under pressure themselves to demonstrate that their funding is well spent. Thus, evidence-based decision making relies not just on collecting and collating information but also on analysis, interpretation, reflection and effective communication of this to inform and guide public decision making. As Streatfield and Markless state:

> The demand for more and better evidence of service efficiency and effectiveness has rapidly extended … target setting, benchmarking and efforts at standardization of services varies from country to country, but the trend towards greater accountability appears inexorable.
>
> (Streatfield and Markless, 2012)

Impact is not about business as usual. Standard performance measures are great for working out if a current activity is operating efficiently within its scope and delivering planned outputs. Impact connects special projects or new initiatives to the people most affected by the change; it either predicts or will show how well served those people are. New initiatives or strategic change requires a refocusing of resources (especially time, money and infrastructure) from other operational activities. Understanding impact allows for continuous assessment of whether innovation is working and how. Impact assessment also allows for the deliberate modelling of strategic planning to deliver the desired impact with demonstrable economic, social and cultural benefits.

Origins of impact assessment and variations on the impact theme

For this book the functioning definition of impact is:

> The measurable outcomes arising from the existence of a digital resource that demonstrate a change in the life or life opportunities of the community.

This exacting and ambitious definition is the basis of the BVI Model (Tanner, 2012). It is used in this way here as an all-encompassing definition considering the highest aspirations of impact assessment. It puts people at its centre and expects that strategies will aspire to make a beneficial change in the lives of people.

Impact as a form of assessment spans both qualitative and quantitative methods, with measurements possible before and during the event (ex-ante) and after the fact (ex-post). All impact should assume that there is an intervention of some form. The effects of the intervention are measured against the potential needs of benefiting stakeholders. Impact assumes change, not stasis or business as usual.

There are four founding *communities of use* which have originated the concept and practice of impact assessment:

- environmental
- social
- health
- economic.

It is useful to consider a basic definition of these, as it provides some insight into the origins of impact as a theme, and thus to understand its scope and coverage. Some further discussion of impact from a political viewpoint, the funders' and foundations' perspective and academic research considerations will add further context and understanding of the current impact agenda.

Environmental impact assessment (EIA)

The International Association for Impact Assessment (IAIA) provides this definition of EIA:

> Impact Assessment (IA) simply defined is the process of identifying the future consequences of a current or proposed action. The 'impact' is the difference between what would happen with the action and what would happen without it ... The Environmental Impact Assessment ... definition adopted by IAIA is the process of identifying, predicting, evaluating and mitigating the biophysical, social, and other relevant effects of development proposals prior to major decisions being taken and commitments made.
>
> (International Association for Impact Assessment, 2009)

In this definition and application impact has a dual nature, each with its methodological approaches. It can be a technical tool for analysis of the consequences of a planned intervention (policy based or specific to a project/programme). It can also be the formative steps for legal or governmental procedures linked to the process of decision making for a planned environmental intervention; for example, the building of new transport infrastructure requiring the compulsory purchase of land or regulatory change.

In both cases, the impact assessment is predictive and seeks to provide information to stakeholders and decision makers identifying the future consequences of current or proposed action. Response to unplanned events, such as natural disasters, war and conflicts may rely on EIA to measure and evaluate the effects on the environment of those unplanned-for interventions. Environmental impact measures will not frequently feature in this book. However, the problematic issues illustrated by environmental modelling with regard to predicting causality and consequence from action will be a point reflected on when considering the feasibility of any given strategy for evidence gathering.

Social impact assessment (SIA)

Frank Vanclay, in his pivotal 'International Principles for Social Impact Assessment', defined SIA as including:

> the processes of analysing, monitoring and managing the intended and unintended social consequences, both positive and negative, of planned interventions (policies, programs, plans, projects) and any social change processes invoked by those interventions. Its primary purpose is to bring about a more sustainable and equitable biophysical and human environment.
>
> (Vanclay, 2003)

Social impact looks more closely at individuals, organisations and social macro-systems. It has a predictive element, but successive tools such as Theory of Change have made it more participatory and part of the process of managing social issues (*Theory of Change Community*, n.d.). For pragmatic purposes, Social Return on Investment (SROI) is included in this section on SIA, although some in the impact community may find this approach somewhat reductive or an unappealing conjoining of investment with social matters. There are many methods and tools for SIA that may prove helpful in considering questions of life opportunities and indicators.

Many social impact measures require some level or form of participatory research method, where the process of engagement directly involves the people whose meaningful actions or life/world are being affected in the knowledge-production process (Bergold and Thomas, 2012). Participatory methods are thus defined in terms of their emphasis on 'collaboration' and frequently involve the participation of underprivileged, often marginalised, groups.

> It seeks to bring together action and reflection, theory and practice, in participation with others, in the pursuit of practical solutions to issues of pressing concern to people, and more generally the flourishing of individual persons and their communities.
>
> (Borg et al., 2012)

Participation is a particularly challenging area of investigation, as it requires the conscious giving up of hierarchies and hegemonic knowledge and accepting that participation may challenge or confront accepted norms, the existing status quo and their legitimacy. True partnerships are entwined, trust based and will assume that participants help to decide how data is collected and analysed.

In the BVI Model, the Social Strategic Perspective and SIA methods and techniques are aligned.

Health impact assessment (HIA)

Definitions of health impacts have changed over time, as described by this useful overview:

Scholars have defined various definitions of HIA over time. HIA is any combination of procedures or methods by which a proposed policy or program may be judged as to the effect(s) it may have on the health of a population. In 1999, the WHO Regional Office for Europe added 'and the distribution of those effects within the population' to include consideration of health inequalities. Further, Mindell et al. (2010) have described HIA as 'the use of the best available evidence to assess the likely effect of a specific policy in a specific situation', leading to comparisons with evidence-based medicine. It is generally agreed that three types of knowledge are combined in HIA: that provided by stakeholders based on their experience; local data; and publicly available evidence, including past HIAs.

Impact can thus relate to measuring the change in a person's well-being through a specific intervention.

Health impacts are generally considered via a range of evidence, and using a structured framework. This evidence can be used to determine population health outcomes or to defend policy decisions. The UK National Health Service uses a tool called the QALY system (Quality Adjusted Life Years). This system assesses not only how much longer a treatment will allow a person to live, but also how it improves the life of that person. The QALY is a measure of the value of health outcomes and, as such, is somewhat more limited than other methods used in HIA, particularly in palliative care. King's College London has developed the Palliative Care Outcome Scale (POS), a tool to measure patients' physical symptoms, psychological, emotional and spiritual needs, and provision of information and support at the end of life (*Palliative Care Outcome Scale*, n.d.). These forms of impact assessment are effective at measuring interventions and have interesting data gathering mechanisms that are worthy of investigation, but generally, they need very clear baselines and large comparable populations to gain significance. HIA will not feature in this book again, although the well-being measures can be instructive methodologically.

Economic impact assessment

Economic impact assessment estimates changes in employment, income or levels of business activity that may result from a proposed project or intervention. There are an enormous range of mechanisms to measure these outcomes. It is helpful to consider *direct, indirect* and *induced* economic impacts. The UK Office for National Statistics summarised these as follows:

> Direct impacts occur when additional demand for a unit generates a corresponding unit of output, e.g. production of a chair.
>
> Indirect impacts arise as demand for materials and fuels used to create that additional unit of output generates, in turn, outputs in other industries, e.g. wood, steel, paint, fabric, electricity, gas, water and other materials, fuels, and services used in furniture production. There will be associated increases in labour, profits and capital.
>
> Induced impacts are felt as increases in compensation of employees lead to increased spending on goods and services in the economy.
>
> (Office for National Statistics, 2010)

Economic impacts accrue when it is possible to show that there is a financial return on investment that is specific and directly or indirectly measurable. The cultural field has used this approach successfully. Chapter 3 includes examples.

Economic impact can provide a focus to consider the wealth or level of economic activity in a given geographic area or zone of influence. It is usually feasible to identify baselines and significant indicators to measure improvement in the economic well-being of an area, such as via increased:

- business output
- value added
- wealth (including property values)
- personal income (including wages) or
- jobs.

New business investment now sometimes describes the Triple Bottom Line, also known as the three pillars: people, planet and profit (Vanclay, 2004). In these, an impact investor seeks to enhance social structure or environmental health as well as to achieve financial returns. The modes of measurement in the Triple Bottom Line are of interest to the evidence-gathering approaches and perspectives proposed in this book.

In the BVI Model, the Economic Strategic Perspective is aligned with economic impact methods and techniques.

Governmental definitions of impact

Further to the above sector- and subject-based definitions, the European Commission (EC) provides an instrumental definition that focuses on how impact assessment relates directly to policy and decision making.

Impact assessment (IA), as defined by the EC, involves a set of logical steps to be followed when preparing policy proposals. It is a process that prepares evidence for political decision makers on the advantages and disadvantages of possible policy options by assessing their potential impacts. The following are the core questions that must be answered in impact assessments conducted by the EC.

1 What is the problem that needs to be addressed by public policy intervention?
2 What should be the objectives of the proposed policy intervention?
3 What are the main policy options for reaching the objectives identified?
4 What are the likely economic, social and environmental impacts of these options?
5 How do the main options compare in terms of effectiveness, efficiency and coherence in solving the problem identified?
6 How can the performance of the preferred policy option be evaluated in the future? (European Commission, n.d.)

The EC's definition of impact assessment relates to a process that prepares evidence for political decision makers on the advantages and disadvantages of possible policy options by assessing their potential impacts. In this latter case, an impact is often considered in both political and economic terms. The most important aspect of this mode of impact assessment is to influence and inform decision makers on future interventions and potential policy pathways.

The US government does not seem to have a single definition of impact and there is a different usage in many branches of government (US General Services Administration, n.d.). The most useful for consideration here is that for US Aid, which has rigorous processes for measurement and also an extensive blog for exemplars of achievement (US Aid, n.d.). The US Aid definitions of impact evaluation are:

> An evaluation that looks at the impact of an intervention on final welfare outcomes, rather than only at project outputs, or a process evaluation which focuses on implementation.
>
> An evaluation carried out some time (five to ten years) after the intervention has been completed, to allow time for impact to appear.
>
> An evaluation considering all interventions within a given sector or geographical area.
>
> An evaluation concerned with establishing the counterfactual, i.e., the difference the project made (how indicators behaved with the project compared to how they would have been without it).
>
> (US Aid, n.d.)

The addition of a counterfactual element seeks a means of demonstrating the differences that the change has generated in the communities affected by showing the alternative circumstances. This is difficult to evidence or authenticate, so may feel more like marketing or public relations than a settled scientific process.

The UK government has a regulatory system for impact assessment. Regulatory impact assessments are a tool to help explain the effects of regulatory proposals that have an impact on consumers, industry participants and social and environmental issues. They do not determine final political decisions, but they form a vital part of the decision-making process. Regulatory impact is thus a structured framework for understanding the impacts associated with critical governmental proposals. The Practical Guidance for UK Government Officials states that an impact assessment is:

> [both a] continuous process to help think through the reasons for government intervention, to weigh up various options for achieving an objective and to understand the consequences of a proposed intervention; and a tool to be used to help develop policy by assessing and presenting the likely costs and benefits and the associated risks of a proposal that might have an impact on the public, business or civil society organisations, the environment and wider society over the long term.
>
> (Department for Business, Information and Skills, 2015)

These regulatory systems demonstrate the importance of impact assessment to policy makers and political decision makers. As such, they create a cascade throughout their societies as more aspects take on the rhetoric and reality of impact assessment as a normal tool of management, strategic planning and policy making.

Academic research impacts

The desire at national levels for evidence and indicators of the significance and reach of academic research drives the academic interest in impact assessment. This is especially prevalent in the UK, where the Research Excellence Framework (REF) acts as an expert peer assessment of the quality of UK universities' research in all disciplines. The REF for 2014 was undertaken by the four UK higher education funding bodies, who use the results to inform the selective allocation of their research funding to universities. Impact made up 20% of the total assessment for each research group in 2014 and is 25% in the REF for 2021. The assessment also provides accountability for public investment in research and produces evidence of the benefits of this investment. These are strong motivators for all concerned.

The REF2014 included four-page impact case studies of societal and economic impact for a research group, supported by impact evidence linking research to outcomes. A total of 6,975 impact case studies were submitted by 154 UK institutions to REF2014 (https://impact.ref.ac.uk/casestudies/). Each impact case study aimed to showcase how research that was undertaken in UK universities over the previous 20 years has benefited society beyond academia – whether in the UK or globally. The case studies outline changes and benefits to the economy, society, culture, public policy and services, health, the environment and quality of life (King's College London and Digital Science, 2015).

According to guidance from UK Research and Innovation, research impact for REF2021

> is defined as an effect on, change or benefit to the economy, society, culture, public policy or services, health, the environment or quality of life, beyond academia …
>
> Impact includes, but is not limited to, an effect on, change or benefit to:
>
> - the activity, attitude, awareness, behaviour, capacity, opportunity, performance, policy, practice, process or understanding
> - of an audience, beneficiary, community, constituency, organisation or individuals

- in any geographic location whether locally, regionally, nationally or internationally …

Impact includes the reduction or prevention of harm, risk, cost or other negative effects.

(UK Research and Innovation, 2019)

Each impact case study is assessed using two core criteria.

1 Reach: How widely were the research benefits felt?
2 Significance: How much difference did the research make to beneficiaries?

Academic research does frequently change people's lives or life opportunities, even if some of those benefits occur over periods measured in years and decades rather than months. It is incumbent on scholars to attempt to engage with these changes, to seek the means to find out more about how research fosters change. Also, if academics are going to collaborate with the cultural, heritage and GLAM sectors, then understanding the issue of impact from that perspective will help to form better-aligned co-research and more useful digital resources. There are ever-present barriers, such as the constraints of funding, the difficulties in identifying beneficial stakeholders and the often long time-scale for academic impact to become fully visible.

The importance of impact to memory institutions

During the 1990s techniques such as cost-benefit analysis prevailed in management techniques. This drive to demonstrate 'value for money' originated from political and commercial pressures. It was further driven by an increased understanding of how information, data and, also, media culture play a strategic role in competitiveness for all strata of socio-economic activity (Badenoch et al., 1994). This brought information, particularly the increasing volumes of digital information, into the fold of resource-management processes that drive towards assessments of cost efficiency and value. This process of increasing managerialism in memory institutions led to increased awareness of cost-related factors and sophisticated management of resources, but for some time issues of value and impact were relatively under-acknowledged.

Early impact evaluations

It took until 2002 for the largest review of impact evaluation for museums, archives and libraries in the UK to take place (Wavell et al., 2002). This breakthrough work identified a series of outcomes that were specific to these sectors, found through analysis of an extensive and comprehensive review of the available evaluations to that date.

For museums, they found evidence of:

- engagement and enjoyment;
- acquisition of new skills;
- trying new experiences;
- encouraging creativity;
- increased self-confidence or changes in attitude;
- higher-order cognitive learning, mainly when individuals are already familiar with the subject on display or with museum environments;
- younger people making connections with existing knowledge, mainly when there is appropriate mediation to facilitate the learning process.

For archives, they found evidence that related mainly to learning in terms of:

- useful and enjoyable learning experience;
- important source of leisure enjoyment and personal satisfaction;
- stimulating or broadening understanding of history and culture;
- increasing abilities, skills and confidence;
- to a limited extent, helping job seeking or workplace skills.

For libraries, they found evidence from library use of:

- enjoyment and choice of leisure reading material;
- reading development in young children;
- academic achievement, particularly in terms of language skills;
- acquisition of skills, particularly ICT and information literacy;
- broader aspects of learning, such as increased motivation for learning, self-confidence, independence. (Wavell et al., 2002)

Markless and Streatfield, in their valuable book on evaluating impact, give one of the first detailed definitions of impact for the library sector:

> any effect of the service (or of an event or initiative) on an individual or group. [Impact can show itself] through discernible changes, such as shifts in: quality of life: e.g. self-esteem; confidence; feeling included; work or social prospects; educational and other outcomes: e.g. skills acquired; educational attainment; levels of knowledge.
>
> (Markless and Streatfield, 2006)

Sara Selwood engaged with the cultural impact of museums with an extremely thoughtful and insightful work that adopted broad working definitions of culture, impacts and evidence, as there was no singular definition with which she was comfortable. She states that:

> the kinds of impacts that museums exert are often perceived very broadly – not least in terms of making places cultural. They tend to report those that comply with generic frameworks, although they may – in some cases – regard such outcomes as secondary to their main purpose.
>
> (Selwood, 2010)

The fundamental presumptions and impact factors explored by Selwood focused on audience reflection on experiences in terms of articulating and exploring sensitive and difficult cultural issues; generating a sense of belonging and integrating the museum within local communities and society; plus, opening up the museums to different attitudes and perceptions. The impact agenda envisioned has been taken further, such that now museum visitors are increasingly bringing new expectations for participation with them when they visit museums both physically and virtually, primarily through social media uses (Ross, 2014).

The impact and evaluation projects that grew up in the 2005–2008 period tended to focus on what can be measured and how to express outputs, rather than on an overarching definition of impact. Notable examples include Massachusetts Institute of Technology's OpenCourseWare evaluation (Carson, 2006), a Berkeley study on 'Use and Users of Digital Resources' (Harley, 2006), the Open Educational Resources Report (Atkins, Brown and Hammond, 2007) and the Log Analysis of Digital Resources in the Arts and Humanities (LAIRAH) project at University College London (Warwick et al., 2008). This focus on the pragmatic was helpful to the needs of the community of users at that time. However, in so doing, it left the value and impact disconnected from other impact strategies/strengths and consequently much evaluation in this sector became inward looking, without necessarily generating the information needed by decision makers. There was a need and a desire for more concrete ways for those in charge of memory institutions (and for their funders) to collect and evaluate data for measuring impact across the entire life-cycle of a digital service offering or digitisation project.

TIDSR

The foremost response to this need at the time was the TIDSR: Toolkit for the Impact of Digitised Scholarly Resources. Originally developed by the Oxford Internet Institute in 2008, the Toolkit was updated several times afterwards, before closing down all web resources sometime in 2018. TIDSR grew out of a JISC-funded usage and impact study that explored the questions: 'are digital resources succeeding at reaching their intended users? Are they having an impact on their community of users? How can impact be measured?' (Meyer et al., 2009). TIDSR resources can still be accessed via the Internet Archive's Wayback Machine (*TIDSR: Toolkit for the Impact of Digitised Scholarly Resources*, 2018) and JISC (www.jisc.ac.uk/guides/toolkit-for-the-impact-of-digitised-scholarly-resources).

The most important resource provided by TIDSR at the time was a set of tools that combine both quantitative and qualitative methods. Quantitative measures include web metrics, log file analysis, scientometric (or bibliometric) analysis and content analysis. TIDSR further recommended using an array of qualitative measures (stakeholder interviews, resource surveys, user feedback, focus groups and questionnaires) that captured information about the whole cycle of usage and impact. Thus, in a later example of its implementation, the academic founders of TIDSR combined usage data, bibliometrics, interviews and surveys to collate the impact of the digital collections Early English Books Online and the House of Commons Parliamentary Papers (Meyer and Eccles, 2016).

TIDSR was a breakthrough moment in academic impact assessment, primarily focused on digital content and tools provision for data gathering.

Let's Get Real

In 2011 the Culture24 action research programme Let's Get Real started its first of what have so far been five phases looking to develop 'effective ways to define, measure and evaluate the success of online activities' (Finnis, Chan and Clements, 2011). Their work has built toolkits for social media analytics and user segmentation and brand building, with a focus on museums and cultural heritage sectors. As reported by the UK National Gallery, the key significance of working with Culture24 is using the 'knowledge gained to better define our goals and success measures going forward in the Gallery's new digital strategy' (Finnis, Chan and Clements, 2011). Culture24 expanded Let's Get Real to include North America in 2014–16, with organisations such as the Getty Museum, US Holocaust Memorial Museum, Portland Art Museum and the Virtual Museum of Canada taking part (Malde and Finnis, 2016). See Chapter 3 for case studies drawn from Let's Get Real.

ENUMERATE

Another important activity at this time was ENUMERATE, an EC-funded project that ran from 2011 to 2014 (www.enumerate.eu). Its main contribution to the impact agenda was the creation of a reliable baseline of statistical data about digitisation, digital preservation and online access in Europe. This was a crucial contribution to measuring change, as there needs to be a clear understanding of a starting condition from which change has occurred. We take the most notice of the speed of our car when accelerating or braking, not when cruising steadily down the highway. The ten core partners in ENUMERATE initiated a Europe-wide community of practice that led to shared approaches to gathering statistical data and to the digitisation progress. Tools such as the ENUMERATE Benchmark offer institutions the service of comparing their data and correlating with similar institutions in their home country.

Some of the important findings of ENUMERATE include their statistical insights into digitisation activity and readiness. In 2014, 87% of the ~1,400 responding institutions had digital collections, while only 35% had a written digitisation strategy. Just over half the institutions measured the use of their digital collections, mostly through web statistics (91%), with a third using social media statistics (Stroeker and Vogels, 2014). These figures give a good sense of the gap between practice and management/impact ideals. More strategic management is needed for digital collections, supported by effective measures of use and value.

Other activity

A major British report was conducted by Tony Travers of the London School of Economics in 2006, assessing the economic, social and creative impacts of museums and galleries: he found economic benefits of the order of £1.5 billion per year, and that over 9,000 people are directly employed by museums, with 3,000 volunteers and over 14,000 'friends' linked to museums (Travers, 2006). This was followed up by an Arts Council England report assessing the economic impact of museums in England, which stated that the museums sector contributed £1.45 billion in economic output and generated 'an estimated £3 for every £1 of public sector grant' (Tuck and Dickinson, 2015).

This summary of the growth in methods and modes of impact and value measurement appears quite Europe-centric. The reason is not due to a lack of activity in the rest of the world, but one of focal points. Europe has concentrated efforts on building models, frameworks and toolsets. The ethnographic-focused impact assessment work from New Zealand is establishing new, narrative-strong models for impact and working with indigenous collections (Crookston et al., 2016).

Other measures elsewhere have been either economically driven or based on expertise/methods already in place, without such a focus on community model building. For instance, the LibValue project (http://libvalue.cci.utk.edu/) looks at academic library value, outcomes and return on investment. Tenopir makes a vital contribution, stating that 'value of the library to its constituents can be demonstrated in many ways – by time invested, by value to purpose, by outcomes of use, and by ROI [return on investment] … libraries need to focus on measuring outcomes, not inputs' (Tenopir, 2013). Diane M. Zorich, now Director of the Smithsonian's Digitization Program Office, has an extensive career at the forefront of evidence-based considerations for digital libraries, museums and digital scholarship. Some of her most significant work has been about the impact of transitioning to a digital world for art history, art galleries and associated scholarly research and the digital humanities (Zorich, 2012). Kimberly Silk, as the founder of the Library Research Network, based in Canada, has done excellent work on economic impact assessment (http://libraryresearchnetwork.org) and has produced a superb book for library evaluation (Irwin and Silk, 2017). Research by Effie Kapsalis on the impact of open access on GLAM institutions is an exemplar of qualitative research supporting significant changes in a community of practice (Kapsalis, 2016).

Chapter 3 includes more detailed case studies and exemplars on GLAM impact assessments.

Development of the Balanced Value Impact Model (BVI Model)

At the same time as the developments described above were taking place there remained a real sense that the impact of digital was under-studied and not well enough understood. In some respects, this reflected a prior sense that all things digital were intrinsically good. While it is undoubtedly true that the 1990s eLib Programme was designed explicitly as a 'let a thousand flowers bloom' exercise (Brophy, 2006), these activities generally did not survive long after the initial innovation phases. However, assumptions continue to pervade, to date, that digitisation equals funding; that all things digital are innovative; that agile development can replace planning; and that if peers, competitors or Google are doing it, then it is imperative that one must also join in. Acquiescence to these mantras was a sign of entering a 'digital death spiral' (Tanner, 2013). There was a need for a digitally focused impact evaluation that could extend beyond these assumptions so as to provide a substantial evidence base.

One vitally important consideration is the sustainability of digitised resources. Support for many digital resources after the initial development period (and therefore the funding) has ended is typically short lived, rendering the impact difficult to assess. The related problem is that many of the studies of the impact of digitised resources attempt to measure change over a short time (1–3 months) and have no baseline metrics against which to assess what may have changed.

The conception of impact for this book is the measurable outcomes arising from the existence of a digital resource that demonstrate a change in the life or life opportunities of the community. The purpose of this particular definition is to allow an overarching view of the impact that encompasses aspects of all the definitions provided in this chapter such as to unify across sectors and disciplinary perspectives.

This book provides a cohesive model (the BVI Model) that will provide a definition and model of the impact that any memory institution with a pragmatic, implementable framework for delivery can use. The BVI Model allows these varied perspectives and sectoral differences to co-exist in one model. It will also bring into the frame something so far still missing in many of these definitions: the digital factor.

Intellectual and administrative journey to the delivery of BVI Model 2.0

The original BVI Model was the result of a funded research commission from the Arcadia Fund (a charitable fund of Lisbet Rausing and Peter Baldwin – www.arcadiafund.org.uk). The goal was to research and test the best methods for assessing the impact of digitised collections, so as to construct a synthesis of methodologies and techniques and resolve these into a cohesive and achievable methodology for impact assessment of digitised resources and collections. This research began as a means of resolving the Arcadia Fund's concern that they were investing significant sums in digital projects but without the same means of assessment of impact that were available for their environmental funding. It soon transpired that the current state of impact assessment in digital resources was nascent, and thus the path to the BVI Model was born.

Evaluation and impact toolsets were inspirational to the development of the BVI Model in 2010–12, and its continued development to date (Tanner, 2012). There is no shortage of tools and excellent guidance on data collection, metrics and usage figures; but there remained a sense that the full panoply and depth of impact assessment was a goal still to be achieved beyond usage figures or web metrics. As an analogy, if the digital ecosystem is an engine, then the BVI Model seeks to find its place as a manual guiding the mechanic to understand the engine better. Understanding the engine means knowing which tools to use, and thus how to plan and to use tools effectively.

The development of BVI Model and its revised version, as provided in this book, starts from this consideration, that working at the methods level was far too low down in the process and there were too many methods to make a process that was cohesive and applicable to all its possible users. The BVI Model thus attempts to step back and consider application models rather than just the methods themselves. Over the years, I have consulted with many experts and those with an active interest in impact assessment to gather ideas, and for their guidance on the feasibility of certain core concepts and ideas. I have further tested impact assessment methods and models in expert practitioner workshops, focus groups and social experimentation. I have consulted for various libraries, museums and archives (not shared here as covered by non-disclosure agreements) and this experience has informed the practice and development of the BVI Model.

Core to the development of the BVI Model to version 2.0 has been participation in the Europeana Impact Taskforce (Fallon, 2017b) to advance the tailored development of a practical toolkit for impact design, assessment and narration (the outcomes of this process are available at https://impkt.tools/). This is a culmination of previous Europeana partnering, beginning in

2012 with the chairing of a wide-ranging Impact Assessment Taskforce considering the means of measuring the impact of digital resources and the creation of a set of principles or a framework to enable the effective measurement of impact for Europeana and its partners. This work had a strong influence on the Europeana Strategic Plan for 2015–20 (Europeana Foundation, 2014b) and the associated White Paper on implementing impact assessment in that strategy (Europeana Foundation, 2014a). I worked closely with Europeana in 2015–16 to clarify their objectives concerning impact. This work put in place practical recommendations for implementing the BVI Model to carry out, measure, document and communicate the impact of the Europeana digital platform for European cultural heritage (Tanner, 2016a). The case study Workers Underground will be reflected on in more detail as an exemplar of impact implementation in Chapter 8 (Verwayen, Wilms and Fallon, 2016).

The BVI Model has been implemented or used as a model in a wide range of instances. Some implementations or adaptations of BVI Model include:

1 Europeana's *Impact Playbook* (Verwayen et al., 2017)
2 the Wellcome Library digitisation programme (Tanner, 2016c; Green and Andersen, 2017)
3 the People's Collection Wales with the National Museum Wales, the National Library of Wales and the Royal Commission on the Ancient and Historical Monuments of Wales (Vittle, Haswell-Walls and Dixon, 2016)
4 estimating the value and impact of Nectar Virtual Laboratories (Sweeny, Fridman and Rasmussen, 2017)
5 a Twitter Case Study for Assessing Digital Sound (Giannetti, 2018)
6 implementing resource discovery techniques at the Museum of Domestic Design and Architecture, Middlesex University (Smith and Panaser, 2015)
7 JISC training and guidance: Making Your Digital Collections Easier to Discover (Colbron et al., 2019)
8 Museum Theatre Gallery, Hawke's Bay (Powell, 2014)
9 Valuing Our Scans: Understanding the Impacts of Digitized Native American Ethnographic Archives, a research project led by Ricardo L. Punzalan at the College of Information Studies at the University of Maryland.

In Chapter 2 the BVI Model is introduced as a conceptual model.

Chapter 2

The Balanced Value Impact Model

Introduction

This chapter introduces the BVI Model. The BVI Model is a cohesive model to provide any memory institution with a useful definition and process of impact assessment. It reflects the broader process of impact assessment and strategic planning. Principles from the BVI Model can be applied in different settings or at a less advanced level. The adoption of the Model challenges organisations to be more evidence based and to investigate the underlying assumptions driving institutional values and strategies.

This chapter will show the underlying assumptions supporting the building of the BVI Model. This focus on understanding assumptions is an essential part of strategic planning for impact. Before embarking, it is vital to bring these assumptions to the surface.

In short, some core questions to address are:

- what to assess
- why to assess it
- how to use the intended results
- the worth of knowing this information.

The BVI Model is a means to structure an activity for the purposes of setting strategic contexts, deciding what to measure and to add purpose, direction and a disciplined approach to the often vague concept of impact. This book argues for defining modes of value for digital culture not solely driven by economics but which contain indicators of other, more intangible values, even including non-use. This balanced approach seeks to show that the digital resource demonstrably made the host organisation grow better, becoming more efficient and effective in reaching its goals, while stakeholders have become more satisfied, finding social, community and educative benefits of tangible worth that enhance society.

Unless there is a clear sense of the purposefulness of impact assessment or of planning to deliver impact, then do not begin yet. An impact assessment process, especially applying the BVI Model, requires time, attention and focus.

Introducing the BVI Model

All impact assumes an intervention. The effect of the intervention is measured against a set of potential beneficiary stakeholder needs. Impact assessment spans both qualitative and quantitative methods, with a focus on measuring change and evaluating the value of that change. As such, impact provides a useful lens through which to consider strategic planning that seeks to achieve measurable change for a community.

The definition of impact offered is the measurable outcomes arising from the existence of a digital resource that demonstrate a change in the life or life opportunities of the community. Each concept in this definition is laden with assumptions that influence the scope and structure of the process model. The BVI Model is indeed a measurement model. The measurement focuses on identifying the change in a community arising from the existence of digital resources that are of proven value to the community. Implementation will be iterative and cyclical, rather than one-off and linear.

The BVI Model has five core functional stages:

Stage 1: Set the context
Stage 2: Design the framework
Stage 3: Implement the framework
Stage 4: Narrate the outcomes and results
Stage 5: Review and respond.

An overview of the five stages of the BVI Model and how they interact is shown in Figure 2.1 opposite.

The concept underlying the BVI Model follows a process that stresses the importance of distinguishing between actions, the outputs and the outcomes of these actions, and ultimately the impact which a memory organisation or its digital presence has on people. Qualitative and quantitative methods to collect

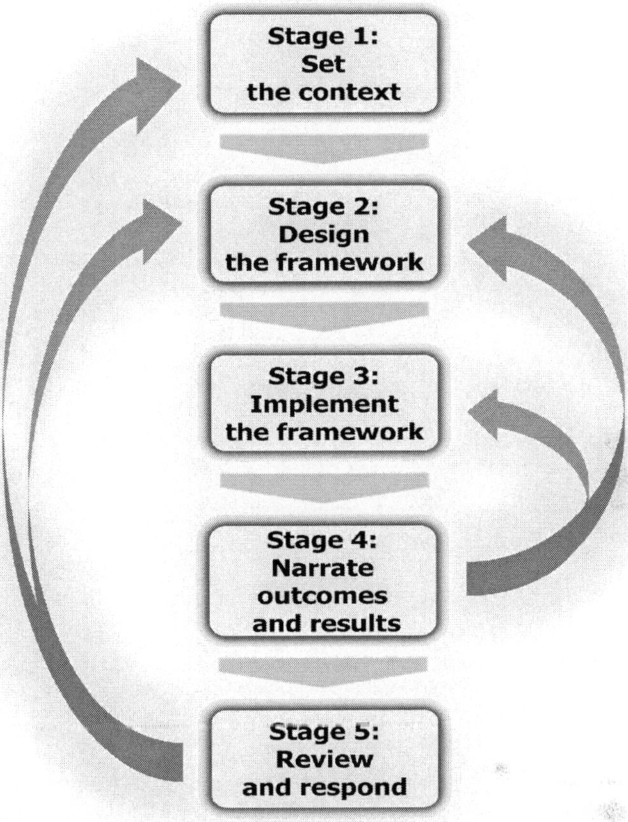

Figure 2.1 *Overview of the BVI Model stages*

data, such as usage statistics, case studies, surveys and focus groups, are at the heart of measuring this impact. The aim is also to challenge implementers to think of more profound indicators of impact. In particular, the BVI Model encourages a continuous assessment to look beyond the immediately measurable 'output' and towards the demonstrable outcome, which leads to defining the real impact.

To enhance the reputation of a memory institution, it must demonstrate impact through evidence of reaching out to a community, having a positive influence on society and showing the significance of its activity to the lives and life opportunities of people in its diverse communities.

Figure 2.2 on the next page shows the high-level conceptual overview of the BVI Model.

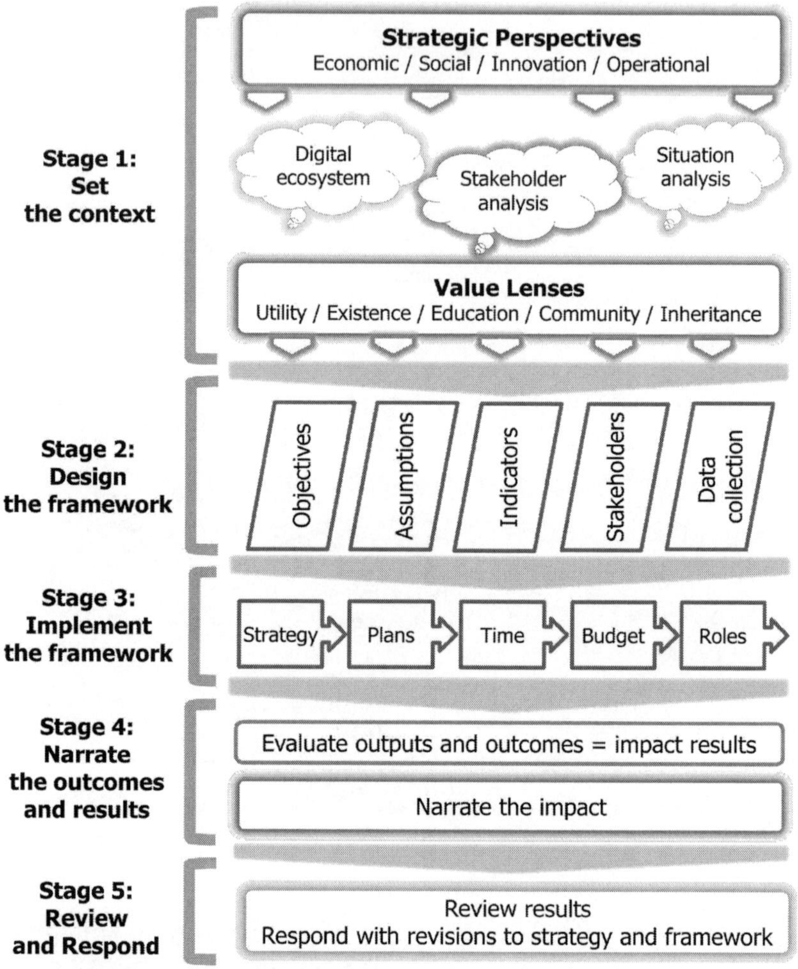

Figure 2.2 *Conceptual overview of the BVI Model*

Stage 1: Set the context focuses information gathered on the organisational and community context through Strategic Perspectives and the Value Lenses (see Chapters 5 and 6).

Stage 2: Design the framework populates a defined logical BVI Framework with decisions about what and whom to measure and how to do that measurement (see Chapter 7).

Stage 3: Implement the framework is the project management phase, where each of the mini-plans set in Stage 2 is set into action and data is gathered that will, over time, become the impact evidence base (see Chapters 7 and 8).

Stage 4: Narrate the outcomes and results collates, analyses and turns the evidence into an impact narrative shared with interested stakeholders, especially decision makers (see Chapter 9).

Stage 5: Review and respond activities should be embedded throughout to establish the iterative and cyclical nature of impact assessment (see Chapter 10). The BVI Model must deliver actionable evidence or information of change that is useful, otherwise it is not functioning as designed.

The structured outcomes from use of the BVI Model should advocate for a digital resource through the Strategic Perspectives. A narrative summary might state the following.

1 Rich digital content is available for existing users and new audiences, placing content in every home and hand to share and make new personal experiences. This resource has changed our stakeholders' behaviour in ways that link to benefits in education, social life, community cohesion, a sense of place and improved welfare. (Social impact)
2 Because of these changes we are also delivering substantial economic benefits to our stakeholders that demonstrate the worth and value of our endeavours in clear monetary terms. (Economic impact)
3 Innovation in the building of the digital resource and its functionality means that we are gaining a strategic advantage in a vital area of activity for the future sustainability of services and engagement. (Innovation impact)
4 This digital resource enables our organisation to be more effective and efficient in delivering change and resultant benefits to stakeholders, both internally and externally. (Operational impact)

Providing a strong narrative backed with clear evidence of the change achieved will ensure that decision makers can make better-informed decisions and are more likely to follow the recommendations made. Each organisation can learn from its activities and thus become better at planning for the future so as to make the most significant impact and benefit for its stakeholders.

The assumptions driving the BVI Model

Seven core underlying assumptions drive the adoption of the BVI Model as a model containing a nested Framework for measuring impact. Recognition of these assumptions enables the reader to:

- make the most effective use of the BVI Model;
- allow for partial or adapted implementation; or
- allow for independent use of the embedded concepts, outside of the BVI Framework.

The impact Framework is nested within the BVI Model

The BVI Model name reflects its components: the balanced scorecard approach; the importance of modes of value; and that it represents an impact model. The concept of 'model', in this context, is a representation that indicates the construction or formulation of a method of organising an impact assessment activity, rather than circumscribing the activity itself. For instance, a conceptual model allows for the resolution of major design decisions – much like an architect deciding with a client between building a domestic house, industrial factory or castle.

Use of the BVI Model produces an impact framework as an immediate output. The BVI Framework structures and guides the process to manage the gathering of impact evidence. Returning to the architectural metaphor, a framework would be the equivalent of a structured plan for how each room had a purpose (e.g. kitchen, bathroom, lounge) and how the house was furnished. It is only once the house is built and lived in that the metaphor moves from a model, through the framework, to implementation and action. The BVI Framework thus provides the overall structure of any proposed impact assessment process, while the BVI Model as a whole explores the specific methodology of establishing the impact work.

The advantage of a framework nested within an overarching model is that it allows flexibility for those tasked with its practical implementation. As long as the conceptual model is recognised, then the actual delivery of any one aspect is not prescribed or required. Thus, anyone using the BVI Model should feel free to rename or revise the functional parts to suit local needs or to aid cognition or acceptance in their organisation or community.

The model-to-framework approach also accounts for the range of fuzzy elements within an assessment of impact. A high-level conceptual BVI Model allows for a representation of the thinking, context and perception, while the BVI Framework allows the products of this thinking to be controlled, contained and then utilised.

The BVI Model uses a DPSIR approach to suggest causation

The DPSIR (drivers, pressures, state, impact and responses) environmental impact assessment model strongly influences the BVI Model. As articulated by Danish scientist Peter Kristensen the DPSIR model establishes causal relationships across drivers, pressures, state, impact and responses that in turn structure the interactions between society and a defined ecosystem (Kristensen, 2004). The DPSIR model itself is an adaptation of a broader framework of relationships (pressure-state-response) adopted by the Organisation for Economic Co-operation and Development (Giupponi, 2002), which can be seen applied in the Better Life Index (www.oecdbetterlifeindex.org/topics/life-satisfaction).

Figure 2.3 shows the DPSIR impact model. DPSIR assumes a causal chain starting with D:driving forces (BVI Model: Value Lenses, stakeholders) affected through P:pressures (BVI Model: Economic, Social, Innovation, Operational Strategic Perspectives) related to an S:state (BVI Model: ecosystem) that records an I:impact (BVI Model: data on changes recorded), eventually leading to strategic and evidence-based decisions R:responses (BVI Model: review and respond).

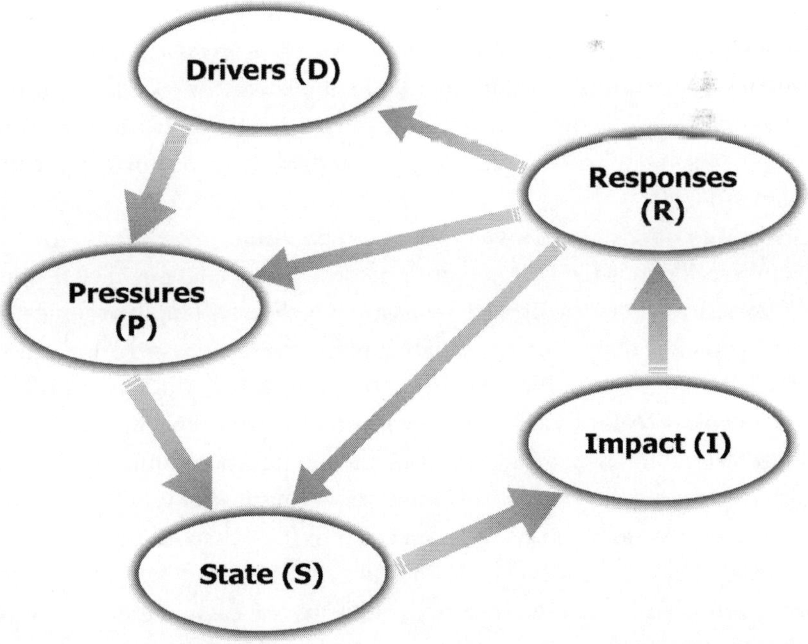

Figure 2.3 *The DPSIR Model*

The BVI Model considers impact holistically and engages with multiple methods. The Framework and Model are influenced by insights from DPSIR and other methods (Bell and Morse, 2008) seeking to unify the diverse processes into a coherent chain of activity while allowing the context of the drivers/pressures/state to be accounted for in selecting key indicators, defining beneficial stakeholders and evaluating outcomes.

The BVI Model privileges conceptual thinking prior to and following implementation

The practical use of the BVI Model happens in two distinct phases – conception (Stages 1 and 2) and implementation (Stages 3 and 4) – with review and reflection happening throughout (Stage 5). At the conception stage a holistic overview considering the context of the impact (stakeholders, ecosystem) aids the overall design and initial analysis phase. The output of this phase results in a document that describes the impact process, with additional detail recorded on each impact measure within the BVI Framework (usually represented as a spreadsheet). This document/plan describes and models the impact assessment and lays the foundations for the delivery of impact assessment.

The BVI Framework provides a map for navigating through activities, their expected impact and the data-collection mechanisms to measure that impact. It offers the opportunity to understand at a glance the Social, Innovation, Operational and Economic impact of a planned activity. It is not the impact assessment itself but a means of planning and providing control over the impact assessment.

Once the activity moves from conceptual planning to actual implementation, it is likely that further, more specific plans will be needed. In a circumstance where the impact assessment is discrete (small organisation or specific project), then the only further planning is necessary logistics. For instance, the Wellcome Library wanted to initially limit their attention to one specific project (called Codebreakers); moving from concept to execution required only data-gathering planning and preparation (Tanner, 2016c).

For a sizeable, organisation-wide assessment, or where the impact distributes across many services/projects/activities, then additional planning is essential. In such cases every individual activity should have a short impact action plan. The plans detail the impact objective of each planned activity, the resources required, the expected outcomes and the data-collection mechanisms – quantitative or qualitative – required to assess the impact of the individual activity. This was required for the Europeana impact strategy (Verwayen, Wilms and Fallon, 2016) and would apply to any other assessment that extended over a long period. It could be advantageous in a UK higher education context where individual academic subjects have to produce impact case studies to support their periodic formal assessment of research quality (Digital Science, 2016).

In the BVI Framework, there are objectives set for each Value Lens to be measured. For each objective, an action plan can be described including the organisational strategy it addresses, the planned actions with a budget, time-scale for completion and the roles of those involved. These action plans express the need for mini-plans within the broader Framework. They also show how the conceptual model at implementation is flipped from a global plan to individual mini-plans within the bigger plan controlled by the Framework.

Meaningful timeframes are important factors in measuring change

As stated above, the BVI Model should be flipped when moving from conception to implementation. As time is a factor in measuring change, mini-plans within the bigger impact plan are an effective way of resolving measuring impact over extended periods.

Each activity should have its mini-impact plan that conforms to the bigger plan. This may be as simple as flagging that a particular type of web metrics is needed or doing a small survey of users who have attended a launch event. The point is that everything that is significantly worth doing is worth asking an impact question about – little and often is the mantra. Using the BVI Framework ensures that the measures do not become out of sync or uncontrolled.

Many evaluations of digital resources attempt to measure change over a very short period (such as three months or less), and thus have no baseline metrics against which to assess what may have changed. Also, it is difficult to measure impact if the resource or activity has not been supported for very long after the initial development period (and therefore the funding) has ended, and they have not been evaluated or assessed over time (Maron, Smith and Loy, 2009) (Tanner, 2011a).

In order to measure a change in anything, it is necessary to have a baseline for comparing current/future performance to a historical metric of the situation discovered through the contexts explored in Stage 1 of the BVI Model. Without such a baseline, numeric data may not demonstrate the desired significance. For example, finding that there is a 25% increase in use is meaningful only if a timeframe contextualises the growth. Similarly, having many users the week after a launch event is not unusual, but do they stay as active users for the longer term?

The baseline date is whatever the activity owner wishes it to be. At no point should a time-oriented baseline suggest that previous activity or outcomes that bridge the baseline be discarded, but there needs to be a point of reference set for change measurement. Often this baseline is implied within strategy documents – that things will be different in the organisation's future actions than they were in previous years. Some measures deliver quickly in the first six months or a year, while others deliver over a four- to five-year period. Hence the need for little-and-often measures or the use of relatively passive measures (such as web usage statistics) that do not need constant attention. Also, there is causality in the order of events to take into account: innovation, for example, generally comes first and financial gain usually follows, so align measures accordingly.

You cannot and should not measure everything

While the BVI Model promotes the means of measuring impact, it is essential to state that not everything can or should be measured. Not every organisational activity delivers an impact outcome every time, but all activities may contribute to the overall context that holistically delivers impact. As such, while no impact measure has a one-to-one relationship with activities, every activity should consider evaluation/feedback questions informed by the impact plan.

Digital resources and memory institutions have an impact, whether this is formally measured or not. The purpose of impact measurement is to understand that impact explicitly and to become purposeful in trying to achieve it and to narrate its benefits to the broader community. However, measures must be cost-effective. Being mindful of the feasibility of a proposed action is equally important to pushing beyond current boundaries to explore new methods and areas within which to collect data. For instance, it might be extremely desirable to know about all the school-aged users in the USA and how they are using a specific educational resource; but usage data metrics do not provide this data. Thus, the cost of finding this data out by polling every school in the USA is patently too expensive in relation to the usefulness of the information gained.

Care must be taken to avoid changing those things measured by how they are measured. It is human nature to treat any form of measurement as a target to reach or a performance metric to exceed. Sometimes known as the observer effect or the Hawthorne effect, it refers to changes that the act of observation makes on an observed phenomenon (Ellwood and Greenwood, 2016). As Goodhart's Law succinctly states: 'when a measure becomes a target, it ceases to be a good measure' (Goodhart, 1984); and Campbell's Law speaks to social consequences: 'the more any quantitative social indicator is used for social decision-making … the more apt it will be to distort and corrupt the social processes it is intended to monitor' (Campbell, 1979). Impact measures should seek to influence the strategic context of the organisation only in response to the results gathered, not in response to the act of measurement itself, otherwise gaming the system so as to achieve desired results becomes a real and negative possibility.

Models are guides, with recursive iterations

One distinct feature observed in successful implementations of the BVI Model is the manner in which they vary the model or adapt to local requirements.

For instance, the rigorous definition of impact used in this book is not immutable in order for application of the BVI Model to succeed. It can be adapted to match specific needs. In the case of Europeana, the impact goal was defined as:

> Impact is a heightened form of evaluation that seeks to measure beyond performance or success indicators to demonstrate the measurable outcomes that can demonstrate a significant change for people affected by the existence of Europeana and its activities. These changes would mainly be beneficial and wide-reaching. We expect Europeana to respond to impacts, both positive and negative, within its strategic management processes.
>
> (Tanner, 2016a)

Although the BVI Model in this book proposes a set of named and defined parameters, no one part is inviolate or immune to being renamed or revised. It is thus acceptable to change a value title from 'utility' to 'use' or 'visitors' if that makes it more understandable to stakeholders. The BVI Model and this text hold to certain phrasings as a means of maintaining a consistent, academic rigour; but the practitioner using it is encouraged to be free-thinking, even playful, and to find approaches that best suit their way of working.

A model is intended to guide thinking. The BVI Model allows for such guided thinking to produce a very structured outcome. However, this should not mean that each step must follow an exact sequence. The Kellogg Logic Model is often used with the BVI Model to express the sequence from the original plan to expected impact as a useful way to model a plan so as to induce the desired outcomes. The Kellogg Logic Model approach states:

> 1 Resources/Inputs: specific resources are needed to operate the plan.
> 2 Activities: with these resources then the planned activities can be accomplished.
> 3 Outputs: if these are accomplished then the amount of product and/or service intended will be delivered.
> 4 Outcomes: by accomplishing the planned activities to the extent intended then the stakeholders will benefit in certain ways.
> 5 Impact: if these benefits for stakeholders are achieved, then changes in organisations, communities or systems might be expected to occur and to deliver certain benefits.
>
> (W. K. Kellogg Foundation, 2004)

The end-product of using the Kellogg Logic Model is a staged plan with input resources for activities which, if accomplished, would lead to a set of service/product outputs that can deliver an intended outcome and possible impacts. This linear end-product is desirable for expressing a plan or as a promise to a funding body. However, it is rarely populated in a linear process. Planning could equally start from the desired outcomes/impact and work backwards. Similarly, a set of activities could form the starting point working forwards to outcomes and backwards to the required resources. A cyclical approach would also work. This is illustrative of the approach to all models, including the BVI Model, where the structured end-product is not produced in a purely linear fashion from the model. There are always recursions, loops and diversions on the pathway to the plan. The strength of any model is thus its ability to allow free thought within its segments while enabling structure and cohesiveness in the eventual end-product.

The starting perspective is vitally important for impact assessment

It is evident that perspective is incredibly important to impact assessment.

One person's benefit is another's deficit. For instance, at a workshop, the Codex Sinaiticus digital resource with its 20 million online visitors was described to an expert in economic impact. He replied (with tongue firmly in cheek) that the nation was arguably in economic deficit, as those 20 million people were not shopping online or engaging in a tangible economic activity while they were viewing this treasure. Perspective will always matter to the impact narrative.

The one immutable element in impact is time, and any assessment looking at the change in people's lives or life opportunities has to ask whether that change is beneficial to them and, if it benefits them, whether that benefit comes at a cost/deficit to others. If people are accessing the library, archive or museum collections online, are they no longer spending money in the community local to those places? In return for an improved service or zero travel time, are they reducing the institution's local economic footprint or sense of community cohesion? Assessing impact has at its heart the need for perspective to be recognised and taken into consideration.

An impact assessment, at best, can tell a strong narrative of benefit to defined stakeholders only in certain circumstances at given times. From this perspective, suggestions and extrapolations are made of the wider benefits. If assumptions overreach or over-claim beyond what is tenable and provable, then the whole fabric of the evidence gathered is called into doubt.

Thus, for the BVI Model, the following attributes of perspective are stated.

- Application of the BVI Model is driven primarily by the needs of the memory institution that is responsible for the digital resource. The stakeholders are a crucial part of the context and drivers for why the impact assessment happens, but essentially the BVI Model is intended as an organisation-led tool. The BVI Model is not a community action model.
- The memory institution must acknowledge and describe the values, the objectives and the stakeholders of the institution before agreeing which aspects of itself and its digital resource are included within the scope for the impact assessment.
- Stakeholders should be involved early, and the institution must understand their role in the impact assessment with great clarity and openness.
- Understanding the perspective on innovation and operational change encompassed within the digital ecosystem is vital.

A five-stage process

This section introduces the five stages of the BVI Model and shows how they fit together.

See Figure 2.4 for a full conceptual overview of the BVI Model.

In combination, stages 1 and 5 express the essential novel components of the BVI Model. These stages provide an additional sense of perspective on the overall impact assessment. Perspective drives all assessments of impact, and so the BVI Model intends to ensure that perspective is clearly understood and purposefully decided. Impact derives power from providing actionable

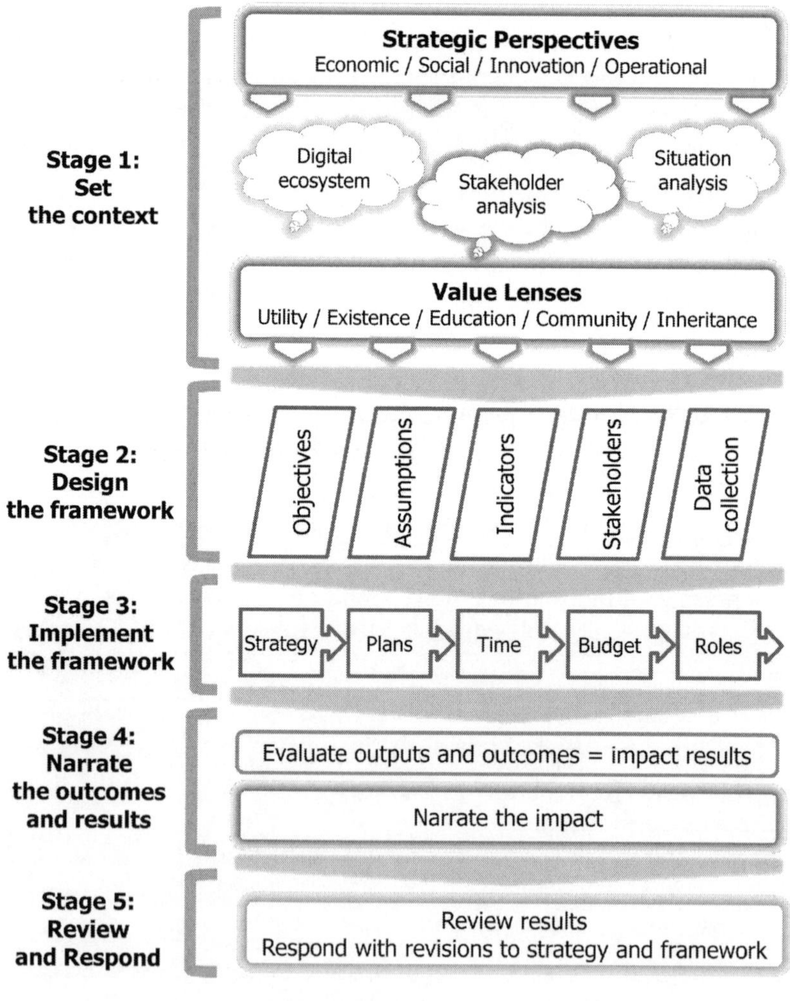

Figure 2.4 *Conceptual overview of the BVI Model*

evidence to decision makers. Without engaging in the process of understanding context and then applying that context to the review and respond stage of the impact assessment, it is highly possible that the impact narrative and results are partial, unusable or lacking in actionable meaning.

The middle stages (2, 3 and 4) are standard activities in almost any assessment of impact. They are required to fulfil the BVI Model. It is notable, though that it would be entirely possible to ignore the first stage and jump straight to Stage 2. Where this happens, then the BVI Model is set aside. However, there are many situations where impact assessment is an exercise of fulfilling a government requirement, measuring a key performance indicator (KPI) or a simple evaluation. In such circumstances, it may be entirely sensible to jump straight to the process from Stage 2 onwards.

The BVI Model is best suited for memory institutions and presumes that the assessment is mostly (but not exclusively) measuring change within the ecosystem of a digital resource.

A user's journey through the BVI Model to Framework might look as follows.

1 In thinking about the memory institution's strategic direction, they map their existent documents/policies/vision statements to the four Strategic Perspectives.
2 They can then use these to focus on their context, investigating the digital ecosystem and the stakeholders and to analyse the situation of the organisation further.
3 These provide a strategic context that allows for decision making about what is to be measured and why that measurement is needed.
4 The practitioner can then use the Value Lens to focus attention on those aspects most productive for measurement in that context. Figure 2.5 on the next page illustrates the measurement goals focused via the Strategic Perspectives and Value Lenses.
5 The Framework (often a spreadsheet – see Chapter 7) can then be completed for each Perspective–Value pairing.
6 This output is built into an action plan for implementation at Stage 3, where the integration of what needs to be measured is related to the practicalities of time, money and other resources.
7 Once all this planning is achieved, then the implementation is phased according to the Framework, and data is gathered alongside any activity measured. The timeframe might be a few months for one

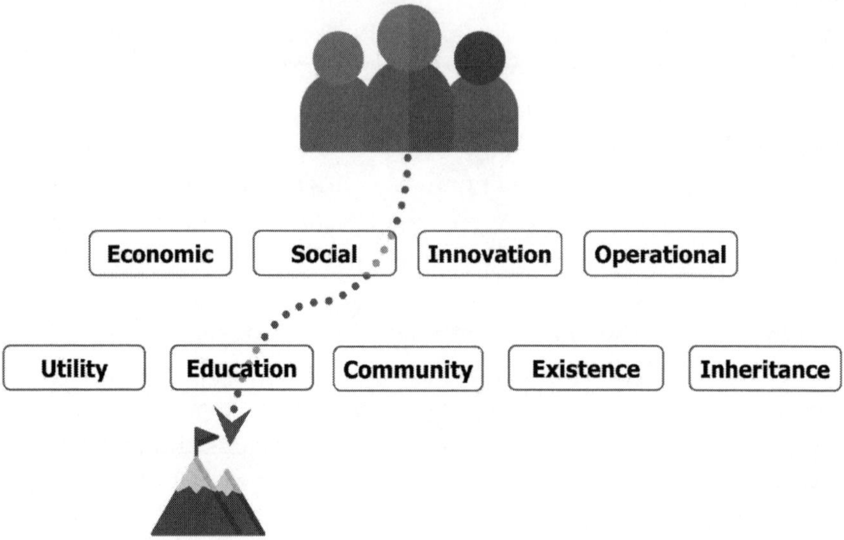

Figure 2.5 *Measurement goals focused via the Strategic Perspectives and Value Lenses*

measure and more extended periods for others – the Framework helps to keep it all in sync and not to lose track of the varied activities.

8 Once a critical mass of data is gathered such that results can be inferred, then the process can start to move into the analysis; narrated via the four Strategic Perspectives: Social, Economic, Innovation and Operational.

9 This narrative acts as a prompt to decision makers and stakeholders to guide future direction and to justify current situations.

10 The stage of revision, reflection and respond assumes that there is embedded continuous learning to allow for decisions made in every stage to be informed by the results and to be modified in response to change, to feedback and to success criteria.

Stage 1: Set the context

Setting the context is made up of the following actions:

1 map to Strategic Perspectives
2 define the ecosystem of the digital resource
3 understand the stakeholders
4 define the appropriate value lens drivers for each strategic perspective.

Chapters 5 and 6 investigate the context steps in detail. Note that the process of designing the Framework in Stage 2 may iteratively influence the context stage. The key elements to consider are summarised here.

Strategic Perspectives

Mapping current strategies or actions against the Strategic Perspectives ensures that the outcomes can be clearly narrated. The understanding gained enables the organisation to review and respond to the results. The BVI Model always applies the following four Strategic Perspectives, defined as:

- **Social impacts**: stakeholders and wider society have been affected and changed in a beneficial fashion;
- **Economic impacts**: the activity is demonstrating economic benefits to society, stakeholders or the organisation;
- **Innovation impacts**: the digital resource represents or enables innovation which is supporting the social, economic or operational benefits accrued;
- **Operational impacts**: the organisation creating/delivering digital resources has been benefited within its internal processes by the innovation demonstrated.

The key benefits of this approach are to align, clarify and gain consensus about strategy in a simple framing that works in many contexts. It further allows for a clear narrative of benefit to be built into the process from the beginning, with two outward-facing perspectives (Social and Economic) and two more internalised perspectives (Innovation and Operational). A holistic strategic context narrates the outcomes and results powerfully as 'our digital resources are benefitting society via these social impacts, leading to economic benefits based in our innovation; while becoming a more effective and efficient organisation'.

Ecosystem

An ecosystem is a set of interdependent relationships among the resources, technologies, hosting organisation, creators and consumers. These must be mapped and described so as to clearly enunciate the ecosystem of the digital resource. The BVI Framework has space to include a summary of the ecosystem of the digital resource. Within the Framework, this is merely a reminder of key aspects of the ecosystem. Behind this must be a broader and deeper set of information to establish the baseline of the technology in question within the assessment.

Stakeholders

This part of the process identifies and characterises a comprehensive, categorised list of stakeholders. In Stage 2, stakeholders are segmented and analysed to identify different groupings to be investigated specifically in response to the needs of the impact assessment. A stakeholder is a person, group, community or organisation who affects or can be affected by the ecosystem of the digital resource assessed.

Situation analysis

Situation analysis (along with the establishment of criteria) assists in defining objectives within the Framework. A 'situation' refers to the context and environment of a digital resource at a specific point in time. It relates to information gathered about the ecosystem, but with an additional process of analysis that defines and interprets the situation, its elements and their relations at a given moment. This element is an audit of current situations. Useful approaches include SWOT or Business Model Canvas, as detailed in Chapters 5 and 6.

Value Lenses

There are five Value Lenses assigned to focus attention on specific assessment activities, reflecting core values measured for their impact. Assign one or more Value Lenses as drivers to any measurement made. The five Value Lenses are:

- **Utility value**: the value expressed and the benefits directly gained by people through active use of the digital resource now or sometime in the future;
- **Education value**: the value expressed and the benefits directly gained by people from their own or others' ability to learn and gain knowledge (formally or informally) from a digital resource;
- **Community value**: the value expressed and the benefits directly gained by people from the experience of being part of a community engaging with or afforded by, a digital resource;
- **Existence and/or Prestige value**: the value expressed and the benefits

people derive from knowing that a digital resource exists and is cherished by a community, regardless of use or non-use of the resource;
- **Inheritance/Legacy value**: the value expressed and the benefits derived by people from the ability to pass forward or receive digital resources between generations and communities, such as the satisfaction that their descendants and other members of the community will in the future be able to enjoy a digital resource if they so choose.

Stage 2: Design the framework

The BVI Model is managed and administered via a Framework that allows a set of impact assessment actions to be recorded in a structured space to enable each element to be planned and completed. By holding all the elements together in one Framework, dependencies between elements can be seen and accounted. Additionally, as some elements may happen in differing timeframes, the Framework allows a bird's-eye view across the entire activity. Impact assessment is partly a matter of asking questions in a structured way and gathering the responses such that they can be understood: much of the process here is about control and organisation.

The BVI Framework is to assist the practitioner to be organised, to be purposeful and to have a common process across all activities. It may be possible and reasonable for actions to be duplicated and repeated across various elements of the Framework (such as data collection, stakeholders or assumptions). This varies according to the size and scope of the assessment.

In Stage 2 the key components are:

- objectives
- assumptions
- indicators
- stakeholders
- data collection.

Table 2.1 on the next page shows an example from the BVI Framework. For each Value Lens, set a separate objective. Objectives will be fulfilled through the assessment of a set group of stakeholders. Assumptions that affect the measurement are recorded. The indicators to measure the objective are defined. For each indicator, a suitable method of investigation is defined, with its method of data collection described.

Table 2.1 *Example of a completed BVI Framework at Stage 2*

Value Lens: Utility				
Impact	**Strategic**	**Indicators**	**Stakeholders**	**Data collection**
Will the resource deliver a change such that new uses and products are made based on the content and/or there is an increase in uptake of services and/or products?	Innovation	Growth in the extent and range of innovative and creative activity	Creative industries, artists, data partners and specialist end-users	• Web analytics • Case studies • Tracking new products • Monitoring social media
	Social	A more socially and culturally aware	Active users of the resource.	• Surveys • Case studies
	Economic	An associated growth in economic activity to indicate that new wealth-	Partner organisations and creative industry businesses	• Surveys • Case studies • Web analytics
	Operational	Growth in usage. An increased capacity to upload new content and respond to user demand	Internal staff and partner organisations	• Management reporting • Statistics • Surveys

Objectives

An objective is an impact outcome that can be reasonably achieved within the desired timeframe and with the available resources. Objectives come from combining the factors explored in Stage 1. Objectives should be expressible in a short, pithy statement that expresses what is to be measured and what the outcome would encompass. The statements are specific to the Perspective/Value pairing and measurable through the indicators and data-collection methods selected.

Stakeholders

Stakeholders are extensively investigated and categorised in Stage 1. There should already be a strong understanding of the stakeholder groups open for investigation. Assign the appropriate stakeholder group(s) to each specific objective. This assignment is a vital ingredient to ensure that the impact assessment produces measurable and meaningful results. Stakeholders are the only group that can transform our understanding of output into a significant outcome, and so investigating a change in the most appropriate, representative group for the outcome explored is critical to success.

Assumptions

No one can measure everything, for all time, in every way possible. As such, there are areas that are deliberately not investigated, or assumptions are made that certain conditions, skills or resources are already in place. For instance, in the examples of objectives given above, the assumptions might include access to an internet-enabled computer or participation in community activities. The listing of assumptions is helpful to ensure that the assessment process is not corrupted from the beginning by an unseen bias or assumption ('everyone has a mobile phone these days') which might either exclude stakeholders or skew the measurement.

Indicators and data collection

Indicators should be specific to the objectives. There should be as few indicators as practicable to demonstrate the change investigated in the objective. Indicators must be SMART (specific, measurable, achievable, realistic and timely), and thus the data-collection methods to support them will be more straightforward to define and design.

Despite the many methods listed at www.BVIModel.org, most data-collection methods fall into a few basic categories: surveys, questionnaires, observation, focus groups, feedback and participatory investigations. The focus of the BVI Model on digital resources also provides some advantages not necessarily available to other impact assessments, most notably the opportunity to reach out digitally to the user base through the digital resource itself or to use web analytics or social media measures to assess change in usage patterns in response to interventions.

Chapter 7 describes Stage 2. There are digital versions of example BVI Frameworks in the resources section of the website that accompanies this book: www.BVIModel.org.

Stage 3: Implement the framework

For each objective, an action plan is described including the timescale for completion, the budget and the specific roles of those who carry out significant aspects of the impact assessment.

Adjust thinking, at implementation, from an impact-centric approach to an activity-centric approach. The BVI Framework is a way of controlling the process – it is not the impact process itself and does not offer a new method of data gathering or metric. Each activity is delivered with an associated impact data-gathering mini-plan to manage that specific process.

The impact mini action plan should state the following:

1. a description of the proposed activity;
2. a list of the resources required to deliver the planned activity, with a budget and timescale;
3. a set of the possible outputs from the activity in terms of an amount of product or service delivery;
4. a list of the expected benefits from the activity;
5. a mapping of how the activity answers impact objective questions in the Framework.

From the beginning, integrate impact measures into the planning and delivery of activities. The Framework allows for control over all those mini-plans to convey a structured process and centralised information hub for evidence of impact.

Chapters 7 and 8 investigate Stage 3 in detail.

Stage 4: Narrate the outcomes and results

Stage 4 focuses on the means of transferring the outputs of data gathering into outcomes that are meaningful demonstrators of impact to be used effectively by decision makers. The direct products of measuring the digital resource are outputs consisting of data in statistical quantitative form and as qualitative evidence. Outputs are therefore often regarded as performance measures or as monitoring information. For instance, a performance measure might focus on how many items were digitised to populate the resource in relation to the expected number predicted in the project plan. Alternatively, the number of online users for a web-based resource over some time is monitoring activity. These are outputs, neither of them is an outcome.

Outcomes are the specific changes and consequences evaluated for aspects such as behaviours, knowledge, skills, status, wealth, well-being or effectiveness. Impacts are the fundamental changes assessed or which occur because the outcomes demonstrate a set of benefits to a defined group in a specific period. Such benefits can be intended or unintended and, most vitally, could be either positive or negative to some or all of the stakeholders.

Evaluating the outputs to find the outcomes and engaging with the emergent impacts can be achieved only with a thorough, in-depth knowledge of the data gathered.

Chapter 9 details the methods and techniques for data evaluation, prioritisation and the narrating of outcomes. The structure provided by the BVI Model means that narration reflects the Strategic Perspectives structure.

Chapter 3 investigates a range of example impact assessments in memory institutions. The source materials demonstrate many approaches and varied media examples for how to communicate impact.

Stage 5: Review and respond

A case having been made for impact through the presentation and communication of the results of the BVI Model process, now is the time to follow through and ensure that the purpose of the impact assessment reaps results. The review and respond aspect of impact assessment is one of the most critical to its success, but is in danger of being the most neglected. Assessment should produce data which leads to action; otherwise, it is purposeless.

Stage 5 is designed to ensure that the results of the BVI Model process are actively used, reflected on and then responded to with an evidence-based response. This stage can help to improve future impact assessments. Further reflection on the possible institutional benefits derived from an evidence-based decision-making process helps to turn ideas into action and promote sustainable change management. Most importantly, this stage should be about making ever deeper connections with stakeholders so as to work with them in response to the evidence and insights gained. This relationship is the most likely means of gaining the greatest benefits for all.

Chapter 10 will guide the reader through Stage 5.

Prerequisites for application of the BVI Model

Before proceeding to an implementation of the BVI Model, consider the following prerequisites of readiness for its application.

- What are the motivations for this organisation to do impact assessment?
- Can the strategic and impact context of the organisation be defined?
- Does the organisation have a definition of impact that works for it and its community? Can one be constructed?

- Is the digital ecosystem understood and is it well defined?
- Are the stakeholders of the organisation well understood and categorised?
- Are the organisation's values understood and can they be mapped to the Value Lenses?
- Does the organisation have sufficient resources to carry out an impact assessment?

The answer for many of these questions may well be a partial yes or a no at present. Chapter 6 will guide on how to become well prepared for planning an impact assessment.

Chapter 3

Impact in libraries, archives, museums and other memory institutions

Framing thinking

This chapter expands on the definition of impact through specific examples of impact in memory institutions.

The use of 'memory institutions' as a collective term for libraries, museums and archives dates back at least to 1994, with the first usage attributed to Swedish information scientist Roland Hjerppe (Hjørland, 2000). In using the term 'memory institution' this book assumes a common aspiration across multiple sectors in preserving, organising and making available the cultural and intellectual records of their societies. It also reflects the confluence with the growth in digital. While this book uses the term as a convenience to refer collectively to libraries, museums and archives it does not assume any primacy in their role as memory institutions, as other places such as schools, universities, media corporations, government or religious bodies are also included within this book's conception of memory institution.

Debate on value and thus on impact in memory institutions has a long history, but became a focal point for strategic thinking in the early 1990s (Griffiths and King, 1994). As definitions of information developed from information as process or knowledge (intangible) to 'information as thing' (tangible) (Buckland, 1991), so too did its valuation. A collection of books or curated objects may be valued as a body of knowledge but not be very meaningful to any tangible measure of knowledge until some person(s) has access to the object or reads the book. This understanding that knowledge is personal and individual is fundamental to value, and thus to impact. The value of the individualised knowledge is attributed by a person and is individually understood, but the outcomes of extended knowledge are collectively shared: thus magnified and tangibly apparent. It is capturing that transition from the personal to the shared that sits at the heart of impact value in memory institutions.

Considering a beneficial change in someone's life or life opportunity means that the intervention in their life through engagement with a digital resource may deliver benefits that are, at heart, advantageous from many perspectives, such as:

- education and learning
- engagement and increase of knowledge
- economy and wealth generation
- health and well-being
- social and community cohesion
- environment and sustainability
- politics and democracy
- technology and innovation
- entertainment and participation
- equality and equity.

Examples of impact in the GLAM sector

A core challenge for the GLAM sector is the difficulty in demonstrating a neat value chain of causality between planned activity and the resulting outputs, leading to clear outcomes and impact. The reasons are often related to scale, the diffusion of the user base and the complexity of the digital ecosystem. However, there are now some exemplars that demonstrate impact.

Case study 3.1: The Wellcome Library's digitisation programme

The Wellcome Library has a very significant digitisation programme, located just down the road from the BL, taking a different approach and integrating impact into a broader framework of evaluation. It is 'developing a world-class online resource for the history of medicine by digitising a substantial proportion of its holdings and making the content freely available on the web' (The Wellcome Library, 2019b). As part of the Wellcome Library's Transformation Strategy (Henshaw and Kiley, 2013) a number of collections have been digitised and included in its innovative and extremely well-formed digital presence. Collections include the Wellcome Arabic Manuscripts Online, recipe book manuscripts, AIDS posters, the very extensive Greater London Medical Officer of Health reports and Codebreakers: Makers of Modern Genetics.

Codebreakers has been the subject of a detailed investigation to evaluate the Library's digitisation programme by measuring four aspects of the project: reach, impact, quality and value for money. The methods for measuring reach, quality and value for money were already in place within the Wellcome Trust (Wellcome). To assess impact, Wellcome worked with the BVI Model to establish their impact assessment framework. Codebreakers is 'an online research resource for the history of genetics, including digitised books and archives from the Wellcome Library and partner institutions' (The Wellcome Library, 2019a). The papers of 22 scientists and organisations have been digitised, including those of Francis Crick, Rosalind Franklin and James Watson.

Wellcome have progressed through stages 1–4 of an initial phase of the five stages of the BVI Model.

Context: Wellcome held a workshop (facilitated by Simon Tanner) to outline the context in which the digital resource Codebreakers is operating; to define the ecosystem of the digital resource and understand their stakeholders; and to agree on the type of impact they wish to measure (social impact, economic impact, impact on innovation or operational processes) and on the type of values they have (Utility, Prestige, Education, Community or Bequest).

Analysis and design: The information gathered in the workshop was analysed and methods for measuring impact against agreed 'value drivers' were discussed, which resulted in the design of a personalised evaluation methodology for Wellcome in relation to Codebreakers. Wellcome created a phased plan to allow for activities over differing timeframes.

Implementation: The plan was implemented to gather data aligned with the types of impact and the values identified. Further data gathering occurs as later phases are implemented.

Outcomes and results: For the initial phases this data is used to give a measure of the impact that is relevant to Codebreakers. It is measured against the types of impact identified in the 'Context' stage.

Review and respond: Wellcome uses these results to review the process, and also to consider potential changes to strategic planning before the process is repeated.

In the Wellcome Library's digitisation programme their Perspective-Value pairings were as shown in Table 3.1.

Table 3.1 *BVI Model Perspective–Value pairings for the Wellcome Library's Codebreakers digitisation project*

Strategic perspective	Value lens
Social	Utility + Community
Innovation	Utility + Community
Operational	Education + Inheritance/Bequest
Economic	Utility

The pairings demonstrate a strategic emphasis on measuring active use and community benefit from the Codebreakers project. Wellcome have a desire to measure value for money, but not to overemphasise the economic element as compared to other priorities. As an organisation, Wellcome also want to measure how they have grown in skills and capacities and delivered on the institutional mission – thus, the focus on Education and Inheritance/Bequest for the internal perspective.

The phased approach at Wellcome means that quantitative measures have produced results, but the more qualitative measures investigating user research and internal impact remain ongoing (Green and Andersen, 2017). Mostly based on web statistics and session metrics regarding page views and time spent, they are indicative and helpful, but will be augmented with more in-depth measures in the future. A considerable amount of work was required to put the measures in place, including, for instance, adding a project code tag in the MARC record to allow for the use of Codebreakers to be assessed separately from that of other sibling resources in the digital library (Green, 2014).

Initial results in 2014 showed that at least 40% of all content in Codebreakers had been looked at one or more times. There was a definite imbalance in usage towards content that had been commissioned as interpretive material (79% of page views), as opposed to the plain digitised source content (21%) (Green, 2014). This suggested both that push modes of engagement were working well and that metadata and guidance on finding source materials could be enhanced to draw researchers deeper into the resource. However, the use of archival content as measured by observing access to the Francis Crick materials demonstrated over 200 times more usage in the digitised content than in the analogue archival collection over comparable periods. Data also showed that Codebreakers digitised content was much used outside the UK and that digitised content gained from partner organisations and contained in Codebreakers was also popular (Green, 2014). These metrics reflect positively on and map closely to the strategic direction of the Wellcome Library. In response to phase one of impact assessment, the Library refreshed its web content strategy to reflect on strategies for enriching metadata (this was seen as a barrier to discovery) and also instigated different marketing approaches based on the knowledge gained to date.

In summary, Wellcome have found the BVI Model a useful framework and a positive process, especially in focusing attention on strategic values and providing a means of impact assessment based on familiar techniques and methods (Chaplin, 2014).

Case study 3.2: Digital library projects in Bangladesh

At a discrete scale, it is sometimes easier to demonstrate causality. For instance, research into sex workers in Bangladesh demonstrates a relatively straightforward causality between the availability of a digital library and the life changes made by those otherwise disadvantaged beneficiaries (Nasiruddin, 2014). The authors report on the Jibon Paribortone Library ('Library for Changing Lives'), a digital library to support 10,000 sex workers:

> Dedicated brothels-based libraries provided them with the opportunity to make their own choices for a better future … to improve the quality of life of the sex workers and their children in a sustainable way through training and learning by the innovative approach of a library.
>
> (Nasiruddin and Nahar, 2013)

They go on to report that in the first year alone some 200 sex workers completely changed profession to other trades (such as making clothes and bags, or working in beauty parlours), while some 300 others had increased their income from trades other than sex work. This is a clear example of how causality is established in the outcomes and impact on those communities targeted by the effect of the digital library's presence.

In a further study, Nasiruddin sought to 'change the lives of the extreme poor children in a sustainable way by the installation of a digital school library in every school of remote rural areas in Bangladesh' (Nasiruddin, 2017). The indicators chosen to show the desired impact are, first, changes in attitude and awareness of the extreme poor, and second, an improvement in the children's enrolment rates. The baselines established provide a tangible target. These are set at:

1. improved pass rate on a standardised test for the poorest children, rising from 10% to 60%
2. increased enrolment rate to 90% (from 40%)
3. increased retention rates to 55% (from 30%) (Nasiruddin, 2017).

The measurement of impact used these quantitative measures plus qualitative survey results. The study results showed dramatic improvements in the ten library project schools for standardised tests and parental awareness and attitude to education. One study cannot solve the obvious challenges of extreme poverty, but the evidence provides a directive to the Bangladeshi government and non-governmental organisations for a successful strategy.

Let's Get Real exemplars

In many respects, the greatest significance of the Culture24 action research has been in the communities of practice and realising the impact of digital engagement on their institutions. This ranges from understanding new things about the audience and participants of the digital services to convincing the organisation to engage differently with digital.

As John Stack, head of Tate Online, stated, metrics 'increased the understanding of the value of social media within the organisation and has helped us to plan our social media content more strategically, by setting objectives for different kinds of posts and evaluating against these objectives' (Finnis, Chan and Clements, 2011).

The Roundhouse performance space realised new things about their audiences through metrics, such as: 'how successful the organisation was in encouraging young users aged 11–25 to access the creative courses offered online ... directly impacted on the organisation's decision to change how these courses are made available' (Finnis, Chan and Clements, 2011).

Elissa Frankle, of the US Holocaust Memorial Museum, reported that they 'uncovered a new truth about working in a digital framework in a physical space: the timelines of digital and traditional exhibition teams are vastly different', and this allowed them to adjust their working practices to enable their exhibitions to be more effective in allowing cross-generational conversations to take place. More fundamental was the realisation that 'we've been putting staff needs and beliefs ahead of visitor needs, and assuming we are our visitors (we're not)', which is a significant shift in understanding for any institution (Malde and Finnis, 2016).

These examples all demonstrate that significant realisations, especially those about organisational culture, are often best fostered by demonstrable evidence to support any narrative for change.

Case study 3.3: Kōrero Kitea project

The Kōrero Kitea project in New Zealand, by studying the impacts of digitised te reo (Māori language) archival collections, recognises the unique position of ethnographic collections on impact. The project focused on the Te reo Māori as a case study, as 'few things represent mātauranga Māori [wisdom] more than the language itself' (Crookston et al., 2016). Te reo archives have been available online for some years, such as newspapers and letters in Māori, and there is a continuing desire to digitise more. This assessment used a narrative-style questioning, committed to understanding impact through studying long-term projects, and put the focus on users, not institutions. The ethnographic approach meant that the survey design prioritised the seeking of narrative responses using open-ended questions. The project were seeking rich qualitative and narrative information, and seem to have been very successful.

The Kōrero Kitea project discovered that 'greater access via digitisation fosters relationships and connections via acts of sharing collections within whānau [extended family], hapū [clans or descent groups], iwi [tribe] and other networks'. Close connections between people, named Whanaungatanga, was a previously unrecorded finding for any digital collection (Crookston et al., 2016). These impacts on kinship, family and community cohesion, cultural identity and legacy for future generations, fostered by digital resources, are very significant to these communities. 'Being able to share and preserve information for future generations was important to respondents and prompts collection providers to be aware of this implication of digitisation' (Crookston et al., 2016). The project were thus able to delineate connections from the digitisation activity to 'macro strategies of the New Zealand government and provide an opportunity for the sector to change how it articulates the value of digitisation in New Zealand' (Crookston et al., 2016).

Case study 3.4: Comparing the impact of two museums

The Museum of Fine Arts in Boston, USA (MFA) and the UK's National Museums Liverpool (NML) published impact assessments within a year of each other, allowing for some comparisons. The MFA has about 1.1 million visitors per year while the NML has some 3.3 million visitors (with free entry). The MFA contributes to the local economy through museum and visitor spending some US$700 million and supports an estimated 1,313 jobs (excluding building projects) (Museum of Fine Arts Boston, 2014; Economic Development Research Group, 2015). NML contributes to the local economy some £97.2 million through similar spending and supports an estimated 1,660 full-time equivalent jobs (National Museums Liverpool, 2013). Both institutions emphasise their community roots and enhancement of the local environment, but the MFA made a stronger case for this in terms of urban regeneration and fresh building projects in their locality. The costs of travel from outside the museums' regions should be factored into the economic spend by visitors – although 60% of the 3.3 million NML visitors come from outside Liverpool (National Museums Liverpool, 2013) the total travel cost inside the UK is far lower than travelling to Boston from other parts of the USA. It would have been useful to have an ROI indicator to show the benefits in those terms and allow for comparisons.

NML show a significant public good in their education programmes, reaching more than 400,000 children in education (National Museums Liverpool, 2013). Both the NML and MFA make strong statements about the impact of their museums on social inclusion and communities. Both institutions make no special mention of digital or web-based impacts from their collections. The areas of focus and priorities in the impact assessments demonstrate the relative strengths and priorities of the institutions. They further demonstrate that impact assessment is always partial, and setting objectives for what outcomes are to be measured will be vital to defining the process and shaping the results of impact assessments.

The British Library: Codex Sinaiticus

Digital projects and resources frequently operate at a much larger scale and in these cases it becomes ever harder to relate the heightened engagement or use to an exacting measure of impact. This is especially true as the digital resources become of less immediately instrumentalist value. For example, the Codex Sinaiticus digital project at the BL reportedly had 20 million hits online in the first 24 hours after project launch, of which some 170,000 turned into continuing visits (Garcés, 2007; First Followers, 2009).

These numbers appear significant, but do they indicate the importance and value of the digital resource to the community or just the newsworthy nature of the project, which was carried by some 450 news organisations? How can we measure the impact in terms of genuine change or enhanced experience when the numbers are so high and yet the user audience and the effect on them is so diffuse?

Case study 3.5: The value of the British Library

The BL assessed valuation for the Library's web services in 2013 as £19.5 million per annum (Tessler, 2013). The total valuation claimed in the same report for BL services was £527.3 million per annum. Compared to the costs reported in 2013, showing that the BL spent £3.6 million on web services out of a total spend of £137 million, those returns on investment for the UK look at first sight to be tremendously encouraging indicators of significant economic impact.

On closer inspection, the means of arriving at these figures is based almost entirely on the time saved and travel costs mitigated for the online user, with an added element of consumer surplus value. The travel and time savings are hard to pin to any one aspect of the BL service provision. Thus, it is difficult to see how these might help to assess an exacting measure of impact other than a statement that online services are a generic good.

Consumer surplus value is the benefit to those who would otherwise never use the BL's resources and is a form of induced demand – effectively, an increase in consumption of a good associated with an increase in supply. The method used to measure it is stated as taking a suggested value from McKinsey (Rausas et al., 2011) relating to 'recreational internet services' of €20 per month and 'used in conjunction with the relative proportion of time spent on the Library's website to derive a consumer surplus value' (Tessler, 2013).

The figures derived from this method are closer to marketing management than impact assessment. Marketing management is defined by Kotler as the 'normative science involving the efficient creation and offering of values to stimulate desired transactions … [the] achieving specific responses in others through the creation and offering of values' (Kotler, 1972). As such, the figures do not contribute to improvements in planning and strategic understanding, as they are a product, an outcome (almost a casus belli), rather than a generator of strategic insight.

Case study 3.6: The economic impact of Canadian libraries

The economic impact assessment of Vancouver Island Regional Library is notable, as it demonstrates not just a positive ROI but also links impact to the Library's mission to 'enrich lives and communities through universal access to knowledge, lifelong learning, and literacy' through four fundamental principles:

- Community
- Collect. Connect. Collaborate. Create.
- Places and Spaces
- Life at Work.

(Vancouver Island Regional Library Authority, 2016)

The study, using an adapted form of market substitution as its method, claims that the Library had a total economic impact of almost C$95 million in 2015. It expresses this as C$5.36 in value received for every dollar invested, or as a ROI of 335% (Vancouver Island Regional Library Authority, 2016). This is quite possibly an underestimation, due to areas in which the Library provides value that could not be measured: 'the impact the Library has on literacy, employment, and social and mental health cannot be measured, but these areas are vital for a healthy, vibrant, successful community' (Vancouver Island Regional Library Authority, 2016).

A market substitution method was used: an approach used in public service sectors to value services by identifying what it would cost to purchase such equivalent services elsewhere. The study analysed three components to calculate total economic impact and ROI:

- direct tangible benefits
- direct spending
- indirect tangible benefits.

For instance, the Library provide free WiFi and logged over 22,000 Gb of use during 2015. They also registered over 125,000 logins by the hour. Using market rates and commercial comparisons, they were able to place a valuation to the public on those technical services of $632,684 per year (Vancouver Island Regional Library Authority, 2016).

When looking at the overall value, one of the most effective narratives of impact was to be able to state that for every hour the Library service is open to the public, they deliver a value of C$1,107 at the cost of just C$277. These are compelling figures and the method used is robust. The one remaining doubt in this method is whether the assumption holds that the service would be bought at equal volume if it were not available free at the point of use as a public service.

The Vancouver study is among the widest and most in-depth of the assessments done in Canada. There is a substantial similarity in the ROI demonstrated across the range of other Canadian public libraries that have done similar assessments (Table 3.2).

Table 3.2 Return on investments demonstrated in Canadian public libraries

Canadian library system	Impact per C$ spent	Return on investment
Sault Sainte Marie Public Library	C$2.36	236%
Halton Hills Public Library	C$4.04	304%
Vancouver Island Regional Library	C$5.36	335%
London Public Library, Ontario	C$6.68	452%
Toronto Public Library	C$5.63	463%
Kawartha Lakes Public Library	C$7.05	605%
Stratford Public Library	C$7.48	648%
Ottawa Public Library	C$5.17	417%

Data source: Library Research Network (http://libraryresearchnetwork.org/).

The Ottawa Public Library advanced their impact narrative by not just adding a ROI of C$5.17 per dollar invested but also showing the benefits per household (C$635), per library cardholder (C$1,038) and per citizen (C$266)(Ottawa Public Library, 2016). They also produced an interactive graphical report to make these impacts easier for their public to understand (https://biblioottawalibrary.ca/en/impact).

These economic impact measures are to be augmented by a follow-up phase to assess social impacts.

Case study 3.7: People's Collection Wales Digital Heritage Programme

The People's Collection Wales (PCW) is a bilingual (Welsh/English) digital service platform for an online collection of Welsh heritage delivered by a federated partnership of National Museums Wales (NMW), National Library of Wales (NLW) and the Royal Commission on the Ancient and Historical Monuments of Wales (RACHMW). They carried out an impact assessment in 2013 adapting the BVI Model with a Theory of Change approach to assess impact across social, innovation, process and economic values (Vittle, Haswell-Walls and Dixon, 2016).

They reported achievements against their strategic priorities as described below.

PCW encourages participation in heritage and improved understanding, knowledge and interest in Welsh heritage. One young person described that 'receiving the training has given me the tools to document my story/my family's story … It's accessible, for all people. You can use the equipment at any time' (Vittle, Haswell-Walls and Dixon, 2016).

People were empowered – there were 'increased skills and opportunities to access and contribute to Welsh Heritage, and to support others to do so' (Vittle, Haswell-Walls and Dixon, 2016).

The life-long learning priority had evidence of progress but not by as much as could have been desired. They saw academics appreciating the research value of PCW and a 'small number of educators reporting positive impacts', while one stated: 'it's so expensive to do transatlantic research, so for academic work PCW is an incredible tool' (Vittle, Haswell-Walls and Dixon, 2016).

The PCW demonstrated the benefits of collaborative approaches to digital issues through the federated partnership: 'People's Collection Wales is the glue that keeps everyone stuck together, e.g. IT, content, visitor experience, hardware' (Vittle, Haswell-Walls and Dixon, 2016). However, the economic, business and tourism impacts were considered to be nascent, but with strong potential.

The PCW demonstrates a robust narrative approach to impact and the report has four detailed case studies to match the areas of investigation. To an extent, it shows how difficult it is to provide a simple impact narrative without a numeric indicator (as shown by the ROI examples from Canada). The impacts are arguably closer to the ideal of demonstrable changes in life opportunities, thus a more nuanced outcome should be expected. For instance, the installation of 'Digital Heritage Stations' across Wales has the aim to 'enable a transformative impact on people's lives through the provision of accreditation, engagement, learning, and digital inclusion'

(Vittle, Haswell-Walls and Dixon, 2016). The effects on the individuals in the study were considerable, with one reporting: 'I've gained a new life skill and a professional qualification which has made career difference. Employers are definitely interested. It has fast-tracked my career' (Vittle, Haswell-Walls and Dixon, 2016).

Europeana implementing the BVI Model

See Chapter 8, written by Julia Fallon, for a user's perspective on implementing the BVI Model through a case study provided by the Europeana Foundation.

The questions focused on in this case study are:

- a reflection on Europeana's implementation of impact assessment with focus on one complete cycle;
- the ideas driving how Europeana developed the *Impact Playbook*;
- how these integrate with the BVI Model.

Chapter 4

Finding value and impact in an attention economy

The challenge of creating digital resources in an attention economy

This chapter will provide the context for decision making about the selection and creation of content for digital resources. Chapters 5 and 6 onwards explore these contexts further, so this chapter focuses on the broad picture of the attention economy and how this influences digital culture. In response to an understanding of the influences and motivators in an attention economy, then a broad concept of how selection and creation of digital content leads towards impactful resources may be considered.

Defining digital resources

The following parameters help to scope what a digital resource is.

- There is a defined resource that is made up of a describable, cohesive set of primary and secondary materials, services, products and activities.
- The resource is accessed primarily through a digital platform (web, mobile or other means).
- The nature of the content within the resource is digital – achieved either through digitisation or as born-digital content.
- There is a definable group of users that the resource is intended to reach by digital means.
- The resource does not have to stand alone; it could be part of a broader set of activities, products or services.

Digital in an attention economy

In the Introduction, the terms 'digital' and the 'attention economy' were both briefly defined. It is instructive that many people can state what digital is with ease, while often not understanding what it does or how it does it. Digital becomes analogous to breathing, in the sense that it has become such a ubiquitous and natural part of our lives to access or receive digital content or technologies that we do so without much conscious thought. Digital does not create a scarcity of *information*. To the contrary, it creates a *digital* deluge that immerses and potentially drowns. The attention economy reflects that the scarcity in a digital domain is not the data or the information. What we are competing for is *attention*, the ability to 'attend to' the information, to take time to spend with a resource. We need to think about that as being one of the leading indicators of success and possible impact.

How much time and attention do we have from our communities, and what does that mean to them? This question is crucial because we will not be able to compete on quantitative numbers alone. Stating we have 100,000 historical photographs in our digital collection when Facebook uploads 350 million photos every day leaves us at a competitive disadvantage. In the attention economy, trying to impress a government minister or major funder with the size of the collection will not work when it can be compared so easily with Facebook and others. However, good, trustworthy, authenticated information is scarce. This is a significant strength that memory institutions have: their resources carry a lot of trust, as well as the attention of their communities. So, instead of competing on numbers we have to compete on the values and benefits of the collections; on the fact that this photograph collection is worth looking at, worth spending time with, and that the community cares that it exists and sees significant benefits in its use. Quality and values are where the small memory institution can compete in the attention economy with the data behemoths. To make this case we have to understand better the digital environment in which we find ourselves immersed.

Digital discoverability

'Try to imagine a culture where no one has ever "looked up" anything,' challenges cultural historian Walter J. Ong (Ong, 1982). Then we can immediately grasp how difficult it is to conceive our culture as one where no one wrote anything down, or one in which we could not refer back to recorded information. Because many of us are now of a generation who have grown up with computers as ubiquitous in our lives, we forget that before their widespread use directly managing information content was limited and very difficult, while managing context was resource-hungry, time-consuming and tended to reflect the narrow concerns of the organisation archiving the content. In many ways, museum collections reflect the historical struggle to provide a context in the material world, and this struggle remains a significant challenge in the digital world. As digital storage and manipulation grew, they biased the equation towards managing content, especially in terms of volume and for textual resources. However, Ted Nelson's 1960s aspiration for his Xanadu system, in which all the books in the entire world would be 'deeply intertwingled' with bi-directional links, has still not been realised (Nelson, 1974). In other words, we understand the principles and the need quite well and have applied them where possible, but rarely are the resources or infrastructure actually available in the digital domain to make contextual information widely shared, usable, robust and powerful.

When people focus on personal benefit, then digital may also be considered analogous to driving a car. We have gained the skills and resources to drive, without many drivers having much, if any, mechanical knowledge. Becoming a safe driver requires a different set of knowledge, and skills that are hard-won for some are relatively easy for others to gain, while the amount of money spent to gain them differs from person to person. The process of obtaining the right to drive (a driver's licence) varies from one country to another, as do the cost of buying or renting a vehicle and the running and eventual replacement costs. Not everyone has a car, and car types and models are very different, often reflecting the owner's wealth. All car users share the three core values on which they base their driving, described as instrumental, symbolic and affective motives (Steg, 2005). The instrumental motive is one of usefulness: can the car transport one efficiently from place to place in an affordable manner? However, we do not drive for utility alone. Steg argues that 'for many people, the car seems to be a status symbol, people can express themselves by means of their car, driving is adventurous, thrilling and pleasurable' (Steg, 2005). For driving, we are not motivated purely by utility and usefulness. Other factors are in play, and we could easily make comparisons to digital culture. Few of these emotions are relative to our understanding of *how the thing works*; rather, they are focused on what it does for or on behalf of us.

Digital is very similar, to the extent that our desire for its use is not directly related to our understanding of how it does that task. The *why* is always paramount in our set of desires for using digital resources. Most users of digital technology, content and services understand enough to obtain the information they think they need or to use technology to create, present or share information. However, with the dawn of digitisation came the opportunity for content (first for printed sources, but latterly for other modes of information carrier) not to be inferred from catalogues and indexes but directly managed, preserved and used. This move has provided a challenge for information workers and users alike, with an accompanying information deluge in which sorting out the useful from the chaff becomes ever more difficult.

This explosion in information, services and resources, whether appropriate to the user's needs or not, consumes attention. Information has to be selected or discarded, read or not read; it cannot be ignored. The actual downside of the information explosion is a deficit of attention, known historically and more popularly as '*information overload*' (Gross, 1964).

What defines a digital resource in an attention economy?

Imagine a visit to Giverny in France. While you are there, your mobile device (which understands your location, preferences and interests) offers information in response to questions such as: 'tell me some historical information about this village and anyone famous who lived here'; 'places to buy Monet souvenirs near where I am now'; 'French gardens and painting'; 'where did Monet live and what colour is his house?' or 'why did Monet paint flowers and gardens?'. In a genuinely digital context-sensitive world, as envisaged by the Semantic Web, widely divergent user needs are supported when seeking this sort of information. These questions are not unusually difficult in human-mediated environments (e.g. libraries, archives or tourist information), but in a digital environment they are not easily answerable unless very rigorous description, and context through metadata, are provided. It is at the point of managing context that our digital plans have provided somewhat frugal results and frustrated our aspirations. In an attention economy, information not being found through these sorts of queries will be tantamount to it not existing for all but experts.

Finding a known object is always going to be easier than finding a range of previously unknown pertinent objects. If the starting perspective of the searcher is unknown because of diversity (e.g. age, education, language), then making a resource findable when it might be text, audio, video, 3D, geographic, database or image based is a challenge to any digital repository. In a known case (e.g. Monet's paintings of Giverny), searches can be constructed by inexperienced users that will almost certainly result in satisfactory retrieval. It is when the user knows only the field of enquiry, and not the precise resource, that searches struggle to be useful. Metadata and tools for resource discovery are needed to allow users to locate the items they seek, whether they know of their existence or not.

Attempts at full interoperability between varied collections, systems and standards, and between communities, have not yet satisfactorily succeeded, and seem unlikely to do so in the near term. Even assuming that technical barriers are crossed, there are political issues of control; resources; legal frameworks; and regional, national and international community differences to overcome. The goal of the worldwide Semantic Web is probably unreachable while the issue of interoperability remains such a major sticking point. The unresolved issues in the transition revolve around money, infrastructure, scalability and sustainability. Frankly, managing content and context in digital resources is a large and unfunded mandate forced on the community. Unfunded mandates are driven by factors such as perceived user demand and the short timeframe in which to take action before digital content will be not just unmanaged but lost to the future.

Reconsidering the digital resource scoping parameters listed earlier, we have to contemplate what makes something a *describable, cohesive set* in an attention economy. Users want the resource and the information; they may be less interested in the format of that information. The format is relevant only when it impedes retrieval or use: if a book is available on a shelf nearby, then that is immediately accessible, but if the book is unique and only available in the physical form many thousands of miles away, then an electronic text will serve the purpose. A significant goal of the memory institution is to find the shortest path between the expression of an information need and its satisfaction. How to provide that shortest path is part of the challenge of how we generate digital/digitised content, deliver it and, most importantly, find the community of users.

The mantra of 'if we build it, they will come' does not work in the attention economy; but equally, not building anything will ensure obscurity. The early history of digitisation has been somewhat blighted by the 'build it' mantra, which reflects the fantasy and wish fulfilment at the core of the story of personal redemption in the movie *Field of Dreams* (based on the book *Shoeless*

Joe). As Wilson opined, 'we build it, hoping people will come, without knowing what we are building, or precisely who will be coming' (Wilson, 2003). It is not access that deters use when building to this mantra, but the resource quality and fitness for a purpose (Rimmer et al., 2008). As Nat Torkington pithily put it:

> You want a massive digital collection: SCAN THE STACKS! You agonize over digital metadata and the purity thereof ... And you offer crap access. If I ask you to talk about your collections, I know that you will glow as you describe the amazing treasures you have. When you go for money for digitisation projects, you talk up the incredible cultural value ... But then if I look at the results of those digitisation projects, I find the shittiest websites on the planet. It's like a gallery spent all its money buying art and then just stuck the paintings in supermarket bags and leaned them against the wall.
>
> (Torkington, 2011)

To combat these problematic assumptions and to build digital resources that will thrive and survive in the attention economy, then, we must understand that context, understand our communities of use with greater precision and be willing to change our perspectives in response to evidence.

Defining the attention economy

The definition of the attention economy used in this book draws heavily on Herbert A. Simon to articulate the concept of attention economics:

> When we speak of an information-rich world, we may expect, analogically, that the wealth of information means a dearth of something else – a scarcity of whatever it is that information consumes. What information consumes is rather obvious: it consumes the attention of its recipients. Hence a wealth of information creates a poverty of attention, and a need to allocate that attention efficiently among the overabundance of information sources that might consume it.
>
> (Simon, 1971)

What we take notice of, and the regarding of something or someone as interesting or important, delineates what we consider worthy of attending to and thus defines our economics of attention.

The attention economy is also an expression of the way the digital domain is inverting centuries of cultures of creation and consumption:

> From photography to news and encyclopedic knowledge, the centuries old pattern has been one in which relatively few people and organisations produce content and most people consume it. With the advent of the web … that pattern has reversed, leading to a situation whereby millions create content in the form of blogs, news, ideas, videos, music, and product reviews, and relatively few can attend to it all.
>
> (Huberman, 2013)

There are marketplaces of attention that express the attention economy, and memory institutions interact with these markets all the time. Content producers and providers – such as magazine publishers, advertisers and broadcasters – are dependent on the viewer's attention that they exchange for money thousands of times per day. When a company talk of monetising content, they generally mean finding the right marketplace to turn attention into cash. This economy responds to the laws of supply and demand. As the volume of information increases, so demand for attention also increases and we can see this driving business decision making to try to gather an ever-greater membership/following to supply attention. This creates a marketplace based on digital content and usage that can be challenging for libraries, archives and museums – their concerns do not necessarily align with the marketplace.

Focal attention

The other foundational principle of the attention economy is that the currency of the economy has to be scarce. The currency here is attention, and, on an individual basis, it is unlikely that many of us can contemplate giving more attention to our world than we currently achieve. In this respect, so as to be more precise, it is worth refining the definition of attention to that of 'focal attention'. As defined by Schachtel in 1959, focal attention is 'man's capacity to center his attention on an object fully, so that he can perceive or understand it from many sides, as clearly as possible' (Neisser, 2014). We can thus imagine the consequences of focal attention. We cannot be in two places at once; we cannot (despite the best assurances of technology) concentrate fully on several things at once; and our performance decreases in states of attention overload when we are asked to multi-task. Referred to as the cognitive bottleneck theory, this shows that when two cognitive tasks are performed simultaneously there will be a decrease in performance in at least one of the tasks (Wood et al., 2012). In short, if attention goes in one direction it cannot be in another; this is the scarcity of resource in the attention economy. The choices we make and how we allocate our attention are crucial factors that determine how a currency is made out of attention.

This assertion may suggest that time is the best proxy for an attention currency. However, time has to be qualified so as to show a value to the attention given. We might assume that 20 minutes of a teenager's seven hours' daily online time is less significant to them than the same 20 minutes for an octogenarian who spends one hour per day online. Davenport and Beck state: 'I don't know if anyone is actually attending to my Web site, but I can measure the total time it was displayed on someone's screen.' However, this is not necessarily a satisfying measurement of attention, whereas if the payoff of attention allocation is 'I can learn something, change something for the better, fix what's broken, or gratify another human being', then the benefits become more tangible (Davenport and Beck, 2001). Measuring impact is one of the most satisfying measures and units of currency for the attention economy.

Examples of the attention economy

In the attention economy, how we spend our time and consume, produce or create with that time matters. It is directly related to value, whether monetary or social. Consider the way that being an aggregator and organiser of content allows businesses to find the market share and to profit by capturing our attention with beneficial, value-driven services. Facebook is the world's largest popular media owner, but creates no content itself; Alibaba is the world's most valuable retailer/marketplace, but carries no inventory (unlike its rival Amazon). Services like Uber and Airbnb are growing into the world's largest taxi and accommodation providers, respectively, but neither service owns taxis or property; they are merely aggregating the material world to provide a service. These are expressions of the attention economy – they are simplifying and concentrating the flow of information for us and using it to direct a value-driven service rather than a content-driven service. People stay and take notice because it adds value to time, productivity and experiences.

Academic attention

Attention is often also the primary currency in many aspects of academic behaviour and endeavour. Research for the Academic Book of the Future asked the question: 'why do academics write books?' (http://academicbookfuture.org/). The reasons for writing academic books are multifaceted, but motivations keep showing a strong relevance to the attention economy and the role of memory institutions. As Jerome McGann asks and answers:

> 'What do scholars want?' Whether we work with digital or paper-based resources, or both, our basic needs are the same. We all want our cultural record to be comprehensive, stable, and accessible. And we all want to be able to augment that record with our own contributions.
>
> (McGann, 2010)

This answer suggests a significant role for memory institutions, including publishers, intermediary booksellers and libraries. For, without them, the attributes of 'comprehensive, stable, and accessible' are very hard to conceive. For the cultural record to be comprehensive, the content must be created, and publishers, whether commercial or open access, have an important role to play. Intermediaries ensure that content gets to a public who can give it due attention and make new content to provide stable growth in the record and our access to it. For the record to remain sustainable and accessible over the long term, then the role of libraries, archives and museums becomes of paramount importance.

The attention economy is relevant as academics publish to augment that cultural record which requires the attention of others (however distant in time from the point of writing). Academics cite the work of others to signal their attention to that work, and so the writers receive attention in turn – not to cite is to commit poor scholarship. Academic promotion and greatness are rooted in the way that an idea or work gathers attention and currency. As Anne Welsh puts it, 'it's not the people who write the book who make the future. It's the people who read the book and implement it' (Welsh, 2015).

Digital cultures

We can also seek to demonstrate the impact of the attention economy on digital cultures of creation and consumption. The most important products for the mobile generation (the 'killer-apps') are the platforms for self-expression and communication. As billions of people use web-based consumer, informational, social and cultural resources/services they also want to share, discuss and re-use content with each other related to their discoveries, interests and ideas. The internet meme is a simple example of this, whether related to current political events, a new provocative piece of writing or a 'cats vs cucumber' video. This leads to the production of new information through immense social and cultural networks that can extend beyond limitations of geography, culture or personal relationships.

There is a significant shift from the broadcast model still clung to by many media and publishing organisations. In this environment the YouTube channel of an individual, such as seven-year-old Ryan ToysReview (18 million subscribers) can compete with a similar weekly viewership when compared to top TV shows such as *America's Got Talent* (~14 million) or *Britain's Got Talent* (~8–11 million) (Broadcasting Audience Research Board, 2019; Nielsen, 2019). Ryan ToysReview earned $22 million in 2018, all without the implicit production costs of those TV shows, nor with any of the supporting promotion, marketing or celebrities (Robehmed and Berg, 2018).

Swedish gamer Felix Kjellberg, known as PewDiePie, has been able to overcome significant scandal to remain the most followed YouTuber (91 million subscribers). Despite a series of nasty anti-Semitic videos in 2018 which caused a loss of sponsors – such as Disney – advertisers are still paying up to $450,000 for a sponsored video (Robehmed and Berg, 2018). Will Ryan ToysReview and PewDiePie still be as popular in 2025? Nobody knows, but they illustrate the disruptive effect of self-expression based content, how people consume media on digital platforms and the attention it can garner.

These examples also reflect, in part, the shift in how time is spent. In 2008 an American adult would spend roughly 2.7 hours a day with digital media. By 2018 that had doubled to 5.9 hours per day, with mobile making up most of that growth (3.3 hours) (Meeker, 2018). Globally, internet penetration has risen in the same period from 24% to over 50%. In China, online advertising revenue has grown fivefold, to US$50 billion, from a baseline of US$10 billion in 2012 (Meeker, 2018).

Considered from a different perspective – that of the share of consumption by media platform – the same trends emerge towards digital media devices, mobile in particular, with print suffering the most in consequence.

The attention economy also functions in a state of 'increasing returns to scale', which, quite unfairly, ensures that the more of anything you have to begin with, the easier it is to get more of it in the future. Increasing returns are thus mechanisms of positive feedback that reinforce that which gains success or aggravate that which suffers loss. 'If I'm a rock star, anything I do will attract attention. If I'm a very well known politician or CEO, any

Table 4.1 Media platform consumption share USA, 2008 vs 2015

Platform	Share of consumption	Share of consumption
TV	44%	38%
Digital desktop/laptop	23%	21%
Digital mobile device	3%	22%
Print	11%	4%
Radio	18%	13%
Other connected devices (e.g. game console)	2%	3%

Data source: Internet Trends (Meeker, 2015).

pronouncement I make will be covered by the press' (Davenport and Beck, 2001). In the attention economy this increasing-returns effect generates not equilibrium but instability – the rock star could get positive publicity one day and be destroyed by the media the next. If a service, product or technology gets ahead, increasing returns can magnify advantage and the product or company or technology can go on to lock in the market. This is part of the process of disruptive technologies, where one part of the market may get a head start on the rest. In terms of attention, it also works in network effects, where the more participation in a given network exponentially increases the overall value of the network – for example Twitter, LinkedIn or Alibaba.

The significance of the attention economy to memory institutions

On the one hand, the increasing returns on scale have worked for some of the very largest memory institutions in an attention economy context. For example, the Codex Sinaiticus digital project at the BL reportedly had 20 million hits in the first 24 hours after its launch (Garcés, 2007). These numbers are significant; they indicate the relationship between the value of the digital resource to the community and the newsworthy nature of the project, carried by some 450 news outlets. However, with publicity and attention come both positive and negative attitudes. The Library of Congress, despite its many successful digital projects, especially in the field of digital preservation and digitisation of newspaper and sound/video archives, has been criticised for not delivering on its early promise. For instance, the Twitter archive at Library of Congress remains inaccessible and is now defunded (Library of Congress, 2017; Zimmer, 2015). The *New York Times* and the *Washington Post* criticised the Librarian of Congress, James Billington:

> The relentless growth of its collections, which top 160 million items, and push to digitize them have strained the institution's staff and budget, making its IT systems that much more important. But instead of adopting recommendations to improve IT efficiency, Billington has a long record of ignoring them.
>
> (McGlone, 2015)

The extensive negative attention forced Billington to retire from his long-held post. The conclusion of his peer Robert Darnton that the 'Library of Congress sat on the sidelines while this digital revolution took place' (Shear, 2015) is an especially damning assessment of the lost opportunities for funding, partnership and impact. The attention given to the new Librarian of Congress, Carla Hayden, and the new appointments she immediately made to important digital roles, have led to a new strategy, including Library of Congress Labs to test projects that use the Library's digital collections in innovative ways: 'the Library is adopting a digital-forward strategy that harnesses technology to bridge geographical divides, expand our reach, and enhance our services' (www.loc.gov/ digital-strategy).

The attention economy can be particularly kind to large memory institutions in enabling increasing multipliers on their returns from scale. Many small to medium-sized organisations would love to be able to attract the same levels of attention from their communities of use and from the media. In many ways, the digital domain offers the chance for a smaller organisation to play on an equal footing with the largest players, as the digital public is agnostic on the host of the resources, and more motivated by the value of the content than by the provider. For example, in 2012 William Noel, then at the relatively small Walters Art Museum in Baltimore, Maryland, gave a TED talk in which he said:

> we have put up all our manuscripts on the web for people to enjoy, all the data, descriptions, all the metadata with a Creative Commons License … the result of this is if you do a Google search on images right now and you type in "illuminated manuscript Koran" for example, 24 of the [top] 28 images you'll find come from my institution.
>
> (Noel, 2012)

This example demonstrates how a medium-sized organisation can excel in the digital domain and find a user base for its unique content in an attention economy. However, with attention comes scrutiny, and if the core activities are not delivering the expected value and impacts, then this scrutiny can be negatively ferocious in effect. It is no use to an organisation to garner attention if it does not deliver the impact desired by its community.

Historically, memory institutions have shunned value, evaluation, economics or impact as a means of defining success or as management techniques for strategic improvement. While the concept of the attention economy has existed since at least the 1970s and possibly can be seen reflected as early as Ranganathan (Ranganathan, 1931), the role of memory institutions as providers of both primary source and aggregated material was not deeply challenged until the attention-grabbing digital medium gained a series of massive boosts in public use. This happened in three main phases: first, in 1994 with the development of the web, then in the early 2000s with the development of social media and easy digital creation/sharing, followed by acceleration from 2010 onwards as mobile devices connected to high-speed networks became ever-more ubiquitous.

Memory institutions' importance and core roles have not changed significantly. Claims of reducing budgets and increased competition are not new. As was stated in 1994, 'since the 1980s there has been a tightening of budgets ... In order to be competitive, libraries have had to provide stronger arguments concerning the usefulness, value, and worth of their services' (Griffiths and King, 1994). Further mandates added because of the growing digital domain remain mainly unfunded, or exist in a hyper-competitive environment where funding and investment of any kind are predicated on a defined Return on Investment (ROI). Such ROIs are set by government agencies (the UK Treasury Green Book, for instance), funding body agendas (see the US National Endowment for the Humanities) or the commercial market's desire for profit. If we cannot demonstrate the value of the work done, nor show that it succeeds within the attention economy, then the funding will not flow.

Finding value in an attention economy

This book will guide the strategic thinking required to deliver impactful digital resources. Understanding the importance and relevance of the attention economy to the impact agenda is a useful first step in planning future activities and reviewing current practices. Later chapters will concentrate on issues of Strategic Perspectives and Value Lenses to keep impact focused on the core issues driving memory institutions.

Some immediate questions to consider include the following.

1 How does the organisation engage in the attention economy?
   a Carry out a basic audit of activities and relate them to the themes in this chapter.
   b Check Chapter 9 for further advice on marketing and positioning with decision and policy makers.
2 How is digital content being used, re-used and actively shared online at present?
   a Consider a basic information audit.
   b Check the digital ecosystem in Chapters 5 and 6 for further advice.
3 Do the current selection criteria for what gets made available online take into account possible impact, and are they evidence based?
   a Can the selection policy be revised for digital content?
   b Can the collection management strategy be reviewed?
4 Does the organisation consult its stakeholders? Proceed by consulting the principal beneficiaries of the collections with a genuine desire to listen to their ideas.
   a Consult the stakeholders, and see Chapters 6 and 10 for further advice.
   b Create a selection advisory board.

Selecting content for digital resources

In this context, selection focuses on collection management rather than acquisition or appraisal. Assume that the items to be considered for selection are already contained in the collection or soon will be. The goal of the selection process is to ensure that any materials digitised or made digitally available will be used extensively and will be well regarded, valued by the user community, cost-effective and legally sound. The organisation may already have digital strategies and relevant collection policies; now would be a good time to consider reviewing them to see if they can be augmented to include a stronger reference to the intended impact goals set out in this book.

The needs and demands of the user base are paramount in selection decisions. Without a good understanding of them, decisions will not have a sufficient evidence base for management of the process, nor is there likely to be an audience from whom to garner attention once the digitisation is completed. There may be a temptation to look backwards to determine selection criteria, using the curator's sense of value to decide on what should be made available, or allowing considerations of popularity to drive decisions. While these are important considerations, they may stifle forward planning for the intended benefits and impacts desired.

Planning for resources and activities such that they will deliver desired outputs is standard practice. Many digital project teams are skilled in delivering millions of digital objects to their communities. What impact brings to planning is the consideration of stages and steps far beyond those outputs. It forces a focus toward the outcomes or benefits that will be experienced by the digital community if the outputs are achieved. Be more ambitious; state the objective of change to the stakeholder community and organisation, such that it is measurable and so as to demonstrate that it has occurred.

Other decisions within this process might include:

- assessment and selection of originals for digitisation;
- feasibility testing, costing and piloting;
- copyright clearance and intellectual property rights management;
- preparation of original materials, including conservation;
- benchmarking of processes and technologies;
- digital capture, including scanning, digital imaging, OCR, digital recording for audio/video;
- quality assessment and assurance;
- metadata for discovery, data management, preservation and administration;
- storage solutions for long-term preservation and sustainability of the digitised content;
- delivery mechanisms to get the end digitised content to the user;
- workflow processes to effectively manage the flow of activity;
- project management (of crucial importance) to ensure time, money, risk and deliverables are well managed;
- physical condition of materials and resources available.

This non-exhaustive list includes just some of the processes. No digitisation activity should proceed without knowing the plan and technologies for each one. Underlying these are a range of other issues specific to each form of original material, to each information goal desired from the digitisation process and the intended functional outcomes. As a rule of thumb, if you are unable to provide the information or answers to support each part of the process as listed here, then do not start until that information is available or the decision has been made.

Getting digital content online is very process-driven. It is treated often as a neutral technology or naturally beneficent activity. A brief consideration of the varied facets and components of these processes demonstrates that digitisation has so many aspects that its impact intrinsically links to the broader context of its application. Digitisation, especially of cultural heritage, brings 'a curious and unprecedented fusion of technology, imagination, necessity, philosophy and production which is continuously creating new images, many of which are changing the culture within which we live' (Colson and Hall, 1992, 75). Michelle Pickover, ex-curator of manuscripts at the University of the Witwatersrand in South Africa, argues that 'Cyberspace is not an uncontested domain. The digital medium contains an ideological base – it is a site of struggle' (Pickover, 2014).

Genuine consultation with stakeholders is essential – never assume that the digitisation or digital delivery of heritage or cultural collections will be a neutral process, or that the custodian/curator/collection owner knows best. Remember that past decisions made about which items should be included in collections still influence decisions made today, but that none of them was inevitable and they often reflect biases at that time. Consult Chapters 6, 9 and 10 for further guidance on how to engage stakeholders towards a more impactful digital resource.

There are persuasive arguments that digital resources have the potential to bring a range of opportunities to some of the world's most marginalised groups. The Australian Ara Irititja project supports and preserves local identities via a database of over 50,000 digital images and sound recordings of indigenous Australian Aṉangu culture (www.irititja.com). One way to further engage with the stakeholder community is to establish a selection advisory board to define selection criteria and to advise on ethical issues and community-based needs.

Other likely factors for consideration in the selection of materials are the following:

- What is the proposed significance of the content? Consider perspectives of:
  - social
  - political
  - cultural

  - heritage
  - economic
  - legal
  - environmental
  - technological.
- What is the chronological coverage, density and completeness?
- What is the geographical distribution, providing a sense of place?
- Novelty: how can the outputs provide a new experience? Few users will keep attending to content that they have viewed already or that is lacking new insights.
- What family content will be provided? Genealogical perspectives on content, putting people into the centre of the search, are fantastically popular with users.
- What is the intended research value, including academic, personal and professional values?
- How will repetition of others' work or collection content be avoided?

By means reflecting on and reviewing the impact evidence gathered (Chapter 10), the collection development can be kept relevant and responsive to the stakeholder community; decisions on digitisation investment will be more evidence-driven and thus will better serve the community of users.

Chapter 5

Strategic Perspectives and Value Lenses

Introduction

This chapter will provide the background and reasoning for adopting the concepts of Strategic Perspectives and Value Lenses in an impact assessment. It will establish the originating foundation stones of theory and influences that underpin the BVI Model. At the core of this chapter is an explanation of the way strategy interacts with values in a broader context, including a focal case study from the SMK to illuminate these strategic issues.

Strategy and values in memory institutions

What is a strategy?

A strategy, most simply, is a plan of action designed to achieve a long-term or overall aim; it is the answer to the question 'where are we going and why?' Strategy differs from the everyday management processes and plans implemented as a procedure, policy or protocol that answers a different question: 'how do we get things done around here?'

As Freedman puts it, a strategy is 'about maintaining a balance between ends, ways, and means; about identifying objectives; and about the resources and methods available for meeting such objectives' (Freedman, 2013).

Technology is accessible to logic and planning, whereas it is always the human factor that provides the greatest variable, the most unknowable link in any chain of actions. Thus, a strategy is also much more than a plan. A plan supposes a sequence of events that allows the organisation to 'move with confidence from one state of affairs to another' (Freedman, 2013), but, as is often stated, no plan or project survives its first engagement with people fully intact. Alternatively, as heavyweight boxer Mike Tyson memorably put it, 'everybody has plans until they get hit for the first time' (*Los Angeles Times*, 1987). This quote also reflects the military origins of a lot of strategic rhetoric that pervades the literature.

The balance between ends (desirable outcomes), ways (plans for achieving outcomes) and means (what resources or inputs can we mobilise) is delicate, requiring a clear sense of the starting situation and the desired outcomes. A strategy usually assumes some challenges, conflict or contest – if the steps to the destination are clear, smooth, low risk and uncontested, then this is hardly worth being named a strategy. It is when there are conflicting needs, competition for scarce resources, contested digital spaces, intangible rewards or high risks that the most effective approach is a strategic one.

A strategy should ideally be able to describe the desired end state, with a set of tangible outcomes delivered for a set expenditure of resources. Resources could be people, time, money, knowledge, infrastructure, materials and other assets that can be drawn on in order to function effectively and achieve set goals. As resources transform, through use in support of a strategy to produce benefit, they may be consumed or made unavailable. As such, strategic thinking has to deal with a large number of variables and usually addresses this through having:

- an overarching vision of the desired outcome based in shared values;
- a clear set of 'ground truths' to establish an accepted group understanding of the reality of a given situation;
- a set of resource-based plans aimed at transforming resource use into desired benefits.

It makes sense to plan strategically, as risk from the inherent unpredictability of people, events, future technologies and the actions of competing forces lends management its drama and challenge. Conflicts may be mild (in macro terms), say between those in an organisation supposedly pursuing the same goals but with differing responsibilities or resources. In every circumstance, understanding the strategic context is a positive step towards clarifying goals and focusing on the benefits and values to be achieved.

In an attempt to simplify this strategic thinking process, some have adopted a logic-model approach and others a business-modelling approach. The W. K. Kellogg Foundation Logic Model Development Guide provides a useful overview of the transition from data gathering, through outputs, to outcomes and impact (W. K. Kellogg Foundation, 2004). The Model is shown in Figure 5.1.

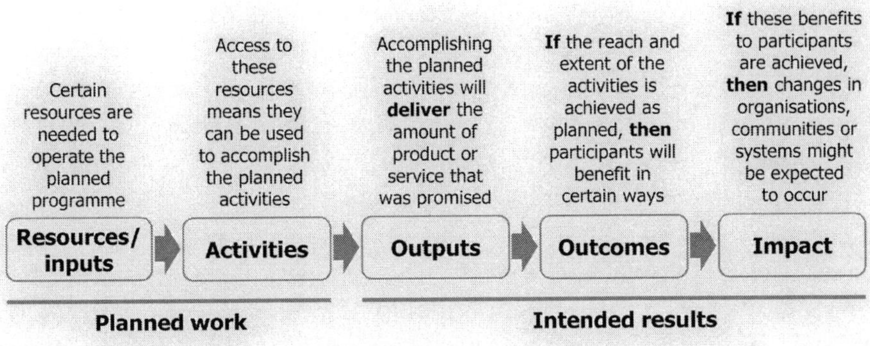

Figure 5.1 *The Kellogg Foundation Logic Model*

The Strategyzer Business Model Canvas (https://strategyzer.com/) is also a useful tool to describe the rationale of how an organisation creates, delivers and captures value. Figure 5.2 shows the Canvas. It translates the complex interlocking elements of an organisation or unit of activity into nine building

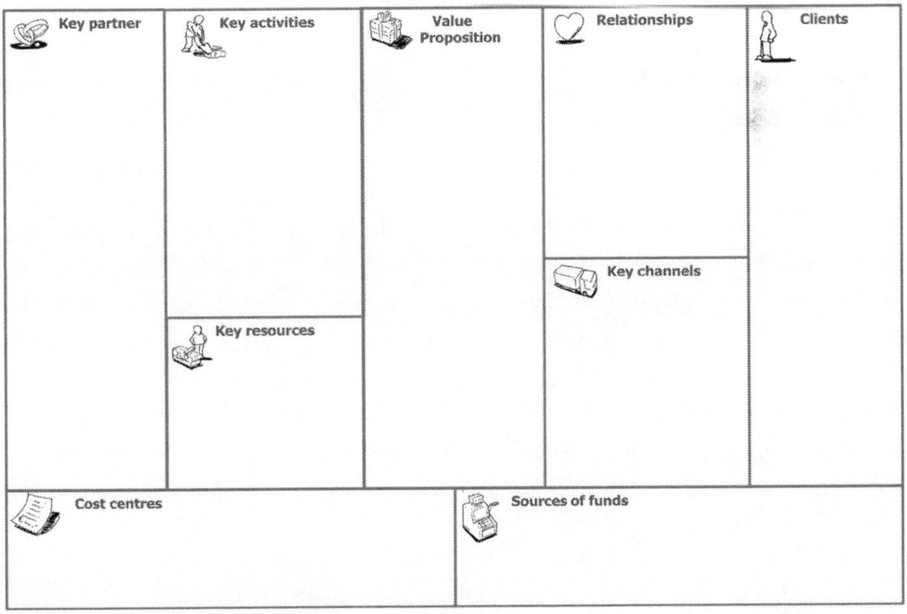

Figure 5.2 *The Strategyzer Business Model Canvas*

Source: Osterwalder et al. (2010)

blocks that show the logic of how they operate and add value and benefit. The primary purpose of the Canvas is to foster understanding and to encourage discussion, creativity and analysis in strategic thinking.

Many organisations have adopted and adapted the Strategyzer Business Model Canvas to meet their specific needs (see Chapter 6). We will return to both the Canvas and the Kellogg Foundation Logic Model later in the book when discussing their use by Europeana in their impact modelling (Chapter 8). Such attempts to simplify and control are a response to complexity in strategic management scenarios.

The BVI Model is a similar response, seeking to bring clarity to the challenge of impact strategy. However, it is still rare that any project or activity of complexity will progress in an orderly fashion to achieve its goals set in advance. As the process evolves, a feedback loop of reappraisal and modifications should support the strategy and its ultimate objectives. All strategy has to be flexible and somewhat fluid, governed by the starting contexts that define what is achievable.

What is value?

Value is individually understood and attributed but collectively shared, and thus magnified.

> We must look again at the relations between knowledge and values, the criteria according to which we say something is good, beautiful or true.
>
> (Smith, 2007)

There is neither time nor space here to work through all the implications of Roger Smith's statement in his seminal book, *Being Human*. These values encompass considerations as broad as the good of a nurse's healing touch, the beautiful dawn's light or the life-long search for enlightenment compared with the good use of a well-built bridge, the beauty of an elegant equation to a mathematician or the true line of a building in its landscape. These examples reflect the complexity of the term 'value', a concept that is deeply ingrained in the human psyche.

> The word 'value' describes an idea about economics, an idea about personal expression and an idea about morality.
>
> (O'Brien, 2013)

O'Brien here summarises the core foci of how the term value is used in cultural contexts. Value is sometimes described as an economic marker for worth or how much a product or service is valued compared to others, as indicated by price or willingness to pay. At other times, value is used as an arbiter for preference, satisfaction, aesthetics or taste at any given moment. Morality means that value sits on an axis of moral and ethical debate against factors such as security, integrity, authenticity and validation. Often these economic and humanistic values are in tension with each other. As the anthropologist Daniel Miller stresses, value when expressed as 'prices' is directly opposed to value understood as 'values' (Miller, 2008).

From an impact point of view, this can become an unhelpful debate about value that concentrates on 'worth' versus 'worthiness'. When focused on worthiness it could be used to posit that museums are more worthy than libraries, and vice versa. Asking whether the Natural History Museum is 'better than', for instance, the Science Museum or the Wellcome Trust Library is an unanswerable comparison if 'better' equates worthiness. Another example might suggest that a digitised collection is somehow more worthy than a school textbook in teaching children, or vice versa. Worth asks only the question 'how much is this worth to me to pay for it?' and solely constructs value as an economic measure ('is it worth my time or money?'). This book considers the outcomes and impact of a digitised resource or a memory institution. As such, worth or worthiness is not a particular point of focus and may be left to others to derive or assume from the impact reported or the outcomes delivered.

Value, as perceived by stakeholders, can be fluid in an attention economy and no memory organisation can set its own value. What is possible is to consider what values are essential to the organisation and its stakeholders and to measure indicators of these values.

> Digital resources are valuable to different audiences for different reasons, and some value may not be realized immediately.
>
> (Hughes, 2012)

Consider a value from a user's or stakeholder's viewpoint. It will usually fit to one of several categories.

- **Transaction value,** in which the value of the transaction is estimated as if it were a purchase or exchange of goods. This may include the willingness to pay for a service or time spent. For example, how much is an hour of free WiFi service in the library worth if charged for commercially?

- **Implied value,** in which the quantitative data about performance is an indicator of value; for example, the equating of an increasing volume of downloads as a signifier of user demand. These are often the basis of a KPI.
- **Relative value,** where the service or product is compared to other services/products to reveal benefits. An example is a comparison of the public archive family history database to a social care Alzheimer's self-help resource.
- **Intangible value,** where the value cannot be tangibly touched and is not recordable as a transaction value or indicated by a set of assets. Memory institutions rely on intangible values such as knowledge, brand or goodwill. It remains hard to determine intangible value because of its fluidity in an attention economy. The next section focuses on intangible value as a vital component of the BVI Model.
- **Cost-benefit value relationships,** demonstrating the value gained from any given investment of time or resources. This could be the benefit received by digitising artworks in a museum such that they can be used many times without further notable costs. The benefit of speeding up finding a digitised engineering drawing to an oil company in saved engineer's time is another example. The cost-benefit value may also relate to ROI. For instance, an investment of £1 million in digitisation of newspapers may be perceived as 'good' ROI because it results in 200,000 users per day.

The missions of memory institutions are reflected in many virtues that are deeply ingrained in human perception. These extend well beyond the purely economic. It is critical to find ways to unchain digital value from solely economic measures and to express value and impact as vectors of a multi-variant environment.

As Bobby Kennedy made so evident in his 1968 speech at the University of Kansas, money is not an adequate measure on its own and without context:

> Our Gross National Product, now, is over 800 billion dollars a year, but that Gross National Product – if we judge the United States of America by that – that Gross National Product counts air pollution and cigarette

> advertising, and ambulances to clear our highways of carnage. It counts special locks for our doors and the jails for the people who break them. It counts the destruction of the redwood and the loss of our natural wonder in chaotic sprawl … Yet the Gross National Product does not allow for the health of our children, the quality of their education or the joy of their play. It does not include the beauty of our poetry or the strength of our marriages, the intelligence of our public debate or the integrity of our public officials. It measures neither our wit nor our courage, neither our wisdom nor our learning, neither our compassion nor our devotion to our country, it measures everything in short, except that which makes life worthwhile.
>
> (Kennedy, 1968)

Balancing intangible values

In theoretical terms, an intangible value is the residual balance of the total value given by the market to any organisation less the total value of its net tangible assets (e.g. buildings, money, infrastructure, objects). In a heritage context, tangible value is often associated with artefacts, historic sites or places that are considered by organisations like UNESCO or ICOMOS (the International Council on Monuments and Sites) as 'inherently and intrinsically of value' (Smith and Campbell, 2018). Intangible value is something that cannot be touched (such as education or social memory) or has a significant information component (such as a patent) and has greater fluidity, possibly changing in value over time and between different groups (such as beliefs, interests or symbolic associations).

Intangible value is an essential concept for memory institutions and digital resources to grasp. They rely on intangible values such as knowledge, social memory, brand or goodwill. It remains nigh on impossible to fix a single price on an artwork, a piece of information or digital culture. However, it is possible to measure their alignment with value-creating strategies. Intangibles have different worth for different people, as they do not have or create value by themselves and are valuable only in context. As the Kennedy quote above states, the quality of education should not be measured solely through the economic success of a country.

This valuing of intangibles is often in tension with concepts of intrinsic value:

> Mozart is Mozart because of his music and not because he created a tourist industry in Salzburg … Picasso is important because he taught a century new ways of looking at objects and not because his paintings in the Bilbao Guggenheim Museum are regenerating an otherwise derelict northern Spanish port.
>
> (John Tusa, 1999, cited in Reeves, 2002)

Mozart did not create the tourist industry, but this does not mean that there is no intangible value for tourism as a result of his music. In the Picasso/Bilbao example, others created the tourist industry or the museum. These efforts are allowed to be valued in their own right, even if they are drawing heavily on the intrinsic value of the music or art. Intrinsic value here means the value that something has in itself, as opposed to an instrumentalist value which is defined by its helping to get or achieve some other thing.

In memory institutions, delivering digital content has traditionally been based on a highly aspirational model. As Dame Lynne Brindley, ex-chief executive at the BL, stated:

> We are sitting on a goldmine of content … to support Digital Britain we need to deliver a critical mass of digital content. Access ought to be the right of every citizen, every household, every child, every school and public library, universities and business. That is a vision worth delivering on.
>
> (Tanner and Deegan, 2010)

There has also been a backlash against this aspiration-driven model, sometimes referred to as 'build it, and they will come'. There may be a sense that it is not delivering on the promises made.

There is a conflicting set of values and measures of success to be addressed when making digital content available. Memory institutions can be very inward-looking about considering their effectiveness or value, thinking that assessing the management systems or processes is enough, rather than investigating their actual impact (Selwood, 2010). The flip side of this is to become too concentrated on the frameworks used by central government or major funders in the absence of other value judgements (O'Brien, 2013).

Such thinking tends to lead to a cultural economics approach:

> Cultural economics, potentially, can in fact provide precisely those guarantees required, by the critics of instrumentalism, that choices about arts funding should be freed from the prejudices which arise if intrinsic value is neglected. 'Good' economics – the rigorous application of cultural economics – can thus reverse a traditional but obstructive line-up which pits economists, cast as architects of instrumentalism and all things philistine, against arts leaders, cast as beleaguered defendants of intrinsic value and all things aesthetic.
>
> (Bakhshi, Freeman and Hitchen, 2009)

This book proposes that a firm grasp of cultural economics is essential, but also too limited. If the community of memory institutions were to harness itself solely to economic measures based on usage, then it would measure only one vector of a multi-variant environment of value and life-changing impact. Therefore, this book argues for defining modes of value for a digitised collection driven not solely by economics but which contain indicators of other, more intangible values, even including non-use. This balanced approach seeks to show that the digital resource has demonstrably made the host organisation grow better – becoming more efficient and effective in reaching its goals – while stakeholders have become more satisfied and have found social, community and educative benefits of tangible worth, and thus society has been enhanced.

Origins for modes of cultural value

A number of modes of cultural value are available to adapt for the purposes of engaging with tangible and intangible value for impact assessment. The use of the term 'modes' is deliberate in expressing that those suggested here are not absolute values. Mode thus relates to a way or manner in which the cultural value occurs or is experienced, expressed or achieved most frequently in a given set of data.

Leading thinkers on the cultural value of art, Bruno S. Frey and the late Werner W. Pommerehne, in their seminal work *Muses and Markets: Explorations in the Economics of the Arts*, propose various modes of value that are more widely applicable to culture (Frey and Pommerehne, 1990). These include the following.

- **Option value** is where an individual may benefit from the supply of culture even if that person does not currently make use of it.
- **Existence value** considers the positive value in the existence of 'art

goods' that 'obtains for those not using them'. For example, a ruined historic building or monument.

- **Bequest value** suggests that future generations may benefit from the preservation of art or artefacts even though these generations cannot 'express their preferences on currently existing markets'.
- **Prestige value** considers the value ascribed to cultural institutions even by those who never or rarely use them.
- **Education value** is, as stated in their book, about how artistic activities 'help a society to foster creativity, to improve the capacity for cultural evaluation and to develop aesthetic standards'. (Frey and Pommerehne, 1990)

Different contextual uses have adapted these qualifiers for cultural value (Pearce and Özedemiroglu, 2002). The key concept is of value existing even when something is not in active use, so that total value comprises the sum of use and non-use values.

This distinction may be further sub-categorised into direct or indirect benefits. A direct benefit occurs directly through use. An indirect benefit may be derived by one person through another person's use. A person may also experience an indirect benefit through the existence of that which is valued but not personally used. A bridge, for example, serves both direct and indirect purposes. Those travelling across the bridge make direct use to travel across an obstacle, usually water. Those who do not travel over the bridge may also benefit, for example, from goods brought across the bridge by others, by the aesthetic beauty of the bridge or by the excellent fishing in the shadowed ecosystem created by the existence of the bridge.

Economists have adopted the non-use option value in methods such as willingness to pay, where the respondent demonstrates their financial commitment to an option's being available to them. Others have used the concept of willingness to define a bequest value that relates to future uses by others (e.g., children or future generations).

Inspired by these concepts, the BVI Model suggests that, to aid and support the process of impact assessment, five new modes of cultural value for digital resources be established (Tanner, 2011b, 2012). When applied in the BVI Model these are known as the 'Value Lenses'. Their purpose is to give a broader range of choices for direct and indirect values than just measures of use or economics. The modes also fully engage the problematic concept of non-use value; this is rarely discussed or defined for digital resources, as generally they are measured from a mainly instrumentalist viewpoint (Meyer et al., 2009; Meyer and Eccles, 2016).

The importance of these modes of cultural value (Value Lenses) in the BVI Model is to provide context to ensure that measures consider not just direct benefits but also intangible value. Digital resources and collections are valued even by those not actively using them; they can have benefits that reflect on the creators and users and their communities. They have benefits that extend well into the future, to the next generations.

The Value Lenses translate into something more applicable to the BVI Model in terms both of scope and of language. Some values, as suggested by Frey and Pommerehne (1990), are condensed and joined; more values are also added to reflect the needs of practitioners who will use the BVI Model.

The five Value Lenses are:

- Utility
- Education
- Community
- Existence/Prestige
- Inheritance/Legacy.

Balanced Scorecard approaches to value and strategy

In the BVI Model, the values desirable to be measured are specific to each impact assessment. So, it proves useful to provide a common framework that would work across many scenarios to control and manage the outcomes. By focusing on a higher level of common purpose it is possible to provide a broad framework that works for all the various memory institutions without significant modification for each.

The Balanced Scorecard is useful for this purpose as a performance measurement and guidance framework that fully engages with intangible value and strategic change. Robert Kaplan and David Norton originated the Balanced Scorecard as a response to the overwhelmingly financially weighted measures that dominated the annual reports of major corporations (Kaplan and Norton, 1996). As financial measures by their nature lag behind or look backwards at past performance, Kaplan and Norton suggest that such measures are becoming obsolete and do not reflect the full complexity of competitive organisational environments. They use the analogy of an aeroplane with only one dial (airspeed) as an example of how measuring only one thing at a time or focusing on only one aspect of performance would most likely lead to a very challenging time for pilot and passengers alike.

> Managers, like pilots, need instrumentation about many aspects of their environment and performance to monitor the journey toward excellent future outcomes.
>
> (Kaplan and Norton, 1996)

Thus, they proposed the Balanced Scorecard, which, although initially developed to fit the needs of for-profit corporations, has found a wide range of applications in governmental, non-profit and – especially – memory institutions (Fox, n.d.; Woodley, 2006; Matthews, 2008, 2013; Town and Kyrillidou, 2013; Europeana Foundation, 2014a).

The Balanced Scorecard creates a holistic set of viewpoints on the central strategic focal point in order to deliver a framework of performance measurement. The use of perspectives is very beneficial for the richly context-driven work of impact assessment. By enabling four core ways of looking at and assessing any strategic opportunity or activity, the Balanced Scorecard provides a much-desired control and nuance to measurement.

The four perspectives in the Balanced Scorecard are financial, customer, internal business processes, and learning and growth. These perspectives are intended to balance each other, including the financial and non-financial; inward-looking processes and outward-facing customer satisfaction; current and future plans; or drivers towards performance and measures of success. These are usually represented in a graphic or tabular format to allow each to include sub-sections of objectives, means of measurement, targets and initiatives (Kaplan and Norton, 1996; Matthews, 2008).

The Balanced Scorecard has much to offer, but there are problems in applying it without modification to the BVI Model. The language of the Balanced Scorecard is too corporate and either mystifying or excluding for those working in memory institutions. The four perspectives of the Scorecard are useful, but they provide focal points for measurement that do not align closely enough with practice in the cultural, media, academic or heritage sectors. Concepts of digital strategy and digital innovation are introduced in the BVI Model to allow for the framing of thinking provided by the Strategic Perspectives. The BVI Model therefore adopts aspects of the Balanced Scorecard framework, but with adaptations to align closely to the needs and expectations of practitioners from memory institutions.

Thus, to translate the Balanced Scorecard into the BVI Model,

- 'financial' becomes an economic impact;
- 'customer' becomes a social impact;
- 'internal business processes' becomes operational impacts;
- 'learning and growth' becomes innovation impact.

Strategic Perspectives in the BVI Model

The BVI Model assumes that the following four Strategic Perspectives exist and are always used:

- **Social impacts**: stakeholders and wider society have been affected and changed in a beneficial fashion;
- **Economic impacts**: the activity is demonstrating economic benefits to society, stakeholders or the organisation;
- **Innovation impacts**: the digital resource represents or enables innovation that is supporting the social, economic or operational benefits accrued;
- **Operational impacts**: the organisation creating/delivering digital resources has been benefited in its internal processes by the innovation demonstrated.

Prior users of the 2012 BVI Model should note that the category 'Internal' has been renamed to 'Operational' to more accurately reflect usage. Figure 5.3 on page 91 shows the latest overview of Stage 1 of the BVI Model.

The key benefits of this approach are to align, clarify and gain consensus about strategy in a simple framing that will work in many contexts. Mapping current strategies or actions against Strategic Perspectives ensures clearer narration of the impact outcomes. The understanding gained enables the organisation to review and respond to the results.

It further allows for a clear narrative of benefit to be built into the process from the beginning, with two outward-facing perspectives (Social and Economic) and two more inward-facing perspectives (Innovation and Operational). The goal is for a holistic strategic context for the outcomes and results. This narrates as 'our digital resources are benefiting society via these social impacts, leading to economic benefits based in our innovation; while becoming a more effective and efficient organisation'. Together, with supporting evidence, this is a more powerful message than any one of these elements can deliver alone.

Value Lenses in the BVI Model

In the BVI Model, the five Value Lenses focus attention to specific assessment activities and reflect core values measured for their impact. One or more Value Lenses are assigned as drivers to any measurement made. The five Value Lenses are:

- **Utility value**: the value expressed and the benefits directly gained by people through active use of the digital resource now or sometime in the future;
- **Education value**: the value expressed and the benefits directly gained by people from their own or others' ability to learn and gain knowledge (formally or informally) from a digital resource;
- **Community value**: the value expressed and the benefits directly gained by people from the experience of being part of a community engaging with, or afforded by, a digital resource;
- **Existence and/or Prestige value**: the value expressed and the benefits people derive from knowing that a digital resource exists and cherished by a community, regardless of use or non-use of the resource;
- **Inheritance/Legacy value**: the value expressed and the benefits derived by people from the ability to pass forward or receive digital resources between generations and communities, such as the satisfaction that their descendants and other members of the community will in the future be able to enjoy a digital resource if they so choose.

The BVI Model presented in this book has adjusted the Value Lens definitions to more closely reflect actual usage and to enhance understanding of the values from the 2012 version of the Model (Tanner, 2012). To see how the Value Lenses fit into Stage 1 of the BVI Model, see Figure 5.3 opposite.

The Value Lenses focus attention to specific assessment activities and reflect core values that are measured for their impact. Figure 5.4 shows how attention is focused from a Strategic Perspective, through the Value Lenses, to enable choices/decisions and planning.

The Value Lenses are not immutable, nor are they the only way to measure value. Values reflect each other, interact and may even be inextricably linked together. As the SMK Director, Mikkel Bogh, has stated:

> Utility values and Education values are almost two sides of the same coin. Education can be just be a pleasure [in] itself, but it can be useful

also. Usefulness is when knowledge becomes competence. So if there is no direct link between Utility and Education then we are missing an opportunity.

(Bogh, 2017).

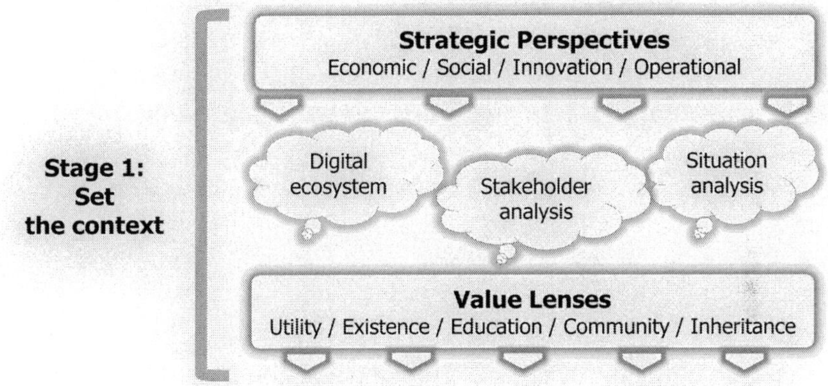

Figure 5.3 *Stage 1 of the BVI Model*

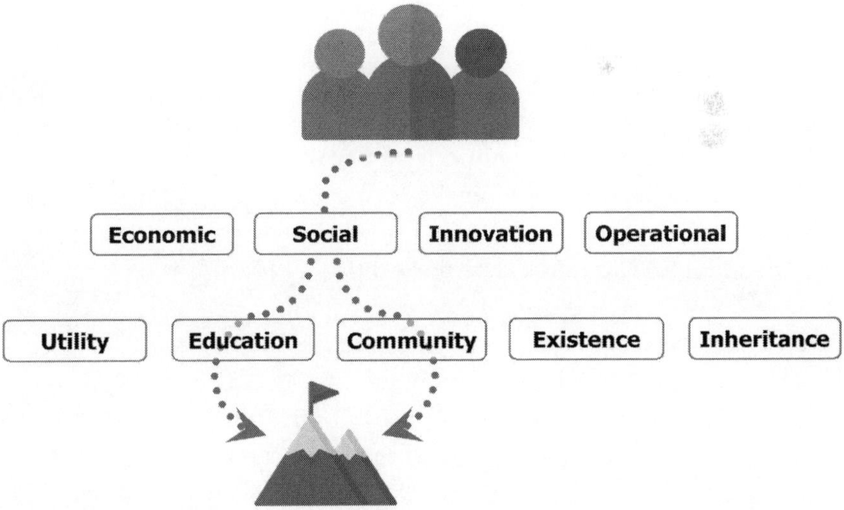

Figure 5.4 *Measurement goals focused via the Strategic Perspectives and two Value Lenses*

There are also other values proposed in the application of the BVI Model – one of the most persistent being leisure/entertainment, which could indeed be added if it were a vital component of the organisation's strategic offering, but which is left out of the model at present. Leisure/entertainment is considered to be well served within the Utility and Community Value Lenses, and somewhat in Education as well.

Case study 5.1: Strategy, values and innovation at the SMK

This case study illustrates the way in which values and innovation fit within a strategic context. The lessons to draw from it relate to framing thinking when building institutional strategy, how digital innovation operates within a group and what digital innovation means to strategic thinking. The SMK has moved on considerably since the time when this case study was researched. This account is also a snapshot of a moment in time and is not intended to express the current state of the SMK.

The Statens Museum for Kunst (SMK) is the National Gallery of Denmark, sited in a beautiful location in the heart of Copenhagen's historic park Østre Anlæg. The museum is a government institution under the auspices of the Danish Ministry of Culture with the objective to build and maintain collections of Danish and foreign art, primarily art from Western culture from the 14th century to the present. Its website states 'we present Danish art to the world and the world's art to Denmark' and 'we want to contribute to redefine the museum as an institution and to help promote a creative and reflective society' (SMK, 2017). In many ways, the SMK evokes the usual expectations of a national art gallery – a great art collection, stunning architecture, high aspirations, public remit and exciting exhibitions. However, when staff were interviewed for this case study a few key features stood out as exceptional. One of these is the research remit as described by Merete Sanderhoff, Curator and Senior Advisor at SMK:

> SMK has a special obligation as the main museum for art history in Denmark to do research; every exhibition we make needs to produce and present original research. This is one of the things that sets us apart … we are very proud and dedicated to our research obligation.
>
> (Sanderhoff, 2017)

The research focus was reiterated by the SMK Director, Mikkel Bogh, in strategic terms:

> We have a healthy professional conservatism ... we have stories we want to tell, we have things we want to research and then the second question

> is how could this be made relevant to a larger public, how to attract a larger audience.
>
> (Bogh, 2017)

The museum has thus built in a spirit of research, experimentation and innovation throughout the organisation. For instance, SMK has been working with participatory practices for many years, being a frontrunner with a young people's art lab (started in 2006 with external funding). Here, the key innovation was to hire young people to develop a community of creatives based in SMK. The SMK also developed a virtual museum around the millennium. In 2008, the Nordeafonden donated 22 million Danish kröne (approximately €3 million) to develop digital museum practice at SMK. Activities – which became known as SMK Digital 1.0 – included a range of education initiatives aimed at the public; a new search mechanism for the collections; an online universe entitled Art Stories; web TV and games; digital presentation and tools within the museum; and the development of MySMK, a creative space for users on the museum website (Sanderhoff, 2014). What is typical of first-generation digital development projects in the cultural heritage sector is how they can become 'stranded once the funding ran out' (Sanderhoff, 2017). However, the inspiration and innovation of MySMK endured and has underpinned the current phase, known as SMK Open.

> Digital is perpetual beta … having to adapt as we go and to adapt to the surrounding world and constant technical development. What is different with SMK Open is we will be experimenting based on a solid infrastructure.
>
> (Sanderhoff, 2017)

SMK Open

> The vision of the project is to make the digitised collection accessible for as many as possible, but that can go a lot of ways … there are many roads to Rome.
>
> (Jensen, 2017).

Christina Jensen is the project manager of SMK Open, a four-year project that began in mid-2016. The museum staff are engaging in deep thought and consideration of what it means to be an 'open' museum: 'not just to open up the digital collections but to be open … it is a paradox that we are opening up and closing down at the same time' (Jensen, 2017). This quote refers to SMK now charging visitors an entrance fee (an edict of the Ministry of Culture), but also trying to be very open via digital offerings. It is the innovation that digital enables which helps to offset that paradox in favour of openness.

Innovation at SMK was reported as being fast and sometimes disruptive, as everyone is working extremely hard, with new ideas emerging all the time. The resultant challenge is to sort out priorities and to decide which of the 'thousand ideas' to pursue and develop technically. For instance, there are consequences to the key objective of SMK Open to provide accessibility to cultural objects and content for everyone. As such, a digitised collection means that each art object must have its own unique identifier. Every aspect of curator interpretation (e.g., an academic essay) must then link through the identifier:

> the physical art pieces are tangible, preserved physically, and they are hanging here and we can see it and discuss it, but the same mindset needs to be transferred into the digitised version of the art piece.
>
> (Jensen, 2017)

The SMK use workshops as a key mode of staff engagement to get people talking about their challenges – especially problems working between IT systems – and to break down any remaining silos of thinking:

> I don't ever see an IT project, it's more I see people, and we build together with the IT infrastructure … there is a positive spirit of development and building upon ideas.
>
> (Jensen, 2017)

The strategic thinking for SMK Open was not integrated across the whole museum – it is a disruptive strategy that may change some jobs and, for some, remove the task entirely, leading to new roles instead. This integration takes time, and it is important to respect the challenges of change management.

On the technology development front, the SMK has a mix of external IT support and internal expertise. Nicholaj Erichsen, SMK's internal API (application programming interface) developer, maintains a constant watch on what other museums and the IT industry are doing, especially in open source, so that SMK can deploy those open solutions rather than developing anything from scratch. At the time of the research, the SMK IT infrastructure was moving to a new collections system, with an indexing solution and an Apache Solr open source enterprise search platform. Thus, by using a range of open APIs, the SMK can add all manner of search functions and metadata to allow for a function such as a search by colour or by form (e.g., Google Vision – image content analysis, https://cloud.google.com/vision/). The SMK plan to utilise IIIF (the International Image Interoperability Framework, http://iiif.io/), which will bring a very rich set of functional capabilities including:

- Fast, rich, zoom and pan delivery of images;
- Manipulation of size, scale, region of interest, rotation, quality and format;
- Annotation – allowing users to comment on, transcribe and draw on image-based resources;
- Assembly and use of image-based resources from across the web, regardless of source, comparing pages, building an exhibit or viewing a virtual collection of items served from different sites;
- Cite and share (IIIF Consortium, n.d.).

A key driving value of technical innovation at SMK is to learn from others: 'we proudly copy from anyone who is doing it right, using open standards and open source' (Erichsen, 2017).

Strategy and management of innovation

Change in museums tends to come from individuals. Thus, digital can be quite disruptive, where senior managers may know that they want digital activities but do not necessarily see all the factors or consequences to ways of working. This is something addressed in the SMK's approach to innovation and strategy.

> Innovation in SMK is very much bottom-up, SMK is a very flat organisation and the directors have huge trust in the staff they hire and we are given permission to be experts in our fields and to do it … if we put together a compelling case, for instance, open data, and work on it and get the experts in and build it they will say 'OK cool, sounds brilliant, go do it', and that has been really interesting and motivated.
> (Sanderhoff, 2017)

SMK has also built in feedback loops to ensure that the digital activities deliver actionable information for managers. For instance:

> The Board [senior management] are also looking to use data to work smarter, and that's inevitably a part of SMK Open because we change or develop the systems that can create the statistics for them so we have to think cleverly so that the system will create the statistics that they need.
>
> (Jensen, 2017)

This approach also means that SMK has to design flow of information across various IT systems so that useful conclusions can be gathered from mutually supporting and interacting data.

The SMK have four-year contracts with the Ministry of Culture, so the strategy is refreshed and revised every four years. The strategy is made within the SMK when the board of directors set the framework for defining a new strategy. Then, a very consultative process follows, including discussing with 'virtually everybody in the organisation … to look at what is actually taking place and what kind of strategies are at stake already, maybe without our being conscious of it or acknowledging it' (Bogh, 2017). From there, priorities can be set and plans made in detail. For instance, 'cultural citizenship' is a crucial priority for SMK, with diversity part of the desired change to be seen in a strategic context. Over 40% of visitors are well-educated women, and these are valued, but diversity means extending voices to many other stakeholders, whether minority groups, elderly people, children and those who are otherwise infrequent users. Thus, by setting a strategic direction to reach out to more diverse and larger audiences it becomes more apparent how to set objectives and activities for digital.

> Digital is a tool without which we couldn't do what we do … making the collection accessible, making the collection a place you can visit and work with after hours is extremely important. Digital as a way of communication, as a platform for sharing and communicating with our audience, has become increasingly important.
>
> (Bogh, 2017)

The SMK has 20% fewer visitors to the physical museum, due to a new entrance charge and various building works, but digital visitors are growing in numbers very quickly (by around 30% per year), which helps to widen the reach of the museum.

> Digital is an integral part of that strategy, we couldn't possibly reach all our audience by inviting them into the museum space only – every visit

> will have an after-life and pre-life in the sense that people will have seen works in WikiMedia or elsewhere and this will feed into a visit or continue a visit later.
>
> (Bogh, 2017)

While mere use of the SMK's web pages is not necessarily building communities, the SMK does report that communities are being built around their Facebook page, Instagram and other social media, and that this is gaining momentum. The SMK has always had a commitment to participative approaches, and this is reflected in the digital strategy. The question of how a digital resource enables a community to coalesce remains a priority, but is a hard to plan for intangible goals.

Planning, building capacity in infrastructure and the right skills in staff, sharing experience/knowledge and providing evidence of success are key factors for strategic development in an innovation environment.

> It means a lot when we, for example, convince a large foundation to send €2 million in our direction that we can say we have built up capacity and resources and knowledge that we will share with a lot of other museums. And so it makes more sense for them to make such an investment in a large museum that has the capacity to share.
>
> (Bogh, 2017)

> Skills are extremely important, you need to have a fundamental understanding of how to do this cleverly … People, man hours, a lot of the open participatory work we do is doable with just a lot of motivated people. If we are allowed to put time and effort into this we don't necessarily need a lot of money. One of the things the OpenGLAM way of thinking opens up is collaboration across sectors; so the museum can be one stakeholder in a bigger picture where start-ups and creative industries and education sectors and so on pool their efforts together.
>
> (Sanderhoff, 2017)

> With the impact work we are doing we are trying hard to build evidence that this [SMK Open] is working. In a lot of the digital innovation that I have been a part of we have experimented without evidence but with indicators and best practices from other parts of the cultural heritage sector, but knowing that this is such a young field that we just have to get hands on and try it out and fail forward as Shirley Bernstein

> beautifully puts it. So I would say that has been very much the way we have been working with innovation for many years … we learned a lot of lessons.
>
> (Sanderhoff, 2017)

> [For some projects] we don't have to build the technological components at all, but we need to deliver our knowledge, our expertise, our passion for art history, our open data and so on.
>
> (Sanderhoff, 2017)

One further interesting feature of senior strategic management that felt quite specific to Denmark is the national leadership forums that exist, where cross-sectoral meetings between chief executives meet some six to eight times per year in groups of 20–40 to share experiences. These meetings' cross-sectoral nature means that private corporate leaders are interacting with cultural and civil service leaders, which helps to share everyday experiences across broader business and management practice. Having a network of peers from a bigger context to broaden the discussion and viewpoints can counter-balance a monocultural dialogue within the cultural sector. Museums may consider themselves very distinct from libraries, for instance, but from a large corporation's perspective they are operationally very similar organisations, and thus the conversations refresh perspectives and strategic insight by getting an outsider's viewpoint. Sometimes this is powerful as a way to reframe internal strategy to answer questions from those external to the museum, uninformed in the specifics, but well informed on strategy, leadership and the need for persuasive strategic objectives (Bogh, 2017).

Latest developments at the SMK

In August 2018 the SMK launched its new website. This development is part of the SMK Open project, supported by Nordea-fonden (www.smk.dk/article/smk-open/). The project aims 'to make the SMK collection digitally accessible, relevant, and useful to as many people as possible' (Smith, 2018).

The website achieves many of the goals set at the time of the case study research. For instance, it implements a connection to the asset management system with an IIIF viewer for large reproductions of artworks. There is also a fully functional API to enable machine-readable interactions with the collections. The SMK strategy is available in Danish; its vision statement states:

> As a visible social actor, SMK will bring art and artistic reflections to all people in Denmark and the whole world. We will inspire more people to use the museum and its collections and to develop the museum in a vibrant dialogue with the society we are a part of.
>
> (SMK, 2018)

The SMK continue to be one of the most innovative and open collections, with a continuous stream of clever ideas to open up engagement with the collection. For instance, SMK have selected 16 different details from the paintings in the collection to freely download as background wallpapers for mobile phones (www.smk.dk/en/article/baggrundsbilleder/).

SMK also work to develop a social and creative community for young people aged 15–25, collaborating with local Young People's Art Lab in workshops:

> Young people create visual expressions of the difficult emotions to do with mental and physical health, social challenges and stigmas, by discussing, clipping and remixing digitised artworks from the SMK public domain collection. Preliminary impact research indicates that creative work supported by open art enables young people who are struggling in life or who are trying to understand how others feel to express their own feelings in different ways, and to find ways to cope with and digest their impressions.
>
> (Fallon, 2019)

SMK is engaged with the Europeana *Impact Playbook* as a means of measuring the ongoing impact of its digital collections. See Chapter 8 for more information about the *Playbook*.

Chapter 6

Planning to plan with the BVI Model

BVI Model Stage 1: Set the context

Figure 6.1 on the next page shows the Balanced Value Impact Model and its five stages.

1 Set the context (Stage 1) focuses information gathered on the organisational and community context though Strategic Perspectives and the Value Lenses.
2 Design the Framework (Stage 2) populates a defined logical BVI Framework with decisions about what and whom to measure and how to do that measurement.
3 Implement the Framework (Stage 3) is the project management phase, where each of the mini-plans set in Stage 2 is set into action and data gathered that will over time become the impact evidence base.
4 Narrate the outcomes and results (Stage 4) collates, analyses and turns the evidence into an impact narrative shared with interested stakeholders, especially decision makers.
5 Review and respond (Stage 5) activities should be embedded throughout to establish the iterative and cyclical nature of impact assessment.

The importance of context, ground truths and baselines

Stage 1 is about finding a holistic lens through which to map the relationships across the organisation and its users; to respect the mission and strategy of the whole organisation ecosystem; and to communicate a clear narrative of direction. It is important to continually reflect on what will be measured, why that is worthwhile measuring and what purpose the measurement is serving.

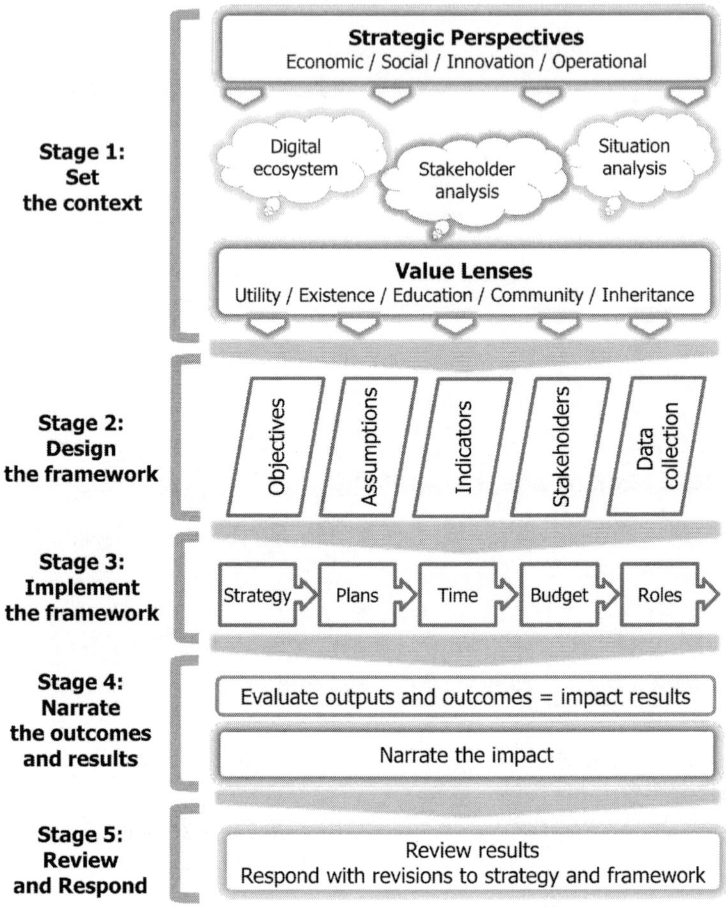

Figure 6.1 *Conceptual overview of the BVI Model*

Impact planning will have to balance available resources with desired activities and programmes. Thus, when considering the purpose of setting context a useful outcome would be the development of a shared, agreed set of information or knowledge relating to the planned impact assessment of digital products or services. Sometimes this is referred to as establishing a set of 'ground truths'. Ground truth refers to information collected on location by observation to establish an accepted group understanding of the reality of a given situation. If such established contextual understanding is not achieved, then the impact assessment and any strategic outcomes will be forever in tension with competing perspectives both within and outside the organisation.

At this point reflect also on the assumptions stated in Chapter 2, remembering in particular that it is not possible to measure everything, nor to measure equally. Choices will inevitably have to be made, and Stage 1 is about supporting choices with useful evidence.

Baselines are also critical to impact assessments. Many evaluations attempt to measure change over a very short period (such as three months or less), and thus have no baseline metrics against which to assess what may have changed. In order to measure the change in anything, it is necessary to have a starting point, a baseline. Baselines are time-oriented and set to whatever the activity owner wishes. Alternatively, set the baseline against something like service level provision, such as 'our school-age education events are engaged with by ~230 people a month', and measure from that baseline concerning the planned change. At no point should a time-oriented baseline suggest discarding that previous activity or outcomes that bridge the baseline. The baseline just needs to be a point of reference for change measurement.

As an example of how this can be useful, consider how the current state of a memory institution's collections dataset may at present be accessible only through desktop web interfaces (possibly providing a measurable baseline of expectation, experience and user data). Assume an intervention, such as the introduction of a new mobile platform, which will change that status quo. From such a baseline the impact indicators are a comparison of the prior state in terms of qualitative measures (satisfaction, knowledge) and quantitative measures (numbers of users, the reach of the resource) with the new state. Knowing the current state allows for better measurement of the change implied by new activity, products or services.

Digital ecosystem

An ecosystem is a set of interdependent relationships among the resources, technologies, organisation hosting, creators and consumers. These must be mapped and described to enunciate the ecosystem of the digital resource. The process could be looking at the digital resource in detail, as suggested here, or it could be describing the ecosystem as community action. A community action is trying to 'get many people to bring their creativity together and accomplish something more important than they can do on their own' (Moore, 2013).

Figure 6.2 overleaf imagines the world as a digital ecosystem. Without understanding the digital ecosystem, it is hard to contemplate the full capabilities of the digital resource and its relationship to stakeholders or to

Figure 6.2 *Imagine a digital ecosystem*
Artwork by Alice Maggs

know the starting point, the baseline, from which any change has occurred or will be measured. Contemplating the digital ecosystem enables a deeper understanding of the driving forces that have brought the organisation to this point and the challenges that are intrinsic to the context of the organisation. Every organisation has a unique digital ecosystem – a set of attributes that are, so to speak, 'baked into the cake'. Some organisations will have enterprise-grade systems, some outsource extensively and others have the in-house skills to allow them to rely on open source solutions. These differences will be formative in considering what is measured and how to measure it.

To understand the context of a digital resource the BVI Model scopes it against a set of parameters. These parameters consider the set of interdependent relationships among the resources, content, stakeholders, technologies, infrastructures, organisation hosting, legal and payment structures, creators and consumers. The BVI Model provides an opportunity to map and describe the ecosystem of the digital resource to provide a baseline for measurement and to establish some accepted ground truths.

Parameters to scope what a digital resource is, include the following.

- There is a defined resource that is made up of a describable, cohesive set of primary and secondary materials, services, products and activities.
- The resource is accessed primarily through a digital platform (web, mobile, virtual reality, exhibition console or other means).
- The nature of the content within the resource is digital – either achieved through digitisation or as born-digital content.
- There is a definable group of users that the resource is intended to reach by digital means.
- The resource does not have to stand alone; it could be part of a broader set of activities, products or services.

Those leading an impact assessment should have a report of the ecosystem to act as a continuing reminder of the critical aspects of the ecosystem. Behind this must be a broader, deeper set of information to establish the baseline of that which is within the assessment.

Questions to be answered in establishing an ecosystem of the digital resource include the following.

- What is the digital resource or service/product that is to be the focus of the assessment?
- What does the digital resource do and how does it behave?
- What does the digital resource explicitly not do?
- Via what platforms (web, mobile, other) is the digital resource primarily experienced by its users?
- What types and extent of content does it carry? What is the lifecycle of the content carried? For instance, is it ephemeral or for long-term preservation; dynamic or relatively static?
- What sort of underlying infrastructure and architectures is it operating within?
- How does this digital resource relate to other digital resources or services? What dependencies and technical connections are required to make the resource function?
- What are the minimum technical specifications required by the user to experience the digital resource as intended by its creators?
- Who hosts the digital resource? Is the organisation/service that hosts the resource the same as that which created it?
- Who are the expected users of the digital resource? (See also the stakeholder section below.)

- Does the user have to pay/subscribe or otherwise trade (e.g., personal information, advertising, membership or subscription) to gain access to the resource?
- Are there any legal or legislative frameworks to be considered, including:
  - intellectual property rights (IPR)
  - digital rights management (DRM)
  - E laws (GDPR in Europe)
  - issues of managing personal data
  - contractual constraints or obligations
  - legislative frameworks of different geographic regions?
- How is the digital resource intended to sustain itself and grow in the future?
- What mechanisms and tools are available to view user behaviour for this digital resource? Is it feasible to add more tools for data collection, if the impact assessment should suggest these?

In some cases, this task will be short and straightforward but, as the complexity of the ecosystem and its relationships to stakeholders grows, the task of describing it such that it aids decision making will take more time to achieve.

Having this report of the digital ecosystem is a significant step to answering the question 'what am I measuring?' It provides an accepted ground truth that will be useful for strategic thinking in any circumstance. It provides a means of establishing a baseline of what is normal or steady state and, as such, provides a point of departure from which to measure any change.

Stakeholder discovery and categorisation

This step will establish as complete a categorised list of stakeholders as feasible. In later stages, the information gathered here will be further segmented and analysed to identify different groupings for investigation specifically in response to the needs of the impact assessment. At this point, the core concern is to identify an extensive list of stakeholder types and characterise them to inform planning processes and identify gaps in knowledge.

A stakeholder is a person, group, community or organisation who affects or can be affected by the ecosystem of the digital resource.

Identifying and grouping stakeholders

Actions to take in establishing and identifying stakeholders include the following.

1 List all primary stakeholders.
   a Primary stakeholders are those directly affected by the ecosystem of the digital resource.
   b The attributes of these stakeholders might include: user, influencer, paymaster, funder, champion, vocal opponent, internal or external.
2 List all secondary stakeholders.
   a Secondary stakeholders are those indirectly affected by the ecosystem of the digital resource.
   b The attributes of these stakeholders might include: potential user, indirect influencer such as a context-setting body (e.g. a government agency or NGO) or opinion leaders, relative of user, potential supporter or opponent who is unaware of the resource at present.
3 Identify and list all potential supporters and opponents.
4 Identify the interests of vulnerable or minority groups.
   a Many impact assessments neglect groups that do not match their core assumptions, and these are often the vulnerable, disadvantaged or those from minority groups. There is a moral and ethical imperative to include these groups.
   b Challenging assumptions and being sure to include these groups will benefit the assessment. When assessing social factors, it may prove easier to demonstrate a measurable benefit and change for these groups – but only if they are identified.
5 List all new primary or secondary stakeholders likely to emerge as the impact assessment progresses.

Working from the list of stakeholders previously identified, in their primary and secondary groupings these can now be segmented into defined groups that can serve impact assessment purposes through a stakeholder analysis. Identify by this process the major stakeholders who can have a significant influence on or will be essential to the perceived success of the digital resource. Note that 'essential' in this sense refers to those stakeholders whose needs and interests are the priority of the digital resource. It could refer to direct users of the resource or direct beneficiaries of use of the resource. Refer to these as the core beneficial stakeholders.

The kinds of broad categories to consider include:

- consumers: those who will use the resource regularly;
- one-stop consumers: those who may use the resource only once or twice;
- partners and collaborators: those relationships required to deliver the digital resource;
- paymasters: those who hold financial sway over the digital resource in one way or another;
- producers and creators: those contributing to the content of the digital resource;
- commentators: those who have opinions on the digital resource that set the context for other stakeholders and may possibly change opinions in the sector;
- marginalised or disadvantaged groups: those groups, whether primary or secondary stakeholders, that it is essential to specify so as to achieve equality of opportunity to participate. This grouping may include, for example, the impoverished, religious or racial minorities, women or indigenous peoples;
- leavers: those no longer in touch with the digital resource who have previously used it;
- non-users: those who are within the target user group but have never used the digital resource;
- champions: those who actively promote the digital resource and can affect the outcome of the impact assessment;
- competitors: those with competing products or persons leading competing activities;
- decision makers: those who have control of resources or who are policy makers.

Allowing for the fact that some stakeholders may reasonably be assigned to more than one grouping, it would be sensible to continue sub-categorising stakeholders until they fall most clearly into one stakeholder grouping over the remaining possibilities.

Using stakeholder information to plan impact assessment

Within the BVI Model, each Value Lens measure will have one or more stakeholder grouping assigned to it as a target for data gathering.

The vast majority of impact assessments will not be able to canvass all possible stakeholders, or even every representative grouping. A choice is thus required to identify or classify groups of stakeholders that can be considered usefully representative of the broader community of its grouping. Stakeholder-related risks are significant influencers on the success, timeliness and cost of projects. If these are got wrong, then resources may be expended chasing data that is not usable or that may be so diffuse or vague as to be unhelpful. Careful, precise and targeted planning for those stakeholders with the highest priority for assessment at this stage is vitally important, as this may influence every other element of impact assessment planning and design.

Risks to the project and any impact assessment assumptions are identified by understanding stakeholders. Risks are then mitigated in the design of the impact assessment. An example might be the measurement of school children's responses to a digital exhibition or a learning resource. Children are challenging to engage with individually or in groups, with many risk parameters; the results of surveying children are also hard to quantify or assign significance to, as many other factors may be driving responses. There is also little opportunity for longitudinal study. As such, the representative group often engaged with as a proxy is teachers or parents. These kinds of considerations and choices are clarified by mapping stakeholders to groupings.

The groupings suggested above also include those who are not users, those who were users and now have left the user group of the digital resource, plus the marginalised or disadvantaged in society. Even though they may not be active users or may have only partial access to the resource, they are important to consider for possible inclusion in an impact assessment.

Engagement with the marginalised is essential, otherwise lack of recognition of their state removes them further from equality of participation. It is also possible that the digital resource may effect a more significant change in their lives than in those of other groups. Non-users and leavers should also not be forgotten, as much can be learned from the experience of primary stakeholders who are no longer using the digital resource (however negative their responses). Non-users may merely not know that the resource exists, or may value it even though they never use it. It is in these groups that the most significant change may be mapped; do not ignore them for convenience or cost reasons.

Once decided, assign the categorised stakeholders (as many and with as much overlap as required) against each of the Value Lens lines in the Framework. The BVI Model assumes that leadership in assessment comes from the memory institution. As such, an implicit hierarchy is built into any choices. In other words, the impact assessment is happening because the memory institution is leading or commissioning it for purposes driven, at least in part, by its objectives and needs. Recognise the risks and assumptions of the BVI Model memory institution approach. There are other methods and techniques, such as the Triple Task Method, which place the stakeholder at the very centre of the process, allowing the stakeholder to define the values and indicators of success (Bell and Morse, 2008).

Stakeholders remain critical not just for the data-capture portion of an impact assessment but also at the latter stages, both when reflecting on the outcomes and as potential points for dissemination of the results.

Situation analysis

In the BVI Framework there is an objectives field for each aspect of the impact assessment and these objectives will need to be established. Situation analysis, along with the establishment of criteria of measurement, will assist in the definition of objectives within the Framework.

A situation refers to the context and environment of a digital resource at a specific point in time. Situation analysis relates to information gathered about the ecosystem, but with an additional process of analysis that defines and interprets the situation, its elements and their relations at a given moment. This step is an audit of current contexts that will affect the impact assessment.

A SWOT analysis is often a significant part of a situation analysis.

Strengths are those attributes or activities related to the digital resource that are expected to perform better than most in the organisation's environment. At this stage, building the selection of strengths is based on the organisation's normal, expected requirements for success. A short and non-exhaustive list of strengths may include, for example:

- a well-established group of benefiting stakeholders;
- an innovative model of digital delivery;
- a proven mechanism of delivering value to the core audience;
- a sustainable financial model already in place;
- close linkage to existing strategies – for instance, digital preservation, internal mission, curatorial concerns, collection or product development, or educational perspectives;
- an experienced and skilled workforce with knowledge of or expertise in evaluation or impact assessment;

- a senior-level champion in the organisation who will ensure that impact assessment gets adequate attention and prioritisation.

Weaknesses are those attributes or activities related to the digital resource that could be improved to increase the probability of success. Identify the predictable weaknesses that would affect the probability of 'success' for the digital resource. These may be known if the assessment starts after the resource is established, or may be predictable in the context of an upcoming implementation. Weaknesses may include, for example:

- poor evidence gathering, resulting in a lack of information for the best decision making;
- lack of expertise in any critical area of endeavour;
- lack of a clear strategy or clear linkage to other strategies in the organisation;
- being out of touch with the benefiting stakeholders;
- inadequate marketing or advertising of the digital resource;
- a digital delivery mechanism that is uninspiring or lacking in technical innovation;
- inadequate infrastructure to deliver the resource into the expected user base in a satisfying way.

Opportunities are those externally focused attributes or activities that may affect the future success of the endeavour. These are likely to be an area of great interest for impact assessment and are often likely to be the product of underlying trends or conditions developing or appearing within the ecosystem for that digital resource. Two suggested activities to help with this process include maintaining a continuous review of the literature and benchmarking inside and outside the organisation to identify and evaluate potential opportunities. Opportunities may include, for example:

- funding through aligning with a funder's programme or priorities;
- reframing and refreshing relationships with key stakeholders through the process of assessment and engagement;
- opening up new relationships with partners in sectors or stakeholder groups that are fresh to the organisation;
- having better, more actionable evidence to aid decision making;
- more visible alignment of plans and strategies to the actual needs of the community;

- the establishment of automated measures and data gathering to allow for continuous, passive, longer-term evidence gathering at low cost;
- prospects to lead the sector.

Threats are those attributes or activities related to the digital resource that are obstacles to the accomplishment of goals. What will or is getting in the way of success? Threats differ from weaknesses, as they may be beyond the scope of an easy solution or change in reaction to the threat, which is usually external. Threats may include, for example:

- changes in government regulation – for example, data protection or privacy regulations;
- changes in funding models that may have a bearing on the sustainability of the service or change the goals of the impact assessment;
- the effect of disruptive new technologies changing the domain space during the assessment. For example, consider the changes that mobile or tablet devices brought as the technology matured. Consider that augmented reality or virtual reality could be the next major disruptor for culture;
- the effect of new business models or practices that change service expectations – for example, WiFi ubiquity or the way that Amazon changed book-buying habits, forcing changes in the way services are offered;
- external competitors syphoning off stakeholder attention – for example, the effects of social media or casual gaming on available attention.

Recognition of real or perceived threats helps to develop situational analysis to assist planning, and is critical to avoiding surprises that may hinder achievement of the impact assessment.

Situation awareness starts to link the information from context to the planning process. For instance, it can help to suggest how potential stakeholder behaviour might reveal the likely effect of different assumptions on the impact measures. It is advantageous to keep a holistic viewpoint, to recognise risks and to see possible opportunities.

Assigning Value Lenses to Perspectives in the BVI Framework

Decisions are now needed. Matching, or pairing, Strategic Perspectives and Value Lenses is the next step in the process.

Impact assessments operate on a spectrum. While balancing all four perspectives is ideal, some will dominate more than others during the assessment. The choice of Strategic Perspectives and Value Lenses will influence the questions to pose and how to narrate the answers. The five Value Lenses allow focus on the types of value most commonly connected with the experience of interacting with digital culture and heritage. The BVI Framework can record each Perspective–Value Lens pairing.

The Value Lenses are:

- Utility
- Education
- Community
- Existence/Prestige
- Inheritance/Legacy.

The Europeana *Impact Playbook* (which applies the BVI Model, see Chapter 8) has a useful summary:

> So, you are asking yourself: what is the value of what I do for a specific person or group of people? Did it make their job easier? That would classify as 'utility' value. Did they learn something from it or did it make them feel more connected to a certain community? That's 'learning' and 'community' value. The 'legacy' and 'existence' lenses are special in the sense that they describe value that people can derive from your work without even personally using your services. The fact that we preserve our heritage for future generations is incredibly valuable to society and is valued by people who never set foot in an archive.
>
> (Verwayen et al., 2017)

For example, in a community digital library collection with a strong social focus, the Perspective–Value pairings for Social impact might require an investigation of the Lenses shown in Table 6.1.

Table 6.1 *Perspective–Value pairing for a community digital library*

Strategic Perspective	Value Lenses
Social	Community + Existence + Education

Whereas, if considering a university with a digital collection relating to a famous historical figure, then the Perspective–Value pairings for Social impact might require the investigation of the Lenses shown in Table 6.2 below.

Table 6.2 *Perspective–Value pairing for a university digital collection*

Strategic Perspective	Value Lenses
Social	Education + Prestige + Inheritance/Legacy

Immediately, this reveals that the data-collection methods and SMART indicators to be used for the social perspective on the impact assessment would be quite different from each other in these two examples. This reflects the differing values inherent in the nature of the collections, the stakeholders and the digital presence of each.

Guidance on Perspective–Value pairings

As there are four Strategic Perspectives and five Value Lenses, there are 20 primary Perspective–Value pairings. Twenty measures are generally too many. The purpose of the BVI Model is to aid focus and choosing, not to propagate endless modes of measurement.

Measuring no more than eight Perspective–Value pairings will be more than adequate for most purposes. There should ideally be at least four pairings to cover the full gamut of Strategic Perspectives. In practice, most applications do not pair more than two Value Lenses per Perspective. Figure 6.3 visualises focusing via through the Strategic Perspectives to two Value Lenses. It is also entirely possible to apply a Value Lens to multiple Perspectives. The following are some examples of common Perspective–Value pairings.

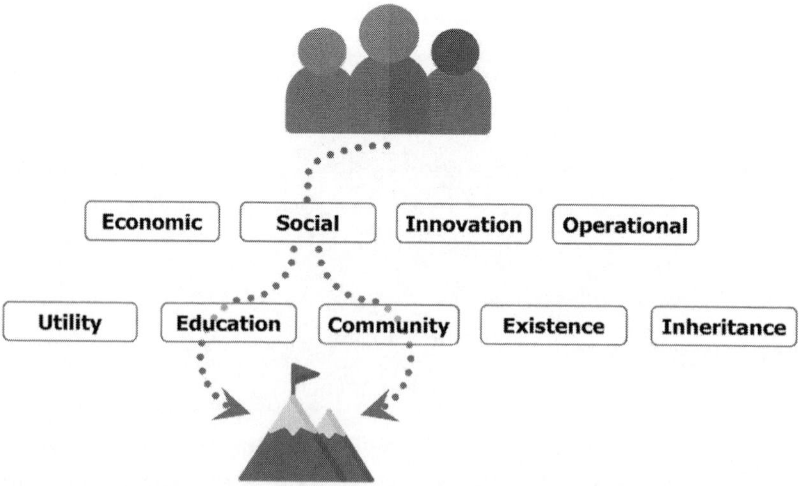

Figure 6.3 *Measurement goals focused via the Strategic Perspectives and two Value Lenses*

- Utility, by its nature, is likely to be paired with any Perspective. Most frequently, it is paired with Economic or Operational Perspectives. Care should be exercised to ensure that it is applied purposefully to deliver actionable data rather than because it is easy to assign.
- Education most often focuses outward onto Social and possibly Economic Perspectives.
- Community is broadly applicable, but almost certainly pairs with Social Perspectives.
- Inheritance/Legacy or Existence values are often usefully applied to Social and Operational Perspectives. They measure outward for Social and inward, to the organisation, for Operational in terms of data gathering.
- Innovation changes according to the nature of the organisation and projects, such that an open access project may pair Innovation with Community, whereas a project for a MOOC (Massive Online Open Course) would pair Innovation with Education. The Utility value is also often paired with Innovation.

See Chapter 3 for a case study of the Wellcome Library that discusses their Perspective–Value pairings.

Moving to Stage 2: Design the framework

Once the Perspective–Value pairings are complete and the context stage is complete, the next phase of enacting the impact assessment begins (described in Chapter 7).

For every activity planned there will be a mini-plan recorded in the BVI Framework. Integrate impact measures into the planning and delivery of activities, preferably from the start. In most cases the resources needed to achieve many of the impact measures may well already exist (web metrics from Google Analytics, for instance). However, as planned activities grow in scale or scope, then it becomes likely that specific impact measures for an activity will be planned for cost-effective evidencing of impact.

The BVI Framework is merely a way to structure the activity of impact assessment (see Chapter 7). It is a way of controlling a process that has many moving parts as expressed by the Perspective–Value pairings. The Framework itself will mainly be of use to those who co-ordinate activity as a means of tracking activity and measures against impact indicators and objectives.

Using Stage 1 for strategic goals not associated with impact assessment

Completing the context-setting stage may identify broader issues of strategy and planning that the organisation needs to address outside of the planning process for an impact assessment. Changes may be identified, new ideas may have emerged and corrective actions may move into focus. These should be addressed as part of a change management process, rather than being bundled within an impact assessment.

Using the contextual information for immediate gain as suggested below may thus demonstrate early success and tangibly beneficial outcomes. The BVI Model can be used to test, record and narrate the success of these activities, but is not the engine of the change itself.

Mapping strategic plans and gap analysis

From the information gathered so far, a mapping document should be easy to produce. It will identify the following.

1. Objectives: what plans and objectives are already stated that any strategic planning must respect?
2. Content ideas: what content or collections strategy and content resources exist that should be addressed/referenced through strategic planning?
3. Audiences and stakeholders: what is known about the relevant audiences and stakeholders? How are these segmented and what measures are in place to record their usage and needs assessment?
4. Resource: what resources are already in place (funds, budgets, people, income/revenue, equipment and infrastructure)?
5. Timeframe: over what timeframes are activities and plans set to occur?
6. Ecosystem: what is the digital ecosystem, and how does this map to the strategic plans of the organisation?
7. Measures: what measures of success are already in place? Are there any KPIs or targets to be met by strategic plans?

This mapping will identify aspects that are already going well, and gaps or areas of under-performance and possibly under-investment. The mapping document acts as a prototype for making recommendations towards a strategic plan and a baseline from which any change is measured.

Such a mapping document can be used to fact-check assumptions internally with colleagues and to gather more detail and different viewpoints on the strategic plan.

Stakeholder analysis and mapping

One instrumentalist strategic task is to create an active change plan. One approach is to use the stakeholder categories to map against criteria to plan for change.

Map stakeholders on a matrix of knowledge against influence/initiative. Figure 6.4 shows an example of a blank matrix with some explanatory text of how each area might promote action and where on the matrix some types of stakeholders often appear.

In this matrix there are four areas, defined by the two axes of Knowledge and Influence/Initiative. The Knowledge axis relates to how much the respective stakeholders know about the area of activity or the specific service/product/project/resource in question. The Influence/Initiative axis focuses on the amount of influence or capacity to act, to initiate, of a group of

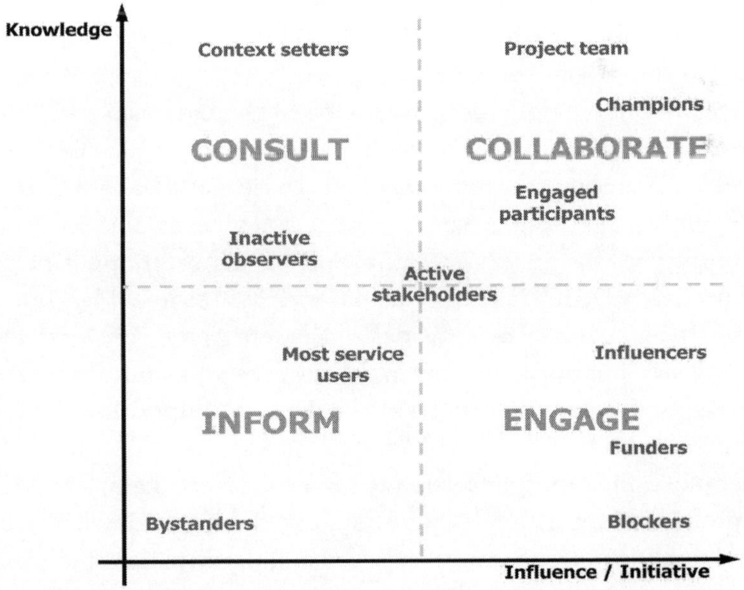

Figure 6.4 *A stakeholder mapping matrix*

stakeholders. The example shows where typical stakeholders often locate for digital resources in memory institutions. It also shows (in the lighter text) the sorts of actions usually associated with each section.

Inform: the bottom left area is for those with little knowledge nor interest in being active. At the extreme, these are bystanders. Most service users and audiences are relatively passive and thus fit here. They have some knowledge and take some initiative but are not necessarily being active in their use and interest. The action to take for stakeholders who fall into this sector is to inform them of the availability of services or products: to increase their knowledge as a way of encouraging and initiating action.

Consult: the top left sector is for those with a lot of knowledge but who are not necessarily active specifically concerning the service or resource in question. A leading institution could be a context setter, a significant commercial company could set the context for a technology platform, or an academic could provide research that sets the tone for professional practice. For instance, in the USA the Library of Congress could be a context setter for video conservation and digitisation practice without being an active participant for the mapped activity. In the UK Tate or in Australia the Powerhouse Museum are often seen as context setters for social media and online presence in museums and may be touchstones for such activities. The key action to take for these stakeholders is to consult them: to gain information and to share experience.

Engage: the bottom right sector is for those who hold positions of influence or the capacity to act but are not yet informed or knowledgeable about the specifics of the service or activity planned. These could be future sources of funding, those who influence government policy or even those who are a block to progress, as they have significant influence in opposition to the desired direction. Do not just to seek to inform these stakeholders but engage with them to persuade them to the desired action. At the very least, the hope is that they will not oppose plans; in the best scenarios influencers become champions. Government departments or regional authorities often occupy this sector.

Collaborate: the top right section is where to locate the project team and any champions of the activity. They should be the most knowledgeable and active in initiating plans. The most engaged and participative of the users will also reside here. These stakeholders do not just use a service but also actively seek to understand it, press for change or adaptation and look for changes that will benefit their community. Collaborating will be a pivotal action to ensure that all these knowledgeable, active and influential persons are working together and toward similar goals.

Movement across boundaries often happens along the diagonals. Thus, bystanders can become active stakeholders, who could be engaged participants through having their awareness stoked by being informed and partnered with. Context setters sometimes become active policy-setting influencers or may have the power to initiate new activities, usually through funding. Examples of champion influencers and context setters are the Andrew W. Mellon Foundation in the USA, and in the UK the Arcadia Foundation for open access to research and public domain works.

Example of stakeholder mapping

The following brief example of stakeholder mapping is based on an actual case, anonymised for publication. In this example a large library whose collections contain long runs of 19th-century scholarly journals in various non-English languages wished to engage in an ambitious digitisation programme. These journals are unusual in that they represent the fullest conception of scholarship, including some of the first published poetry, music, political writing, philosophy, science and medicine of the era by very renowned creators and authors. However, the regional and national governmental bodies were not inclined to digitisation projects at that time and a suitable funding stream did not exist.

As part of the long-term planning for the library, stakeholder mapping aided the plan of action to gain funding as an outcome. The stakeholders were mapped in their current positions (as shown in Figure 6.5) and then their pathways to where they would need to be to facilitate the funding of the project mapped. These destination paths should be listed in the order they need to happen to achieve the set goal. The list, with dates and actions, thus formulates a strategic plan.

From Figure 6.5 on the next page showing the stakeholder mapping in action the list of actions is derived:

1 Project team to develop the technical plans, the conceptual ideas for the resource and to propose deliverables and a possible budget.
2 The chief executive of the library to be deeply informed, to agree to plans and to actively become a champion for this activity.
3 Government seen as context setters and influencers deciding on cultural policy and expenditure on digital activity. The chief executive initiates

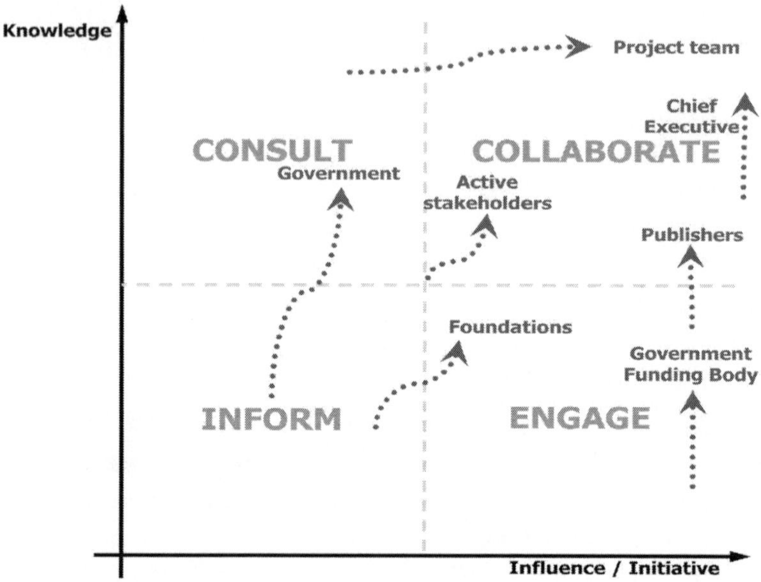

Figure 6.5 *An example of stakeholder mapping in action*

informing and lobbying government as a means of ensuring there are support and interest in the project and the field of work in general.

4 The chief executive and the project team seek to influence the relevant government funding body to consider digitisation of scholarly content a desirable priority for expenditure. The library collaborates with context setters and user champions to show the value of such work and to create a sense of demand and justification for such governmental support. Since actions 3 and 4 occur over a long period, they are placed earlier in the plan as a critical dependency for success.
5 The project team work closely with and seek to collaborate with a major stakeholder group: the publishers. They need to secure the permissions, and agreement to the project in principle. A full project concept, plan and budget are now ready in case of any arising funding opportunity.
6 The project team also engage with active stakeholders (e.g. user groups) to fully assess their user needs and to garner support for the project.
7 The chief executive informs foundations and other private sources of funds about the project concept. Fortunately, they offer matched funding (at 30%) to anything offered by government funding.

8 The government releases a call for proposals for funding, including a category that is relevant and appropriate to the project which the library wishes to achieve.
9 The library project team bid for funds, using the support of their users, stakeholders, partners and other funders as evidence of the feasibility of and demand for the project.

In this case the library was successful in raising the funds needed to digitise hundreds of thousands of pages in relatively minor languages that have enhanced that community's sense of place and identity, widening understanding of a significant historical context. Language training and schools use the digital materials. This process cannot guarantee the outcome; in this example the funding was won in a competitive process, but using this process can optimise the planning and emphatically improve the chance of success.

Using the Business Model Canvas to plan strategically

As mentioned in Chapter 5 the Strategyzer Business Model Canvas (https://strategyzer.com/) is also a useful tool to describe the rationale of how an organisation creates, delivers and captures value. The Canvas translates the complex interlocking elements of an organisation or unit of activity into nine building blocks that show the logic of how they operate and add value and benefit. A Canvas is a way to visualise a ground truth and may be a good outcome of the investigation of the digital ecosystem and stakeholders. Figure 6.6 over the page shows an example of the Canvas completed for the digital imaging and media activity of a museum.

The Canvas can be helpful to visualise a current state and a proposed future state. Adding new or changing current clients would have a ripple effect back through the relationships to the value propositions to activities. Similarly, any change in partners or activities will flow change through value propositions to relationships, channels and clients.

The Strategyzer Canvas also comes with an extension known as the Value Proposition Canvas (https://strategyzer.com/canvas/value-proposition-canvas). The above mappings and stakeholder information can be used to test, visualise and track understanding of a specific user group for whom a service, product or values are proposed.

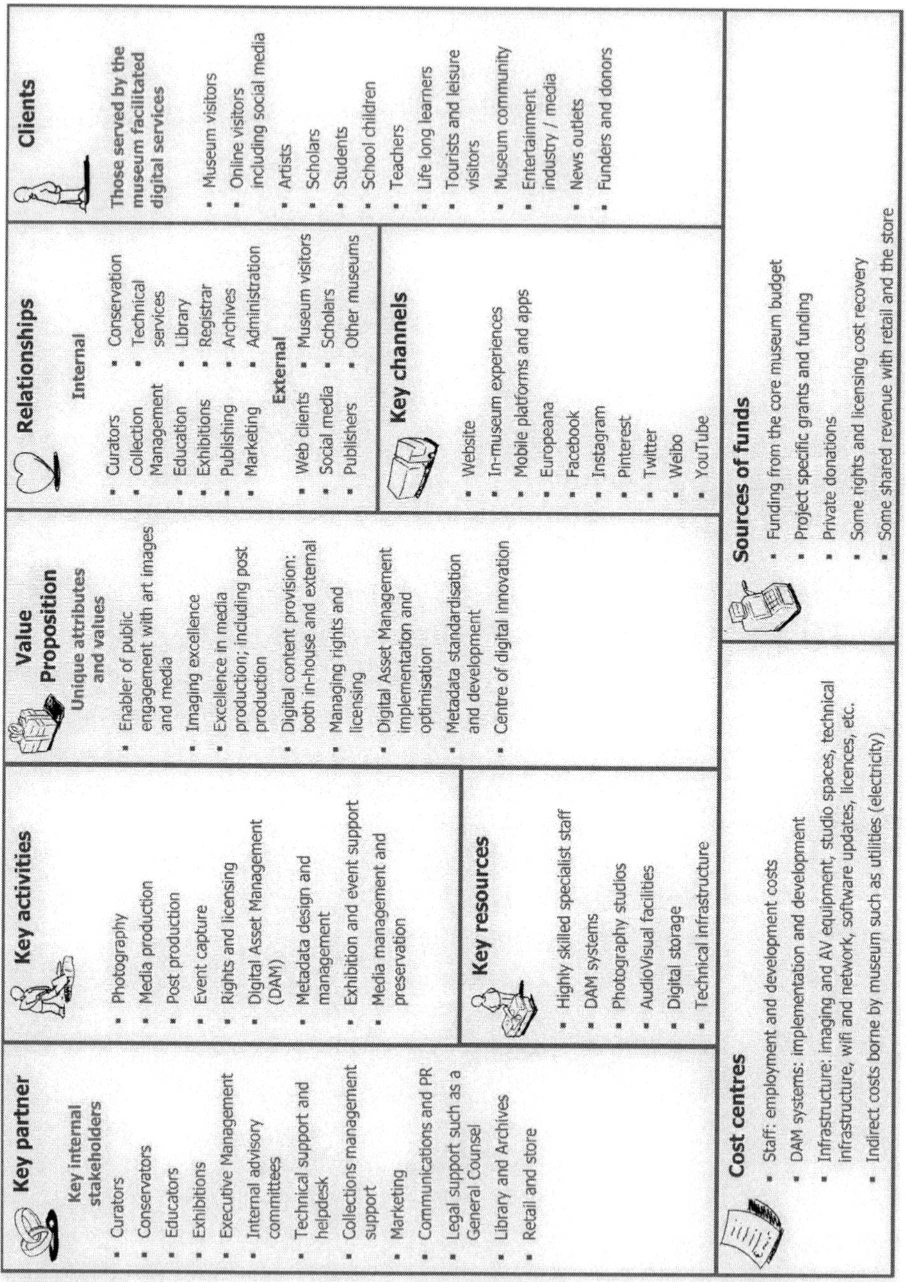

Figure 6.6 *A generic museum digital imaging and media activity on a Strategyzer Canvas*

The Canvas also maps to the Strategic Perspectives on the BVI Model.

- Social impacts equate to the Relationships, Clients and Key Channels sections of the Canvas.
- Economic impacts equate to the Cost Centres and Sources of Funds sections.
- Innovation impact equate to the Value Proposition section, as any changes or new initiatives will be driven by changes in the value propositions.
- Operational impacts equate to the Key Partner, Key Activities and Key Resources sections, as these are the most inward-looking and operational aspects of the Canvas.

Using these aspects together can assist the strategic planner in seeing how the BVI Model will be able to reflect on the current organisational make-up and how change is visualised and shared.

For example, in the above Canvas example museum images are still being made available to the public as licensed objects with rights reserved. One possible outcome of considering the needs of a stakeholder group might be to assess that these reserved rights for works in the public domain are a significant barrier to access, use and re-use (Sanderhoff, 2014; Wallace and Deazley, 2016). Using the BVI Model to consider the outcomes and impacts of a change in policy can be reflected backwards through a change in activity and value proposition in a Canvas. An intervention planned, such as moving to Creative Commons Zero (https://creativecommons.org/publicdomain/zero/1.0/) for images in the collection, would be considered from the stakeholders' perspectives and measured accordingly to provide evidence of the success/failure of the change.

Moving from plan to implementation

Stage 1 delivers the outputs of completing the definition of the digital ecosystem, stakeholder groupings, situation analysis and choosing the Perspective–Value pairings. The next phase, enacting the impact assessment, begins as described in Chapter 7.

Using this context setting stage will allow you to improve overall strategic management and understand the organisational context for delivery of the digital resource. All organisations have individual quirks and subtle differences of emphasis in funding, resource management, infrastructure and decision making that it will be significantly advantageous to understand. See also Chapters 9 and 10 on influencing decision makers and policy makers for how to use this context information as a means to obtain a change in management or executive decision making.

Chapter 7

Implementing the BVI Framework

Introducing the BVI Framework

Memory institutions and digital resources have an impact, whether it is measured or not. The purpose of impact measurement is to understand that impact explicitly and to become purposeful in trying to achieve it and narrate its benefits to the broader community and decision makers. This chapter is about the implementation of impact assessment within a framework to control the activity.

The BVI Framework is not the impact assessment itself, but it structures the activity and plans of impact assessment. It acts as a way of controlling a process that usually has many moving parts that may be occurring over differing timescales, with possibly different teams, resources or points of focus. The Framework itself will mainly be of use to those co-ordinating the activity to track activity and measures against impact indicators and objectives.

Implementation of an impact assessment is achieved best through mini-plans developed within the bigger plan. For example, the mini-plan may be as simple as flagging the need for a small survey of users attending a launch event. The organisation should be in the habit of asking impact-related questions whenever possible. Little and often is the mantra of impact data gathering. Use the Framework to keep the measures and the data collected synchronised and controlled.

Every activity planned will come with a mini action plan that states the following:

1 a description of the proposed activity;
2 the resources required to deliver the planned activity, with a budget and timescale;
3 the expected benefits from the activity;
4 the likely outputs from the activity in terms of an amount of product or service delivery;
5 how the activity will map to the Perspective–Value pairings and the organisation's strategies;
6 how the activity can be measured to answer as many as possible of the Framework's impact objective questions.

It is then up to management to decide if the activity is worthwhile. In most cases, the resources needed to achieve many impact measures will already exist (web metrics, for instance). As planned activities grow in scale or breadth, then specific impact measures for an activity will need to be designed.

Documentation for the BVI Framework

The BVI Framework is available as a digital template in MS Excel spreadsheet format at www.BVIModel.org. For a large-scale impact assessment it is recommended to keep each Strategic Perspective on a separate sheet of the workbook to make the information easier to manage and more accessible. This book refers to 'fields' as a way of identifying the spreadsheet cells of the BVI Framework. See Table 2.1 on page 40 for an example of a completed Framework at Stage 2.

Each field of the Framework is a summary statement. It is not necessary to include all the information for the impact assessment within the constraints of the spreadsheet. Thus, a field stating 'online survey' for a data-collection method should have a set of accompanying documentation stating relevant information, such as the survey method and format. If more than one mechanism is used, then the field contents should use simple, unique identifiers to distinguish them.

Not every field has to be completed at the beginning, nor in the order presented. Pre-set budgets and timescales mean that impact activities may have to be fitted to them, which is far from optimal. Alternatively, the budget may have to be agreed by another group or body, so it will not be set until the activity has been thoroughly planned out. Thus, an iterative approach is optimal, and may depend in practice on how teams or groups make decisions in each organisation.

Content may be duplicated in some Framework fields. For example, the same data-gathering approach may work equally well for more than one measure. Likewise, in some cases the Value Lens may be measured identically across all the Perspectives. For instance, an example Inheritance/Legacy indicator might read as:

> Measuring the increase in the way the public cherish and derive benefit from knowing that the cultural organisation is providing digital resources/services. Measurable differences in significant engagements such as bequeathing or creating content, increases in interest to share with the cultural organisation.

Such an indicator for the Inheritance/Legacy value could apply to all four Strategic Perspectives, with a shared and simple data-gathering approach of:

> Case study approach supported by survey data and interviews with a detailed narrative of benefits.

Fields in the BVI Framework

The core fields of the BVI Framework are:

- Strategic Perspective
- Value Lens
- Objectives
- Assumptions
- Indicators
- Stakeholders
- Data collection
- Action plans
  - Timeframe
  - Budget
  - Roles.

The BVI Framework can be visualised as a simple hierarchy, as shown in Figure 7.1 on the next page.

There are one or more Value Lens pairing per Strategic Perspective. Each Value Lens requires a separate objective. Objectives are short, pithy statements of what is to be measured and what the outcome would encompass. The following is an example objective:

Perspective–Value Lens Pairing: Innovation + Education

Objective: To measure the benefits of using our digital collection to demonstrate a change in teaching and learning through its innovative use.

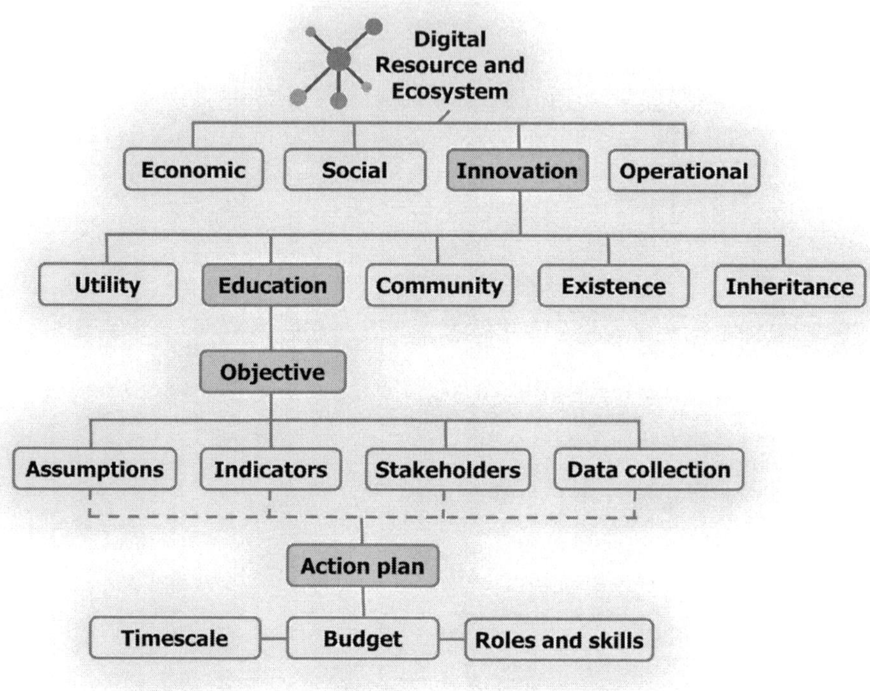

Figure 7.1 *The BVI Framework visualised as a hierarchy*

Note any assumptions that will affect the impact assessment. The following is an assumption:

Assumptions: Educational change and innovation align with the use of our digital collection.

The indicators that will measure the change which the objective seeks to explore will be defined. Fulfil the indicator through the assessment of a set group of stakeholders specific to each objective. A suitable method of investigation is defined for the Indicator with its specific means of data collection also clearly described (data collection). For example:

Indicator: Measuring the lifelong learning enabled by our digital services and products is a significant possible indicator of social and cultural benefit.

Indicated by new or increased use of teaching resources/packs and usage of new technologies in teaching/learning like MOOCs.

Stakeholders: End-users and/or re-users of the digital collections and MOOCs.

Data collection: Qualitative measures: case studies. Survey to identify participants followed by individual case studies, through interviews with stakeholders, delivering a detailed narrative of change and benefits.

For each objective, detail an action plan including the organisational strategy it addresses, the planned actions and a budget and timescale for completion. The plan also specifies the roles of those who will be carrying out the main activities of the impact assessment. For example:

Timeframe: Survey feedback after six months of new content release. Structured interviews to follow for case studies, completion within 11 months of new content release. A report in month 12.

Budget: Survey requires three days of staff time in total, using a free survey tool to set a survey, distribute, then collect and collate results. Interviews require ten person-days to complete 15 structured interviews and record the results in a usable format. Consider possible travel or venue costs and possible consultant costs for interviews.

Roles:
- Impact co-ordinator role tasked in defining questions for the survey and structured interviews. Possibly to carry out interviews.
- Administration role tasked to deliver survey creation, distribution and collection plus setting up of structured interviews.
- Management oversight to support work progress and resourcing.

BVI Model Stage 2: Design the Framework

Generating ideas to build the Framework

A key challenge in building a BVI Framework is generating new ideas and coming up with the best options for fields such as Objectives, Assumptions, Indicators and Stakeholders. The challenge is to ignore the status quo and put

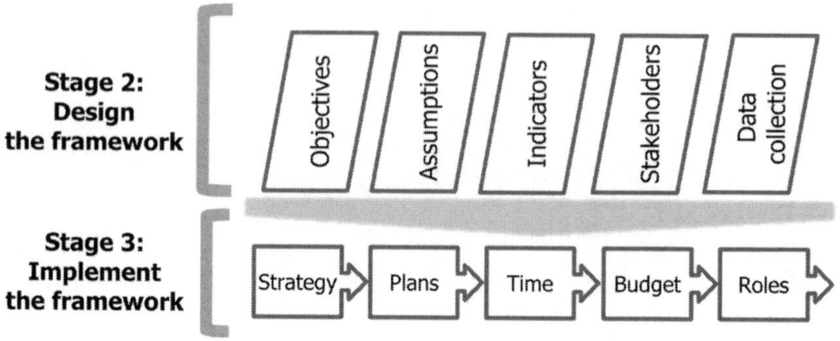

Figure 7.2 *Stages 2 and 3 of the BVI Model*

concerns about resources and operational matters to one side for long enough that new ideas can flow. The process needs to be reflective enough to respect past activity, benchmarks, measures, strategies and values without being shackled to them. Thus Stage 1 is to generate information and inspiration for ideation that will enable Stage 2 to find new questions and approaches to the assessment.

The process of ideation has two phases.

1 the generation of many ideas: quantity and the willingness to challenge any orthodoxies matter the most;
2 refinement and synthesis: combine, discard and thus narrow ideas into a set of viable options.

Generating ideas is about asking 'what if?' questions, especially to challenge assumptions, to provoke fresh thinking and to broaden the scope of assessment indicators and data-collection methods. The narrowing of ideas thus generated is given shape by the Framework, and the constraints that it provides deliver structure to the ideas generated.

The following are some key considerations in ideation.

- Is the team generating the ideas sufficiently diverse actually to generate fresh ideas? Consider adding people from areas not usually included in strategic or planning processes. Include stakeholders and outsiders to challenge assumptions. Ensure that the ideas-generation team represents

the target audiences with both demographic diversity and a range of expertise and experience.
- Use Stage 1 to produce a clear, well-defined statement of what is needed. The statement could be documentation provided as background reading; or the Perspective–Value pairings can provide the point of focus and thus the clarity of purpose for idea generation.
- Brainstorming is the most frequently used ideation method, but there are many ways of doing it. Those which involve some level of visual involvement (e.g., sticky notes on walls or windows), sketching ideas or building/physical representation (e.g. using kids' building blocks) tend to be more immersive and creative (Osterwalder et al., 2010). Other approaches, such as the Open Space approach or Unconference, can also be powerful tools for focused discussion in a participant-driven process (Owen, 2008). The key is getting ideas noted and shared such that everyone can see and contribute iteratively, with each idea begetting new ideas.
- Defer judgement and encourage wild ideas. There will be time for narrowing later; the first iteration is about quantity.
- Have a leader of the activity who is good at facilitation but also understands very well the desired outcomes of the process.
- Give the process time. Creativity rarely happens in those short gaps between major meetings; it needs time to ferment. Similarly, any exercise with lots of people will take time to bed in, to generate trust and thus to become productive.

The ideas generated can be narrowed through the focal lens of the Framework's fields and its structured requirements to deliver a set of viable options.

Setting objectives

An objective in the Framework is a measurable impact outcome achievable within the desired timeframe and available resources.

Objectives are best expressed as short, pithy statements that say what is to be measured and what the outcome will encompass. Derive objectives from a combination of factors explored in Stage 1 and explicitly related to each Perspective–Value pairing. They will be measurable via the indicators and data-collection techniques defined. The objectives for differing Perspective–Value pairings will provide different outcomes to be measured.

Consider this brief example. The digital resource is a national digitised newspaper resource that operates within the ecosystem of a web-based full-text newspaper collection that is free at the point of use.

Perspective–Value pairing: Social + Community

Objective: To measure whether the use of the newspaper resource in local communities (such as public libraries, museums, clubs and schools/colleges) fosters a sense of place and a sense of community cohesion and understanding.

Perspective–Value pairing: Economic + Education

Objective: To measure the educational benefits that have (or will be) accrued through the use of the newspaper resource and to monetise those benefits in comparison to other potential methods of achieving the same outcome to demonstrate the ROI.

As can be seen, each objective suggests slightly different modes of exploration in the method of data collection and the stakeholders investigated (although a survey may encompass both). Most importantly, the analysis of the resultant collected data will be very different. Objectives are thus vital to ensure that the focus remains on measuring outcomes, not mere outputs.

Objectives are also the criteria against which a judgement or decision is made. They provide a basic standard or test of whether the impact is measurable. For example, the Imperial War Museum have used these impact assessment objective criteria in past equality strategies:

> For each of the key functions and policies, the Museum will consider the impact of current policies and procedures associated with equality of opportunity. For each policy the following criteria will be applied:
>
> - Is there any evidence of higher or lower participation of different groups?
> - Is there any evidence that different groups have different needs, experiences or issues?
> - Is there an opportunity to promote equality of opportunity or better community relations by altering the policy or working in partnership with others?
> - Have consultations with relevant groups or individuals indicated that particular policies create problems which are specific to them?
>
> (Imperial War Museum, 2007)

An objective may map directly to the impact assessment from an organisation's mission, a project's purpose, the digital resource's *raison d'être*, or will be defined partly in KPIs or other metrics already in place. It is best if the objective is focused on outcomes: intended and direct, short- and medium-term effects on the target stakeholder groups. The objective must lie within the scope of the digital collection or activity assessed and must be directly attributable to them.

In practice, it is often difficult to distinguish outcomes from outputs or activities. A trap frequently fallen into is to 'prescribe activities instead of objectives – what they will do to get there rather than what they want to achieve' (Streatfield and Markless, 2012). A feature of a well-formed impact objective is the focus on measuring the benefit to the stakeholder through measurable outcomes. These are often stated in terms of improvement/change/increase/growth concerning knowledge, actions taken, capacity, skills, attitude, behaviour or condition (Irwin, 2017).

Objectives need to be something that, if they are met, can be stated with confidence and are checkable via an audit trail to demonstrate the validity of the met conditions or criteria. The following example objectives explore impact in its broadest conception.

- Make improvements in the health of children in the poorest parts of the community via access to the health information source and services.
- Stakeholder communities have better access to formal and informal education through digital services and activities. These lead to demonstrable improvements in education outcomes.
- Students demonstrate improved independent learning skills in their use of the Virtual Learning Environment.
- Local schoolchildren will increase the amount read, and read more extensively for pleasure.
- To foster the increased understanding of works of art in users of our museum app.
- Socially disadvantaged people will be better informed and empowered to more decision making or influence in the community.
- Small and medium enterprises will use our digital images to create more products or services of tangible economic benefit.

These are just some illustrative examples. The best ones start by naming the stakeholders. The benefit of working in an actual impact assessment is that the objectives will be less generalised and can be more precise and tightly focused than these examples.

Objectives are worthwhile spending time and effort on, as good questions tend to lead to better answers and more natural planning.

Assumptions

All impact assessments accept that they cannot measure everything, for all time, in every way possible. As such, there are areas that are deliberately not investigated, or there are assumptions made that certain conditions, skills or resources are already in place. For instance, assumptions might include access to an internet-enabled computer, participation in community activities or the availability of a museum or library in the locality.

The listing of assumptions helps to ensure that the assessment is not corrupted from the beginning by an unseen bias or assumption which might either exclude stakeholders or skew the measurement, such that these remain unaccounted for in the design of the data collection or the subsequent analysis. Keep the adage of correlation not equalling causation at the forefront of your mind in this process.

One widespread assumption is that 'everyone has a smartphone these days', and thus will access digital content via those devices and apps. This assumption is frequently confirmed by statistics showing very high mobile phone ownership in many countries. However, ownership of a data-connected device does not mean that a person has data to spend. Mobile data costs are often significant barriers to accessing information or online resources, yet in many communities with no hard-wired internet the only access to data is via mobile technologies. Consider the choices confronting an economically disadvantaged person. Would they spend their precious 100Mb of data on browsing museum image collections or downloading audiobooks? Would they not be much more likely to spend it on Facetime with family, and to use it to search for jobs, make payments or engage with health or care services? I live in England, where I can download audiobooks for free from the library, access free high-resolution museum images from across the world and delve into free family history archives – but only because I am wealthy enough to afford the data without a second thought. Public memory institutions that offer free Wi-Fi are great equalisers in data access, and should be lauded for their efforts (and not even requiring a coffee purchase in return).

Considering assumptions can sometimes reveal a mode of investigation that was not previously considered but which may show a more substantial change than similar measurements within mainstream stakeholder groups. For instance, assuming that all users can read English excludes not just the non-English readers but possibly those with a learning disability – and yet it is possible that both these groups could benefit in ways that can be measurably larger than the mainstream, in certain circumstances. Making a list of assumptions, if viewed from the proper perspective, will protect the impact assessment process and open up opportunities for better measurement.

Indicators

An indicator is 'a piece of information that indicates something useful to you' (Streatfield and Markless, 2012). The essential thing to bear in mind in the selection and use of indicators is that they are a measure of a tendency in certain conditions, a measure of a state of being, and never an absolute value. Thus, indicators provide clues to answering the questions posited by the objectives within each Perspective–Value pairing.

Canary birds are an everyday example of an indicator in action. From 1911 to 1986 canaries were used in British coal mines to detect carbon monoxide and other toxic gases before these could injure the miners. A canary is an excellent early detector of carbon monoxide because they are vulnerable to airborne poisons and their anatomy allows them to get a dose of oxygen when they inhale and another when they exhale (Eschner, 2016). An ailing or dead canary would indicate the presence of potentially dangerous levels of carbon monoxide or other gases. So, while the ill health of a canary was not absolute proof of gas danger, it provided an excellent indicator that such danger was extremely likely and urgent action was needed. The metaphor of the 'canary in the coalmine' persists long past the birds' replacement by electronic gas monitors because it clearly expresses the idea of causation: where one event is statistically highly likely to result from the occurrence of a prior specific event.

In setting indicators, the search is for the useful 'canaries' to apply to certain types of 'coal mines'. There are many possible measures, but some are not convincing enough, while others may be tangential to the purpose of measurement. The digital domain can be a challenging area in which to find suitable indicators. There can be a lack of effective baselines, or the data may not have a long enough history to be meaningful. Using visitor numbers or hits alone is usually only of partial usefulness, as these often do not tell enough about the value placed on the interaction or the benefit derived. However, while quantitative measures are often not particularly satisfying on their own they can be potent when accompanied by other supporting contextualising information.

Impact indicators generally should focus on showing a change for those in the community that the resource serves. Change can be on many dimensions, usually defined as behavioural, knowledge-based, competence-based or attitudes. If people do things differently, if they know more, are better able to do something, or if they think or feel differently about it, then the impact can be claimed.

Case study 7.1: Impact at the Corning Museum of Glass

The Corning Museum of Glass in the USA records over 1 million hours of viewing time per year on its YouTube channel (www.youtube.com/user/corningmuseumofglass; Kritzeck, 2018). This indicates a high level of engagement, as viewers are watching videos multiple times and commenting very frequently:

> on average, over half of our videos are viewed for longer than 25% of their total run time. This is remarkable considering that our livestreams are typically an hour or more long.
>
> (Kritzeck, 2018)

Because the Corning Museum offers videos on glassmaking, they found that the best indicator of this core stakeholder group's engagement with the museum is through their length of time spent and amount of interaction as part of the audience. The Museum also know that the videos are used by instructors in the decorative arts in their curricula, and so the Museum constructs playlists for teachers every year. Generally, this is more powerful than relying only on the number of views as an indicator of impact (although a guest artist video, featuring James Mongrain, went viral to the tune of 4.2 million views!).

As Mandy Kritzeck, digital media producer/project manager, states:

> The most effective way that we engage our audience is through livestreams. We are constantly listening to viewer feedback and implementing suggested changes where it makes sense to do so. One of the most immediate ways is through actively commenting and responding to viewer questions during the livestreams. When someone is watching our stream on YouTube or Facebook (it is simulcasted to

both) there is someone from our team on site at the demonstration who is responding to questions and comments online, and we have a narrator who explains what is happening in the glassmaking hot shop. We average about three comments per minute ...

YouTube is a good platform for engaging with our audience because of the commenting features, how easy it is for us to livestream at a high quality and because people can subscribe to our channel. We recently surpassed 100,000 subscribers, earning the coveted YouTube Silver Play Button Award.

(Kritzeck, 2018)

SMART indicators

Indicators are the points of evidence to demonstrate that the conditions sought in objectives are met. All indicators should adhere to the SMART criteria: specific, measurable, attainable, relevant, timebound.

The following are essential considerations in establishing useful indicators for the Framework.

1. Ensure that the indicator will, as directly as feasible, provide evidence for the objective set in the Framework.
2. Focus the indicator on measuring change. It may be necessary to define a benchmark or a baseline from which change is measured.
3. Choose as few indicators as possible to achieve the objective. For the Framework, no more than two per Perspective–Value pairing is desirable.
4. Establish SMART indicators, considering whether the data:
   a. is available or attainable
   b. comes from a credible source
   c. is large enough
   d. is gatherable in a suitable timeframe.
5. Do not over-commit to quantitative indicators. Remember that a mixed model of quantitative and qualitative approaches generally provides more powerfully persuasive evidence.
6. Test the validity of the indicator. Consider the question: if all these factors were true, would that satisfy that the measure of success is achieved?
7. Create a shared understanding of what an indicator will measure and demonstrate. If stakeholders or decision makers do not accept the

significance of the indicator, then the results will not be trusted.

8 Check the fairness of the indicator. It is important to measure that which the memory institution has some modicum of control over and which provides a reasonable narrative of the complete story. It is not a fair measure to attempt to show that an archive made a great historian or a gallery a famous artist. For instance, no one should credibly believe that Nicholson's café or The Elephant House, both in Edinburgh, were responsible for J. K. Rowling's success as a writer.
9 Spend time and resources on research to demonstrate that an indicator will generate a sense of causality between action and effect. It is tempting to assume that causality will exist in all other areas that are merely similar to the first indicator.
10 Never assume that an indicator that works well in one circumstance will be meaningful in a different environment. The temptation to stretch indicators to fit different situations is strong. For example, measuring children's satisfaction with a digital resource in a rural school classroom is unlikely to be an adequate indicator of their satisfaction at home or in different regions. It will have value, but more likely the indicator is not so easily transferable.
11 Be prepared to review indicators in response to changing circumstances or finding that the data provided is not matching the objective's criteria.

In short, indicators are the most critical part of the impact assessment. They decide if it is an accurate assessment. It should thus be possible for data gathered from indicators to show both negative as well as positive results. Poor indicators can easily lead to bad assessments where the results are corrupted by data which gives a false impression or incentivises disruptive or counter-productive actions such as target chasing.

A brief list of possible indicators

Indicators are never absolute measures. However, significance can be assigned if the indicator is clear enough. To illustrate, using street noise as an example: if a source of noise measured over time continually exceeds the legal limits, then this will be a significant indicator of negative noise impact.

Indicators of a beneficial change in someone's life or life opportunity through engagement with a digital resource may be in areas such as:

- education and learning
- engagement with and increase in knowledge
- economy and wealth generation
- health and well-being
- social and community cohesion
- environment and sustainability
- politics and democracy
- technology and innovation
- entertainment and participation
- equality and equity.

The focus should always remain on measuring change and evaluating the value of that change.

The following list suggests factors that make good indicators.

1. Metric approaches
   - How large is the group of active users of the resource? Possibly a measure of reach and significance.
   - Where are the active users and other stakeholders located? Does the digital resource save them time and money over attending in person?
   - What times of day do the active users utilise the resource? Time of day may indicate leisure or work uses.
   - How do stakeholders spend their time? How much of their time is spent being part of the resource's group of active users? This may indicate the significance of the resource if they spend a lot of their discretionary time being part of the audience.
2. What is the level of engagement by the stakeholders, possibly measured through the length of time engaging or the conversations held (particularly in social media)?
3. What is the level of enjoyment, enthusiasm or motivation in the stakeholders?
4. Does the resource enrich school curricula or other learning environments?
5. Are stakeholders stimulated to learn more? This may be indicated by return visits, recommendations to others or uptake of activities or courses.
6. Can the level, depth and breadth of subject knowledge be measured?

Possible indicators would be the ability to recollect memorable facts, e.g., by using quizzes to test knowledge before and after an experience.

7 Have the stakeholders acquired new or improved skills?
8 What change is measurable in the stakeholders' sense of self-confidence, self-esteem, community or attitudes, including:
   - social cohesion
   - community empowerment
   - local culture and identity
   - imagination and creativity
   - health and well-being?
9 What are the measurable changes within the organisation, including:
   - staff attitudes
   - staff skills and abilities
   - quality of decision making
   - changes in efficiency and effectiveness
   - economic measures, such as ROI or cost-benefit
   - ability to innovate and respond to change?
10 What indicators of economic change can be measured? Include both direct and indirect measures, such as:
   - income growth or diversification;
   - size of audience or market share;
   - capital funds spent in the local community, such as building projects;
   - employment: increases in permanent jobs, wages and salary payments;
   - contribution to Gross Domestic Product (GDP);
   - the incomes and jobs that result from active users of the resource in local businesses – known as the supplier and induced effects, using economic multipliers;
   - tourist spending levels: spending by the stakeholders in the local economy;
   - stakeholders expressing a willingness to pay for services;
   - the value of time for active users in travelling to a physical service point as compared to using a digital resource;
   - ROI;
   - cost versus benefits.
11 Contribution to the preservation of heritage and culture.

This list is purely indicative and not a complete and definitive list of the possible things that could make interesting or useful indicators.

The digital template at www.BVIModel.org provides some further examples in the context of the Framework.

Stakeholders

Stage 1 resulted in as complete a categorised list of stakeholders as feasible (Chapter 6). Use this in conjunction with the idea-generation process to assign stakeholder groups to each of the Objective/Indicator lines in the Framework. Give primary stakeholders precedence, but always consider other stakeholders.

Categorised stakeholders can be assigned as many times as necessary, and with as much overlap as required. There can be more than one stakeholder group per indicator. Avoid overly vague group categories, such as 'the general public'. It is good to be specific in assigning stakeholders even if this leads to overlap, such as assigning schoolchildren, teenagers and university students as separately named stakeholder groups. It is also fine for the same stakeholder group to be represented in multiple indicators – teachers, for instance.

Most of the time it will not be possible to research all possible stakeholders, or even every representative grouping. A critical choice is thus to identify or classify groups of stakeholders that can be considered broadly representative of the community within the specific indicator. The validity and worth of data gathered may well rest on whether the stakeholder group is considered convincing as a proxy or exemplar for a broader community.

Most methods for data gathering and indicators will fall into a few basic categories: surveys, questionnaires, observation, focus groups, feedback and participatory investigations. The BVI Model's focus on digital resources also provides some additional advantages, most notably the opportunity to reach out digitally to the user base through the digital resource itself or to use web metrics or social media measures to assess change in usage patterns in response to interventions.

The BVI Model assumes that leadership in assessment comes from the memory institution, with an implicit hierarchy thus inbuilt. To avoid conflicts growing from the process, adhere to the basic principles of successfully engaging with stakeholders. Know the audience intimately, meet with them on their terms and have a conversation or other interaction that creates opportunities for meaningful participation.

Data collection

The core methods of measuring impact will by necessity revolve around a mixture of quantitative and qualitative measures. These feed into an impact narrative as the outcome. Despite the many available methods, most data collection will use mechanisms for which memory institutions have some prior experience; thus the task is to organise, structure and deploy them strategically to serve the plan.

Data collection is mainly about surveys, questionnaires, case studies, web metrics, observation, focus groups, feedback, market research and participatory investigations. For any given indicator collect some quantitative data first to help identify the scope, range and participants of the activity. Follow this with qualitative measures, such as case studies, to provide a stronger narrative evidence base to demonstrate the extent and depth of the impact achieved. The layering of evidence and data is essential to provide a fully contextualised impact outcome.

A glossary of the many methods of data collection for impact assessment is provided at www.BVIModel.org.

At implementation of data collection, thinking flips from a design-centric Framework approach to activity-centric planning and action. Each activity needs an associated impact data-collection mini-plan, made to manage that specific process. The activity being measured has to happen and be successful for impact to occur; thus, the detailed planning will always be activity-focused. The Framework allows for control over all those mini-plans to convey a structured process and centralised information hub for evidence of impact.

Choosing methods of gathering and interpreting evidence

The following are those attributes of a data-collection method or technique that should be foremost considerations in helping to choose the most appropriate method.

- Is the information needed already available, for instance, gathered by current data analytics or by a partner organisation?
- Cost: if the information can be gathered, how much is it worth to know that information?
- In what timeframe will the method allow for results to become available? What time will be needed to gather data?

- Are the methods of data gathering going to deliver usable, reliable, comparable and useful data?
- What is the availability of respondents and what is the likelihood of gaining a good proportion of responses from stakeholders?

Other measurements may also continue to take place in parallel with any impact assessment, such as those associated with marketing or user satisfaction. Impact is not the only reason to measure, and not everything measured will necessarily support impact evaluation, but it may contribute to the context of the organisation's impact. These other measures may include, for example:

- quantitative measures of audience reach
- qualitative/quantitative testing of user experience
- technical delivery: achievement of technical quality targets
- governance/financial management: measured via audit
- amount of value created for partners
- delivery to strategic KPIs.

The following is an overview of some of the popular methods of data collection suitable for use with the BVI Model.

Data analytics and KPIs are the starting point for every data gathering. Where these exist, the advantage is that data is already being collected and provides at least information on reach and scope, as well as context to other measures. On their own, they are not helpful, but as a way of seeing where further investigation can be focused and as a way of segmenting audiences into stakeholder groups they work very well. These are useful for all indicators with mainly quantitative outputs, and can be especially useful for Utility values and Economic perspectives.

Web metrics and referrer analysis are quantitative techniques for tracking the usage of web content and sites/resources. Techniques within web metrics include usage figures, visitor information (location, time on site, demographics of users), web log analysis, link analysis, web mention analysis and blog or social media analysis. Another aspect of this is referrer analysis, a process to determine the ways in which a digital collection and resource is being used.

Links to an online resource can reveal data about its popularity and the most frequently used aspects for certain stakeholders. The advantage of link analysis is that it can be applied to any online resource, rather than needing administrative access to log files (which are also useful for data). Added to referrer analysis, data can be gathered about from where the resources are being accessed. For example, content used in a teaching pack or in an online course module, recommended on social media or cited in blogs, in academic research or as inspiration for new creative content.

Consider adding extensions to this kind of data gathering in web design and implementation, such that data gathering on usage is achieved via API key applications, referrer analysis and demographic and interests data collection. These are mainly quantitative outputs and are useful for Utility values.

Case studies are the main narrative tools for expressing impact. A case study involves an up-close, in-depth and detailed examination of a subject, as well as its related contextual conditions. The personalised narrative and the precision of the change or benefit gained add weight to the claims made for impact. Thus, it is essential for any case study to be backed by other evidential data to provide the context, such that it adds significance. Measures of Community, Existence and Inheritance values will often rely on case study and focus group approaches.

Surveys remain a principal tool for asking specific questions of a defined stakeholder group. Surveys tend to be overused by memory institutions without sufficient focused purpose. They must have rigorous design and professional application to be a success in gaining useful data. The memory institutions must know the stakeholders in order to reach them; otherwise surveys can be an expensive process with low response rates. Surveys are particularly useful for Utility indicators and can produce both quantitative and qualitative data.

Web surveys are a sub-set of surveys, carried out purely on the web. They fall into several main types, such as:

- intercept surveys
- list-based samples
- polls as entertainment
- unrestricted self-selected surveys
- volunteer opt-in panels
- pre-recruited panels of internet users
- pre-recruited panels of the full population.

Intercept, list-based and volunteer opt-in panels are the most feasible to apply. Web surveys are a useful starting point for all indicators, especially for Education values. The outputs are both quantitative and qualitative.

Focus groups are a useful tool for finding out the specific benefits gained by a representative group, so as to indicate a broader beneficial group. Leading a focus group needs high skill levels to gain a meaningful outcome and rigorous identification and selection of representative participants. Focus groups work very well for social and cultural impacts, especially for Community values. The data collected is qualitative.

The structured interview holds a kind of halfway position between surveys and focus groups, as it involves a one-to-one interview where the questions are pre-set in a survey style. The interview can range beyond the pre-set questions. All questions must be asked to allow for comparison of results, but the order can vary. While they are time-consuming, they are an especially effective method for gaining opinions and providing comparable data from a range of interviewees, especially experts, policy makers, decision makers or funders. These can be most useful to Education and Inheritance values. The data collected is qualitative but may also include some quantitative information.

Economic measurement comes with a huge range of techniques. Those featured here are the most likely to be of use to memory institutions, as they combine economic and social/community factors. In every case, they require skills that are unlikely to be present within many memory institutions and thus may require external support or consultancy to achieve. As a result, all methods will be costly to achieve at any level of satisfaction. These methods apply to the Economic, Social and Operational perspectives, with outcomes that are both quantitative and qualitative.

1 **Consumer surplus value** is the benefit to those who would otherwise never use the resource and is a form of induced demand. It relies on effectively increasing consumption of a resource through the increase in supply. In the example of the BL (see Case study 3.5), they relied on a suggested value from McKinsey relating to 'recreational internet services' of €20 per month and 'used in conjunction with the relative proportion of time spent on the Library's website to derive a consumer surplus value' (The British Library, 2004).
2 **Multiplier analysis** is associated with capturing the scale and geographical pattern of expenditure impacts and applying multipliers

to reflect the induced and indirect impacts of these. It is a more loosely applied version of PMA (proportional multiplier analysis), where the economic impact of user-based spending relating to a service/product consists of four stages:

a the initial spending by the visitors in the local economy (known as the multiplicand);
b the direct impacts: the incomes and jobs resulting from visitors' spending in destination businesses;
c the indirect impacts: the incomes and jobs that visitor spending generate as a result of businesses buying goods and services locally;
d the induced impacts: the incomes and jobs resulting from people spending some, or all, of any income earned as a result of the visitor spending.

3 **Contingent valuation** assesses the values associated with the user and non-user's willingness to pay to continue accessing a service, or the willingness to accept if the service were to cease.
4 **Income compensation** is an enhancement and adaptation of the contingent valuation (willingness to pay) approach that seeks to link perceptions of well-being with participation in cultural activities and to assign income values to these.
5 **ROI** seeks to obtain a ratio of the benefit of availability of service against the cost of providing that service, using a combination of user value and multiplier techniques.

Public engagement data collection

Case study 7.2: Public engagement evaluation at King's College London

Public events or moments of public engagement are prime opportunities for gathering data that may indicate impact. However, most surveys or evaluations are too meek or oriented towards 'was the food good' questions to be useful for impact purposes. It is essential to ask bold questions and to ask directly for what is needed.

The answers can be most surprising if there is a willingness to ask the more direct 'how has this changed your life' type of questions. At King's College London the annual Arts and Humanities Festival changed its evaluation in 2016. It included new questions like 'I learned something new to me', 'I feel healthier' and 'I feel like I'm going to make a change in my life'. These were a stark departure from previous year's questions about whether the speaker or performance was good or the amenities suitable. The results were validating. Finding that people coming to a festival run by a university felt that they had learned something new was not surprising and easily explained the 89% positive response rate; validating the mission of the university. The responses of ~10% who 'felt healthier' and ~7% who stated that they 'feel I will make a change in my life' due to attending the festival were more surprising, and particularly significant from an impact point of view. Following up with testimonials allowed participants to further express their feelings about the festival.

Seeking feedback from an event audience should aim to answer impact indicators. The answers thus gathered will show a trend, a measure of tendency, or will provide a point of evidence to show that the event or activity has made a difference or a change to those who have engaged with it. Note that while no single event/activity will provide all the evidence needed to demonstrate impact, it can provide enough of an indicator of impact to be useful when aggregated with all other factors gathered.

The guidance below suggests some ways to gather impact indicators from a public event (whether online or in person) through feedback or survey approaches.

- It will always be a good idea to ask why people have decided to come to the event (establishing their stake in the topic) and whether their original perceptions on the topic have been strengthened, challenged or otherwise affected by the event.
- Depending on the nature of the event, a further question could ask whether the event is likely to impact on the person's own professional or personal practice.
- In events with strong public attendance do not be afraid to ask participants how they feel about or react to the event.
- Methods to gather information could be through questionnaires (but vox pop style). Video mini-interviews are also highly effective and engaging (www.bbc.co.uk/academy/production/article/art20141029111247531).
- Contact details (ideally e-mail) are essential so that potentially interesting responses can be followed up in greater detail after the event. Testimonies are valuable as impact indicators, so being able to ask later to investigate a specific type of response can be useful.

- Ask for information about age, gender, sexuality, religion/belief, race, ethnicity and disability, as this information helps to show the reach of the impact. However, such information may be more relevant for certain events than for others, so ethics and sensitivities must be respected. Some of this information may be gathered from the registration process rather than by direct survey. Be aware throughout of the EU's General Data Protection Regulations (www.eugdpr.org).
- Making a podcast, video or blog of the event and posting it online can be a suitable means of increasing attention to the event/activity still further – especially if the web posting allows space for public comment/engagement. Measuring the online usage and interest in this digital space can then become further indicator data.

The following are some possible questions to ask.

1 Tell us about your experience.
   a What was your reason for using this resource? Have your opinions on this topic been challenged, strengthened or otherwise affected?
   b Is your experience likely to impact on your own professional or personal practice? If so, please briefly say how.
2 Has this resource made you think differently about the subject?
   a Yes.
   b No.
   c We'd like to know how? Please tell us more.
3 Please tell us if you have experienced any of the following benefits? Please select all that seem relevant to you.
   a I learned something new to me.
   b I was entertained.
   c I'm going to plan a new activity/project.
   d I felt a sense of community.
   e I felt happier.
   f I have been inspired.
   g My creativity and/or imagination was enhanced.
   h I feel more connected to local culture.
   i I feel healthier.
   j I feel like I'm going to make a change in my life.
4 Has engaging with us changed your view of [insert organisation name]?
   a Yes.

b No.
c We'd like to know how? Please tell us or add any other comments.

Use responses in two main ways. First, as qualitative information providing evidence of the scope, extent or quality of the benefit through testimonials, comments or other qualitative information. Second, use information gathered quantitatively, especially about the proportions of participants, such as '30% of participants felt they would change their professional working practices in response to this event'.

Remember to tailor questions for each event/activity if this will gather information that will indicate impact more specifically to the BVI Framework. The questions given here are a brief guide only.

BVI Model Stage 3: Implement the Framework

Impact assessment is a matter of asking questions in a structured way and gathering the responses such that they can be understood. Much of the process here is about control and organisation; implementation of the plans that occur within the Framework will be smaller activities controlled within the whole.

At implementation, the focus shifts to mini-plans within the bigger plan. For each objective the action plan in the BVI Framework includes the organisational strategy it addresses, plus the planned actions with a budget and timescale for completion. It also specifies the roles of those who will be carrying out major aspects of the impact assessment.

Action plan: timeframe

The outcomes desired to be measured are the specific changes in stakeholders' behaviour, knowledge, skills, status and actions. Measuring over the very short term would usually be considered as no less than six months from the point of intervention from which change is to be measured. One difficulty for digital collections is how often even this is considered to be a long time. Couldn't the measurement be just for a couple of days or weeks after the launch of the new product or service? This question reveals the core difference between evaluation and impact assessment. In an impact assessment the focus is on behaviour change, not on immediate satisfaction, and, as such, this takes time.

Recalibrate considerations of timeframes to include the immediate but understanding that short-term is more likely to mean one year. Medium-term outcomes are likely to be attainable within one to two years, while long-term outcomes should be achievable after three years or more.

In the BVI Framework, having the measures as individual lines enables out-of-sync data collection to happen. Some measures may take a short time to gather (a focus group for instance), while others may be gathered over more extended periods (such as web metrics). Creating a timeframe for each will control the flow of data and planning of the activities.

Outside of the Framework, a regular set of stop points should be established to assess and analyse all the data that has been captured to date. This data becomes an impact outcome report. Reporting impact is discussed in Chapter 9.

Action plan: budget

A rigorous impact assessment will frequently cost more than the standard evaluations with which a memory institution has previously engaged. However, the budgetary effect can be quite low, depending on the type and availability of data collected, as the BVI Framework focuses effort on the core criteria and objectives to be measured. The reflective, responsive aspect of a rigorous impact assessment may lead to future cost savings, through improved digital content, services or activities, with more efficient use of resources over the longer term. Of course, a core reason for some impact assessments is to provide evidence of substantial value for money, or to justify further investment. In these cases, the required ROI in impact assessment can be calculated to assert that the funds are worth expending for the desired outcomes.

Some measures are passive (such as web metrics) and do not require constant investment once established. Other measures may require external support that comes with a visible cost. However, planning for additional costs, especially in terms of staffing and budget needs, is vital to address the value and worth of doing an impact assessment.

In the Framework, each objective has its budget assigned to it. As different timeframes may apply to each objective, so budgets potentially should plan across many years to achieve the envisaged continuous assessment. Consider the eternal balance of all projects: a project can be cheap, quick or excellent, but rarely all three at once. The balance of these factors is likely to define the choices made.

Action plan: roles and skills

Each memory institution will need to utilise skills from within and may need to bring in other skills and resources from outside as the impact assessment progresses. A range of specific skills will be needed, including:

- strategic planning
- project management
- basic audit skills
- desk research and literature review
- stakeholder analysis and community engagement knowledge
- evaluation expertise
- applied data gathering methods and techniques expertise, such as:
  - — web metrics and analytics experience
  - — survey and questionnaire design
  - — case study knowledge
  - — interviewing and testimonial-gathering skills
  - — market research and segmentation expertise
  - — economic evaluation expertise
- data analytics and visualisation expertise
- narrative, communications and design expertise to deliver results to an external audience.

Remember that implementing the BVI Model can be done very much as a local activity, embedding the principles of impact in the everyday activity, with small-scale monitoring to create evidence and a feedback loop of actionable intelligence. This is achievable within current skills bases by following the exemplars given in guides, such as the *Impact Playbook* (Verwayen et al., 2017). Larger-scale impact assessments, particularly those engaging with multiple regions, multiple organisations or tricky processes such as economic measurements, may need external support. There is a growing cadre of consultants who now specialise not just in evaluation but in impact assessments and who can bring this knowledge into memory institutions.

Each impact assessment is likely to assign or establish the following roles.

- Management oversight: to ensure that work progresses to plan and to budget. To lead the review of results (Stages 4 and 5) and recommend any organisational changes resulting from the impact assessment.

- Impact co-ordinator: to design the Framework and implement and control the impact assessment. To manage the data collected and to lead data analysis, communication of outcomes and review of the results.
- Administration: to administer resources and activities that support the impact assessment. To ensure that the BVI Framework is kept up to date.
- Data analytics: to make meaningful assessments of data gathered that result in tangible outcomes.
- Communications: to lead communication with the stakeholders in the process. To lead the narration and distribution of the impact results.
- Expert panel: to provide expertise (internal and external) to guide the impact assessment in a peer review role. To advise on the suitability of objectives, indicators and data gathering and to provide feedback on the results in a review stage.
- Possible external consultancy: to add skills that are not available in-house.

Defining these roles will enable the task to be distributed appropriately and managed over the long term. A single person may hold more than one role.

Chapter 8

Europeana case study implementing the BVI Model

Julia Fallon with Simon Tanner

Introduction

This chapter presents a user perspective on implementing the BVI Model through a case study provided by the Europeana Foundation.

The questions focused on in this case study are:

- a reflection on Europeana's implementation of impact assessment with a focus on one complete cycle;
- the ideas driving how Europeana developed the *Impact Playbook*;
- how these integrate with the BVI Model.

The Europeana Foundation: history and context

The Europeana Foundation is the organisation tasked by the EC with developing a digital cultural heritage platform for Europe. They state their mission as:

> We transform the world with culture. We build on Europe's rich cultural heritage and make it easier for people to use for work, learning or pleasure. Our work contributes to an open, knowledgeable and creative society.
>
> (https://pro.europeana.eu/our-mission)

Europeana has its origin in libraries (Kenny, 2017). With funding from the EC, the European Library was developed and eventually launched in 2005 as a search engine and open data hub for library collections. This expanded over the following years, but 2005 also saw a call from several heads of state, supported by 19 national libraries, for increased investment from the European Union. By 30 September 2005 the EC adopted the i2010: Digital Libraries strategy, which outlined the vision for the digital libraries initiative.

Europeana was born as a key deliverable of the initiative, and the Europeana prototype went live on 20 November 2008. It was open and inclusive, such that museums, university collections and archives contributed alongside libraries. Europeana created a common point of access to Europe's cultural heritage, with 4.5 million digital objects available on its launch date. It took until the summer of 2010 for this prototype to transition into a fully operational service.

One of Europeana's key innovations was to release all Europeana metadata as a Creative Commons CC0 1.0 Universal Public Domain Dedication in September 2012. This was a very significant strategic move, not just in establishing the principles by which Europeana operates but in guiding and supporting Europeana Network Association members to institute change and thus making the metadata freely available for any use that demonstrably boosts creativity and digital innovation. The move to CC0 also encouraged the making available of much other content under similar provisions. At the time of writing, there are over 13 million open access digital objects in Europeana.

In 2015 Europeana became one of the EC's Digital Service Infrastructures. Alongside this strategic leadership role to open the fullest possible benefits of digital services in culture to Europe's people and businesses came the requirement to build long-term financial stability through business model innovation. Thus, in parallel with growth in the Europeana Network Association to over 2,000 experts and 3,500 of Europe's cultural heritage institutions, Europeana had to renew its strategic focus and provide reliable indicators of impact in order for this shared mission to expand and improve access to Europe's digital cultural heritage. Europeana developed its impact framework as part of Strategy 2020 (Europeana Foundation, 2014b) and has further led the sector with the Europeana *Impact Playbook* (Verwayen et al., 2017) as a critical component in providing ongoing impact evaluation.

At the time of writing Europeana Collections (www.europeana.eu/portal/en) give access to over 58 million digital objects, 12 thematic collections, 35 exhibitions, 151 curated galleries and 632 collections blogs (http://blog.europeana.eu/). The portal regularly receives well over 1 million accesses per month, but these are merely measures of scale and reach rather than significance. As will be demonstrated in this case study, measuring the impact of a digital resource (especially one as distributed as Europeana) is much more than counting users, but is a matter of delving deeper into the importance to stakeholders of what they engage with.

Co-research and co-production perspectives

I have co-researched impact for several years with the Europeana Foundation. The term 'co-research' is deliberately used to express that information and knowledge is not a one-way transference from academic to practitioners but 'often jointly created through dialectical processes of enquiry based on different interests and different perspectives' (Hartley and Benington, 2000). Researchers in favour of co-production and co-research should also seek to *not* reproduce unequal power relations (Durose et al., 2012). As such, it is important to also allow those co-researcher voices self-expression in academic works such as this.

Working together in a co-research method with practitioners has enhanced the BVI Model, and at times challenged it. The process of moving from theoretical idea to implementation is necessarily messy, iterative and recursive. Practitioners add experiential expertise that highlights questions otherwise neglected by academics, and dialogue can enhance research by informing researchers of the practitioner's preferences and needs. This process requires a strong commitment to the process from all participants, clear communications, patience and a willingness to be evidence driven.

The essence of co-research is to research 'with' participants, allowing challenges to embedded hierarchies of knowledge, while negotiating the boundaries of engagement between research and practice.

One challenge ever present in the co-research relationship is the desire of practitioners for workable solutions, which may rush them towards cherry-picking the most readily usable available individual mechanisms without much concern about theoretical underpinnings or conceptual completeness. Certainly, for instance, the BVI Model does not mix well with the Theory of Change models that attempt to induce a specific desired impact in a very directive fashion. Maintaining conceptual and theoretical clarity is clearly of greater academic interest, and yet remained important to the design and process thinking behind practitioner implementation.

Working with practitioners also introduces an element of peer review into the development of ideas, concepts and the testing of the BVI Model's feasibility. While many others have had a role in peer reviewing my research (see Acknowledgements), I would like to thank the Europeana Foundation and its network members for their willingness to co-research, co-produce and collaborate on impact matters for the broader benefit of citizens, memory institutions and the cultural and heritage communities.

The case study that follows has been written by Julia Fallon (Senior Policy Advisor, Europeana Foundation) and has been edited by Simon Tanner to fit the format and style of this book.

Case study 8.1: Europeana BVI Model implementation case study

Digital cultural heritage changes lives ... but how can we show it?

At Europeana we believe that everyone benefits from having better and easier access to high-quality and open digital cultural heritage. In 2019 we celebrate 11 years of working towards this goal. We are immensely proud to have published over 58 million digital objects contributed by more than 3,500 of Europe's cultural heritage institutions. However, our contribution is not limited to digitising and democratising cultural heritage. We have committed to measuring its effects – developing richer evidence of what is behind our mission statement of 'transforming the world with culture'.

During this time we have also been developing the Europeana Impact Framework (EIF), which establishes the principles of our approach to impact assessment and is supported with a toolkit of resources which we believe will help to articulate these intangible, unmeasurable benefits that we all so often talk about.

Since 2012 this work has evolved – from the development in 2014 of the EIF as part of Strategy 2020 (Europeana Foundation, 2014b), through to the publication in 2017 of the Europeana *Impact Playbook* (Verwayen et al., 2017) as a centrepiece of the toolkit that operationalised the EIF. The BVI Model lies at the heart of the *Playbook* and has helped us to frame and debate each step we have taken. At the end of 2017 we completed the first full cycle of impact assessment, which in turn provided the basis for continuing to develop the toolkit as well as the wider framework.

Preparation: the journey from a conceptual framework to operational plan

In 2017 Europeana set out to achieve a better understanding of how we would make the changes we describe in our strategy and business plans (https://pro.europeana.eu/tags/ business-plan). This was developed after the first impact assessment (in 2015), which followed the principles of the BVI Model impact framework and laid more groundwork for developing a replicable approach that the sector could use (Europeana Foundation, 2014a). One example, Workers Underground, explored the social impact of a successful and long-running project: Europeana 1914–1918, which collects, digitises and publishes personal memorabilia from the First World War (www.europeana.eu/portal/en/ collections/world-war-I). The results of the research were documented in a short film, and the process and main learning points in a case study (Verwayen, Wilms and Fallon, 2016).

Through this exemplar we learned about how the Europeana 1914–1918 programme was valued by the people who use it; but also that the results provided us with information that we could use to identify ways to improve and build on the existing activity. Our approach to collecting and analysing the data rested heavily on using five of the BVI Model's value drivers (which we renamed as Value Lenses, as they helped us focus and establish specific perspectives) to reflect on and categorise the data and our reflections on that data.

A significant highlight – articulated through the education lens – was that users did not learn as much as they expected to, and language was the main barrier to the discovery of new knowledge. With this experience fresh in our mind, and with a growing understanding that impact assessments could deliver more than a perspective on the subject of the assessment, we reset our ambition. Figure 8.1 shows the learning gap identified.

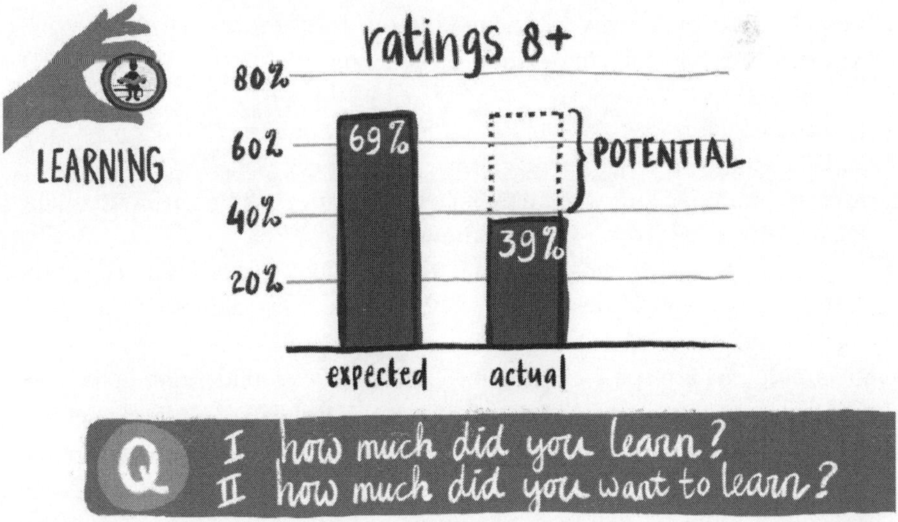

Figure 8.1 *Learning gap identified in the 2015 impact assessment of Europeana 1914–1918*

Our new goal was to enhance the EIF and draw more deeply from the BVI Model in order to undertake a second impact assessment and use that experience to develop and validate a practical working method that others could follow. Here, the BVI Model's Strategic Perspectives helped to guide our decision making; we had already explored a form of economic impact through a cost-benefit study in 2013 (Poort et al., 2013). With impact consultants Sinzer (www.sinzer.org) providing expert support and guidance, we defined the scope and rationale of the impact assessment to improve our understanding of the social impact of Europeana and a variety of the activities that we run or support.

We looked at Europeana's activities as an organisation and mapped them to the changes we wanted to bring about, using the Kellogg Foundation Logic Model (W. K. Kellogg Foundation, 2004). This process validated our strategic plans but also showed us where we could refine our work at either end of the spectrum presented by the Logic Model. We then broke that down in small workshops which we ran with our experts, Europeana staff and stakeholders.

Design and assessment: drawing the dots and connecting them

The workshops addressed Europeana Research and the thematic collections of Photography and Fashion. Each was chosen as a specific user-focused service that in some way used Europeana resources and ultimately contributed towards achieving our business and strategic goals. Each workshop had three elements:

- identifying who was expected to experience a change (main stakeholders and what drives them)
- identifying the changes to be expected or wanted (long-term outcomes we expected our work to contribute to)
- connecting those changes/outcomes with the activities and outputs of the service (and their metrics) that we undertake each week, month and year.

For example, the Europeana Fashion thematic collection identified students of fashion as an important stakeholder group. Europeana would expect to see a change in their awareness and understanding of fashion history, and for them to be inspired by having access to this history through a range of online access points such as Tumblr (http://eurfashion.tumblr.com). A snapshot of an impact workshop is shown in Figure 8.2 opposite.

Figure 8.2 *A snapshot of an impact workshop; showing an empathy map and a change pathway*

Using a range of brainstorming techniques (such as introducing the Value Lenses as wildcards to provoke and stimulate conversation) and the Logic Model to frame our discussion, we set about drawing the connections between the outputs of Fashion, Photography and Research and the changes they sought to bring about, using the principles of materiality: *'Is the change significant?'* and accountability: *'Is the change something Europeana is responsible for?'* to prioritise the findings of each workshop. The next step was to pull it all together again under one umbrella and develop a basic understanding of some of the areas of impact that the three projects shared – using the value lens as a categorisation mechanism – and the places where they differed. This common ground provided the focus for the measures we sought and the data that we subsequently went on to collect. Resource and time constraints meant that we were tied to collecting data solely through surveys.

Through a series of surveys distributed throughout the summer of 2017 we collected a total of 314 responses. The amount of data we collected was below target, but in our planning and preparation for data collection we had identified low response rates as a probable event when collecting data over a summer period. However, the response rate varied between different types of users and the data collected was of a good standard, so we continued with the assessment to see what it would reveal.

The data was collected, cleansed and analysed first in a small group, and then again in a process which included a wider group of stakeholders. Together we identified how we wanted to interpret the data and agreed which of the results were the most significant for us to share. While it did not paint the picture we expected it to, in some places it also surprised us. Just as with our experience with developing Workers Underground, we found ourselves in the position of learning more information, in different ways than we had expected, from the process as well as from the data itself.

Narration and evaluation: reflecting and developing highlights

By this point it was clear that the process was a revealing one. Not only had we developed a way to put the BVI Framework into practice, but we had learned a wide range of things along the way about the services run by Fashion, Photography and Research, about Europeana ourselves and about how we can use this experience to support others in our sector to undertake their own impact assessments. Figure 8.3 provides an insight into the data gathered from members on knowledge and skills.

Looking first to what the data itself revealed about Europeana and the services of Fashion, Photography and Research, we presented our insights into the changes we want to bring about for the stakeholders, both as individuals and as organisations (Fallon, 2017c). As with Workers

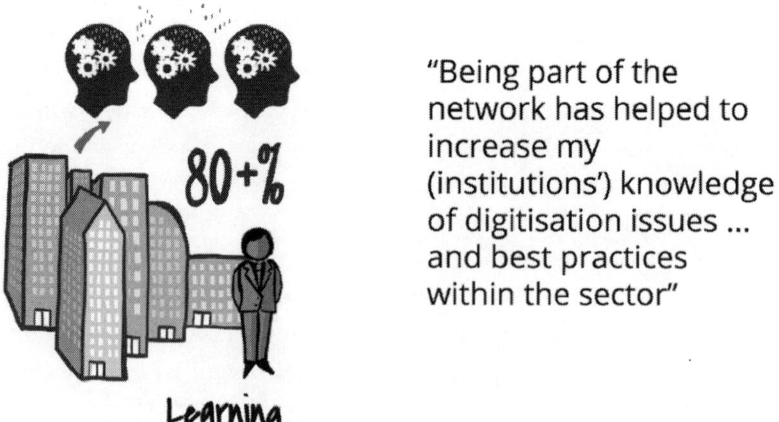

Figure 8.3 *Increase in knowledge and skills through being a member of the Europeana Network Association*

Underground, the Value Lens provided an approach for exploring and presenting the data as we looked for evidence of changes in our stakeholders as a result of our activities. We found indications that Europeana's work does deliver positive effects to our stakeholders, but that we needed to work on refining our approach, such as the questions we ask, in order to really reveal impact measures.

For example, we want EU citizens to discover cultural heritage online and, through that, to gain a deeper understanding of and connection with the world around them. We saw some evidence of that. We looked at the research market and cultural heritage institutions, searching for evidence and examples of how our activities, and those of our partners, led to the development of skills, understanding and knowledge. How has accessing cultural heritage inspired or influenced teaching material, a research topic or the development of a new collaboration? And we looked at how attitudes had changed as a result of interacting with Europeana and our partners. Figure 8.4 shows how cultural heritage institutions responded.

Figure 8.4 *Importance to an institution of openly licensing data and content*

In some cases the data was compelling and validated some long-held beliefs about the impact of our work, and in some we had not met a high enough standard of evidence to make any kind of judgement. Overall, we feel that from this assessment we developed a better understanding of some of the changes that come about from our work in the cultural heritage sector, and that there is much more to research. But it's also relevant to point out that we looked for and found evidence of only positive changes, and that no well-supported examples of unexpected changes were found. So, due to the way that we undertook the research, it served to partially validate our work and provide insights into it.

Early on in the process we decided that we would be open about our experiences, what we learned and how we would take our learning forward in the work that followed. The first observation we made was that our ambition and agile ways of working pushed the boundaries of what we could achieve with the resources we had. It was quite evident, from the wide range of data we collected, that in future we would need to investigate data-collection techniques to enable us to work more efficiently and be smarter about how we collected data. This leads into the second point for us, which was the importance of considering early on in the research what we would do with the results. This was stated in the BVI Model but is something easily overlooked and, on reflection, we did not spend enough time exploring it. Considering end-use helps to refine data collection – in some places changes we made left us unable to measure a desired change properly. We want to find ways to make it easier to draw connections between the data and the results of the change pathways that emerge from the workshops. Finally, we felt that, despite in places being disruptive, our open approach to continuous improvement – being willing to adapt as we went – was a strength that we should maintain by reinforcing the importance of making time to review and refine the process and implementation of the impact research.

The *Impact Playbook*

Concurrently, as we refined our own practices, the components of the *Impact Playbook* began to emerge.

With the support of a task force of cultural heritage professionals, which included Simon Tanner and representatives of the Fashion, Photography and Research services, we identified how our experiences with these impact assessments could be applied to support the uptake of impact assessment across the sector. The process for doing this was run concurrently with the impact assessment and the task force members were willing participants in a number of our experimental cycles. Working together, with knowledge of how the process could be presented and the mutual desire to provide a significant set of resources for those wishing to understand impact better, we formed the basis of an impact toolkit which would contain:

- an easy-to-follow methodology for undertaking impact assessments specific to the cultural heritage sector;
- case studies that demonstrate how impact assessment can bring new insights into our work;
- a place for a community to find and share information about impact assessment.

Alongside the development of the impact assessment we applied these experiences and developed a practical working method for undertaking impact assessment. Intended to be specific to the use of digital resources of the cultural heritage sector, it is founded on a combination of the principles established in the BVI Model, Europeana's own impact framework and other industry standard practices of impact assessment. This became known as the *Impact Playbook*: a set of worked-through exercises and workshops designed to help anyone get their impact practice off the ground. Figure 8.5 shows the Europeana *Impact Playbook*.

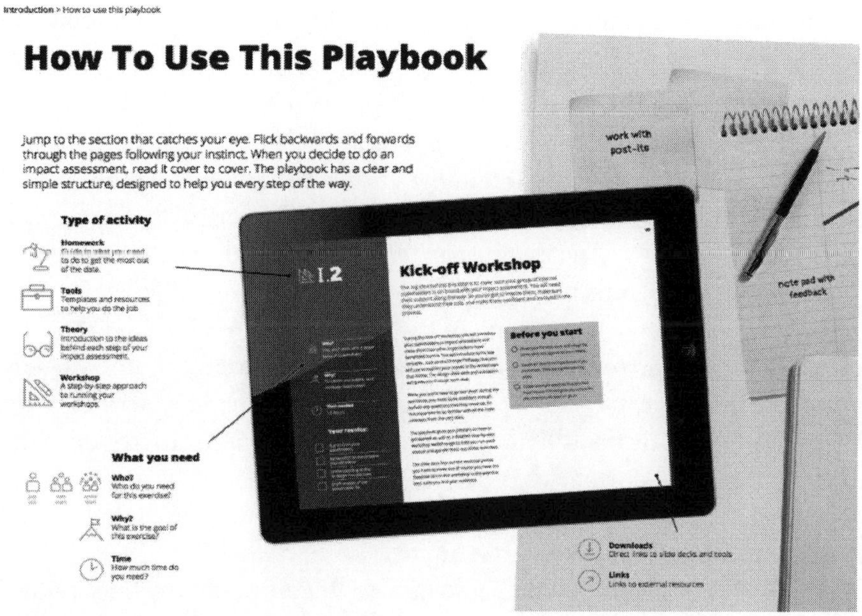

Figure 8.5 The Europeana *Impact Playbook*

The process we followed to develop the *Playbook* was one of iterative development, and it enabled us to validate our work as we progressed

(Fallon, 2017a). Each step, exercise and workshop was tested both on and by our stakeholders. As we ran workshops, we observed what worked well and where adjustments were needed, and then ran them all over again, learning at each stage.

Our goals were for the *Playbook* to mature into a resource that supports those first tentative steps of exploring impact until they become a familiar path to follow and to be a driver for change. As part of that, we also needed to present new vocabulary that enabled this conversation around impact and what it means for cultural heritage organisations to take place. A large part of this language draws from the BVI Model. Through the *Playbook*, we introduce readers to the change pathway – an adapted version of the Logic Model, the Strategic Perspectives and the Value Lenses as tools that can be used to frame discussions around impact. We used this language to start conversations with the growing number of professionals from the cultural heritage sector who share an interest in impact and transform their individual interests into a community.

Work in progress: continuing to develop the *Impact Playbook*, toolkit and framework

In the first nine months since the *Playbook* was launched, alongside our own case studies, we saw marked growth in the practice of impact assessment, in the Europeana community and in the visible discussions around impact in our network. The *Playbook* has been downloaded over 2,000 times and we have heard of a range of ways in which it has facilitated discussions around impact within an organisation. In the case of the National Library of Wales, the *Playbook* has been used to explore the impact of an established externally funded project (Tudur, 2018), as well as to frame an impact assessment of the projects they run through their partnership with Wikimedia UK (Tudur and Evans, 2018). It is used by SMK to explore the impact of their transformative project to fully open their collections, by the Polish GLAM scene and in a Smart Cities project integrating digital art to revitalise a square in Hamburg, Germany.

In 2019 the *Playbook* will be relaunched, with additional resources and guidance, along with a bit of refinement that comes from the feedback we have received and our own experiences in applying it. Alongside this, we continue to showcase examples of impact assessment that are being practised in the sector and to share case studies of how the *Playbook* and toolkit resources are being used so that we can encourage sharing and learning within the Europeana community. Further, we mentor the development of impact assessments which follow the *Playbook* and focus on projects that make use of digital resources, encouraging the sharing of experiences within the community and providing us with valuable insight into the challenges faced during this process.

Looking at our experience, and those of fellow cultural heritage organisations, it is clear to us that resources like the BVI Model and the *Playbook* both enable and facilitate a better understanding of impact – and that the practice of assessing impact should be more widespread. As the environment in which we work evolves, the increase of digital resources leads to greater opportunities to make an impact. We need to encourage open sharing about the challenges of developing our understanding and practice of impact. There is more experimentation to be done, looking at what measures we can take individually and as a sector to demonstrate the changes we contribute to, as well as finding better and more efficient ways to collect data.

From Europeana's bird's-eye view, we have seen that the absence of standardisation in approach, assessment or reporting creates a landscape that's challenging to navigate. As society, sectors and countries continue the drive to move towards a sustainable and socially responsible future, the role of culture as a driver for well-being and social cohesion is becoming more evident. And, in this, there is an opportunity to make stronger connections between the impact of cultural heritage and the strategic goals of regional agencies such as the EC, with its wide range of initiatives supporting the evolution of the sector, and the global visions laid out through the United Nations' Sustainable Development Goals. To respond to these challenges, we see a vital need to refine the BVI Framework as a strategic tool for both policy makers and practitioners to use, so that it helps to raise the standards, accessibility and frequency of impact assessment.

Chapter 9

Using the outcomes of the BVI Model

Transitioning from outputs to outcomes to impact

Outputs are the direct products of the digital resource measured. They consist of data in both statistical quantitative form and qualitative evidence modes. Outputs therefore often talk to performance measures or monitoring information. For example, a measure of the number of items digitised in relation to the number predicted in the project plan. Likewise, keeping track of the number of online users for a web-based resource over time is monitoring activity. Neither is an outcome until it is evaluated in such a way as to show the specific changes that have occurred to the community of stakeholders.

The Logic Model example in Figure 9.1 provides a neat way to visualise the transition from activity, through outputs and data gathering, to outcomes and impact.

Outcomes are the specific changes and consequences evaluated, such as behaviours, knowledge, skills, status, wealth, well-being or effectiveness, to mention a few instances.

Figure 9.1 *Example Logic Model for the Europeana 1914–1918 collection*

Impacts are the fundamental changes that occur because the outcomes demonstrate a set of benefits to a defined group in a specific timeframe. Such impacts can be intended or unintended and, most importantly, may be either positive or negative to some or all of the stakeholders.

The inherent risk in finding undesired impacts, or of not having changed things significantly enough, is a possible reason why impact assessment is not being done frequently or effectively in the cultural, heritage, academic or creative industries. Especially as there has been a strong presumption that all things digital will be positive in performance and therefore will deliver positive impactful outcomes. Outcomes must also be adjusted to account for changes that would have occurred in any case without the intervention of the digital resource. It is the essence of impact to identify the causal links between the change in people's lives and the intervention represented by the digital resource.

The BVI Model's focus on measuring changes in people's lives and life opportunities means that it reflects this need to observe and assess outcomes, not mere outputs. As reported by Paola Marchionni:

> Millions of pounds of public funding have been spent in digitisation so far. However, this is still, on the whole, an activity which only pays partial attention to the users for whom the content is being digitized, and their relevant needs.
>
> (Marchionni, 2009)

The findings of other reports support this conclusion (Tanner and Deegan, 2010; Finnis, Chan and Clements, 2011; Malde and Finnis, 2016). Attempts at evaluation of digitised resources have mainly focused on outputs (such as number-crunching visitor numbers or items digitised) without much segmentation or analysis, and relying on anecdotal evidence or limited short-term surveys to show value and benefit.

Therefore Stages 4 and 5 of the BVI Model focus on the means of transferring the outputs of data gathering into outcomes that are meaningful demonstrators of impact, to be used effectively by decision makers.

Remember that not all data gathered will be immediately useful to impact, but that does not negate its worth in other managerial contexts. Some data is only useful as an indicator of activity effectiveness (for example, 'we digitised 10,000 items this week'), but this is still useful for progress reporting, project management and operational efficiency purposes. It may also be that data gathered now may not reap rewards until many months or years hence, and only once aggregated with or compared to other data. Using the BVI Framework keeps the gathered data well structured and organised, and thus manageable over extended periods.

BVI Model Stage 4: Narrate the outcomes and results

Throughout the BVI Model a founding principle is that data or numeric measures alone do not usually have the power to represent the entire impact that has occurred. It is in pairing quantitative and qualitative measures that a sophisticated picture is best painted. Matching those points of evidence with people's experience of the difference a digital resource made to them is at the heart of narrating a convincing impact narrative.

As Sam Knowles states in *Narrative by Numbers* (Knowles, 2018):

Analytics + storytelling = influence

Evaluating outputs

In assessing the outputs and outcomes from the BVI Model, it should not be terribly surprising if the impacts are not turning up immediately, even for digital resources. There are too many variables to give a one-size-fits-all answer, but the impact is highly unlikely to be significantly measurable in timeframes of a few days or months, nor will one or two events reveal all the data needed. One reason why the BVI Model has four Strategic Perspectives is so that impacts which happen over differing timeframes, with various interventions, can be assessed as they occur and then brought to the fore as those impacts accrue. The BVI Framework is a mechanism for controlling the management of the impact assessment and co-ordinating the various moving parts.

Evaluate data collected from the impact assessment and narrate the results at a point pre-selected for maximum effect. For some quantitative measures, such as web statistics, the outputs may appear on a rolling basis; collate this data into a specific report only when needed. For qualitative data, such as surveys and interviews, the raw data has to be categorised and recorded accurately and then interpreted or summarised such as to have value in an impact narrative. Qualitative measures are thus less likely to be continuous or passive measures and will mostly result from a targeted activity with a pre-set, impact-related purpose.

If the BVI Framework has been used, then the data collected will be associated with a specific Perspective–Value pairing. These pairings will make the next stages of prioritising, choosing and selecting content easier. Each set of data should answer the objective set for a specific stakeholder group. The data gathered should be listed simply, as in the following example.

- **Perspective–Value Lens pairing:** Innovation + Education
- **Objective:** To measure the benefits of using our digital collection to demonstrate a change in teaching and learning through its innovative use.
- **Stakeholders:** End-users and/or re-users of the digital collections and MOOCs.
- **Data collected:** Qualitative measures: case studies.
  Survey to identify participants, followed by individual case studies, through interviews with stakeholders, delivering a detailed narrative of change and benefits.

Before continuing, consider the quality of the evidence and the suitability of the data. These considerations include the following.

1. Does the evidence collected reflect the desired impact assessment goals and objectives as set out in the chosen BVI Framework pairings for Strategic Perspectives and Value Lenses?
2. Are the data and evidence collected complete and in a useful form?
3. Has information been collected from the full range of the most relevant stakeholders?
4. Does the data collected conform to established norms for quality in the sector and was the method used for the collection rigorous?
5. Has some level of peer review or independent assessment been possible for some or all of the evidence, so as to add further validation?

When considering the established norms for quality and rigour consider criteria such as:

- transparency of design and method;
- appropriateness of data-gathering method;
- ethics;
- cultural sensitivity to stakeholders, noting any context-specific cultural factors that may bias the findings;

- conceptual framing, acknowledging other work and research in the same field;
- indicator validity: whether the indicator measuring outcomes is the best and most appropriate;
- replicable results: whether the findings would be replicable in other similar organisations or contexts;
- reliability: for instance, whether web statistics are always reliable and comparable over time;
- logical outcomes: whether there is a logical reason for the outcome achieved, assuming the activity and data gathered;
- limitations: whether the limitations on what is gatherable or data that is missing have been acknowledged.

The more the individual components or sets of information across Perspective–Value pairings demonstrate these features and share similar findings, then the stronger the evidence base.

For instance, in a Social–Education pairing, if the web statistics show high usage of a collection by young people, plus feedback surveys show evidence of young people gaining learning benefits from that use and further investigations demonstrate an increase in knowledge and re-use of that knowledge, then these varied evidence points are correlating to provide a convincing picture of the claimed education impact.

It may be necessary to discard data if it is of low quality/validity or to rethink the approach if there is not adequate data to support authoritative conclusions. There may also be ways to fill gaps in evidence or to instigate activities that will induce more visible evidence if needed.

Prioritising outcomes

Not all data gathered is useful for every purpose. A defined set of data allows it to be prioritised to the narrative purpose desired. Five core measures form the basis for prioritisation for the worthiness of impact evidence:

1 **accountability** for the impact
2 **plausible causality** leading to the impact
3 **the significance** of the impact
4 **differential impact** on stakeholders
5 **the narrative** worth of the impact.

Ideally, there will be data that correlates closely enough to all of the priorities, such that it may be readily selected. Where there are gaps this might identify an area for further data-gathering work or where there is insufficient data.

Where the data is not matching every criterion, then the prioritisation process should work down the list, from accountability as the top priority to narrative worth as the lowest.

Accountability for impact

Is the memory institution responsible for the outcomes claimed? The most important aspect of the data gathered is its ability to evidence that it was the organisation's intervention, resource or activity that was accountable for the impact claimed.

There are many reasons why an individual may demonstrate a change that might look like impact. They may have become passionate about the subject, due to a television show, a book or following a friend's example, and their arrival at the digital resource is not when the change in behaviour occurred but a reflection of some other impactful factor.

If the digital resource were, for instance, an opera or Shakespeare MOOC, are people engaged with it because they were already self-selecting as opera or theatre buffs, or has the digital resource genuinely drawn in new audiences for that content and widened the base of interest? Even if people are already interested, this does not mean that the learning gained loses worth, but maybe it has to be contextualised so that the part for which the host organisation claims to be accountable is clear.

In the case study for the Europeana 1914–18 collection, a challenge would be to identify whether people were already interested in the First World War because it was generally in the media and the public memory, due to the centenaries. How much of the increase in awareness or knowledge, as shown in surveys or other data collection, is claimable by Europeana as their specific contribution? This understanding can be achieved by carefully crafting the questions asked and the data gathered, in addition to sifting the evidence rigorously in search of the strongest correlations that demonstrate the pathway to impact.

Equally, there are aspects of the impact claimed that are not the responsibility of the organisation to claim. It is not necessary to claim the basic digital literacy of the user base just because they use the online resource – unless it has been explicitly designed for that purpose. Publicly funded institutions do not have to apologise for receiving public money when making an impact statement. Public bodies are accountable for the value delivered to the public, not for the way that tax and spend is regionally or nationally decided. Thus, when the BL states that 'the economic value the Library delivers for society is £5 for every £1 invested' (The British Library, n.d.), the Library is not directly responsible for the £1 invested, but it is wholly accountable for the claimed value derived from that public investment.

Plausible causality leading to impact

Very much akin to accountability is plausibility. Ask the question: how plausible is the claim that the activity evidenced by the data has a visibly causal link to the outcomes measured and the impact claimed?

Since a range of methodologies may have been used to assess whether an intervention caused or contributed to an impact, then some may be more likely to demonstrate causality than others. These are more likely to be higher-cost approaches: either through large-scale, quasi-experimental approaches or more in-depth, qualitative-based studies. The objectives within the BVI Framework are useful in assigning criteria for success. Using the Logic Model summary provides a narrative of the way that activity is intended to lead to outputs, with outcomes and impact measured as a result. Finally, always bear in mind that the correlation of data is not the same as proof of causation.

Another way to interrogate causality is to consider what would have happened if the service did not exist or the activity had not taken place. How much of the change measured would have happened without these inputs? It can be a harsh realisation to see how small the increment of change may be, but that does not negate its effect or purpose. It may also lead the organisation to rethink its activities so as to serve the community better.

The critical consideration relates to 'additionality' and being able to differentiate the additional effect that is due to or caused by the intervention. In terms of plausibility, then, this might be considered as having levels that increase as the worth and rigour of the evidence increases.

Lowest: assertions that show a logical reason why the intervention had an impact and the benefits that accrued. Augment this with evaluations or post-hoc assessments (usually surveys and testimonials) that show some change among those receiving or using an intervention. This change or benefits received may be relevant to the recipient but lack some dimensions for demonstrating direct impact causality.

Mid-level: where the evaluations and evidence can demonstrate that an organisation's intervention is causing the impact. The more robust the method, for instance, including control groups or using external evaluators, the more this leans towards plausibility. One way of demonstrating this is by showing less benefit among those who do not engage in the activity or do not receive the service.

Evidence that allows organisations to explain why and how their intervention has the impact they have observed, and any indication it can be replicated elsewhere or act as a model for that approach, will strengthen the impact claim made.

Highest: usually this requires some form of independent evaluation to validate the impact. The impact claimed should be replicable and could even be operated by someone else, somewhere else. The activities or interventions claiming the impact should be robust enough to survive changes in circumstances or contexts, while continuing to have a positive and direct impact on beneficiaries. This is a very high level of evaluation and rarely achieved.

Memory institutions will tend to find themselves generally operating in the low and mid levels of this scale. This is normal; the levels described here are a method to prioritise the best evidence. The highest levels require significant investment, time, skilled people and a commitment to scientific approaches that may not be suitable to any but the largest organisations or the most complex projects.

Significance of impact

Sufficient evidence of impact having been established, then, the extent or significance of that impact can be assessed as a way to prioritise the data collected. Out of all the evidence, consider which evidence shows the highest degree of impact in enabling, enriching, influencing, informing or changing the lives or life opportunities of the communities served. Change may be felt deeply by an individual or a small focal community. This result may be just as significant as a smaller change that is distributed evenly across a broad and diverse community. In digital terms, this illustrates why numeric measures alone are often unsatisfying – knowing that there are 100 or 100,000 users is not particularly helpful unless the extent, depth and meaningfulness of the change experienced by those users are also understood.

Endorsements are usually key signifiers of impact for memory institutions. They may appear directly through responses to surveys, testimonials, focus groups and other feedback. Indirectly they may also be visible through recognition-of-esteem indicators, such as awards, policy influence, funding success and sector leadership.

Match the significance against each of the five Value Lenses. It may thus be possible to think of the worth of the change reflected in results such as increased productivity, reduced costs, increased activity and engagement (Utility). Other behaviour changes may indicate an increase in knowledge, skills or understanding (Education) or changes in attitudes, an increased sense of place or community (Community). Aggregating these outcomes provides evidence of how people value them and their relationship to the memory institution (Existence). Other behaviours may demonstrate significant engagements such as bequeathing or creating content (Inheritance/Legacy).

Prioritising the available impact evidence will, in part, be about considering that which demonstrates the greatest significance, matches the narrative goals of a given reporting requirement and demonstrates most clearly why it is a valuable outcome for the reader to understand.

Differential impact on stakeholders

A further way to prioritise the impact evidence is to consider who, among the stakeholders, benefit most directly and who do not. In order to meet the impact objectives there may be certain stakeholder groups that are much more important to focus on than others. There may also be bias in the results, as some stakeholder groups may be more accessible to gather evidence from but not be a focal point for the impact objectives.

All interventions will lead to winners and losers in a social or economic conception. Consider differential effects and be able to disaggregate analysis to focus on different socio-economic groups. For instance, a library that digitises its newspaper collection so it becomes accessible from home or school will create one set of 'winning' stakeholders about which they may care deeply. If the library sends those physical newspapers to storage, then there may be direct 'losers' among library users – such as academics – for whom the physical copy will still hold additional value. There may also be indirect 'losers' in the local economy (such as shops and cafés) if fewer people are physically visiting the library. Again, this relates to accountability already addressed above.

The most robust impact assessments will seek to better understand the effects on different stakeholder groups, including, especially, disadvantaged and marginalised groups.

Narrative value

Some evidence is more suited than others in telling a clear story of impact. Data may be convincing, but is so complicated to narrate that any claim made could easily be criticised or misunderstood. Thus, does the evidence narrate clearly and as unambiguously as possible to demonstrate the outcomes and impact claimed? Sometimes the more complex evidence narrative will work better in internal reporting or where there is the opportunity to add an appendix. The narrative worth and ethics of narrating impact are returned to later in this chapter. For current purposes, this is the lowest level of prioritisation.

The features of strong evidence that works hard to convey the impact

All this effort concentrates on looking for excellent evidence or the singular piece of information that will convey maximum meaning. It is hard to achieve. Most people find data and statistics confusing. Offering a lot of unfiltered data out of context will be entirely unhelpful to communicate impact. Facts or figures are also inherently unmemorable, which is why narrative approaches are considered more effective. While we may have a flotilla of evidence, it is vital not to blind the audience with science, and thus to be selective in the evidence presented. Make detail accessible, if needed, in an appendix or associated document.

The core features of a strong impact message include:

- simplicity
- significance
- reach
- no need for further explanation
- compounding of values with ideas or proposals
- repeatability and easy sharing.

For example:

> Without access to the information in their public library, 23% of the business users indicated that they estimated their costs would increase between $500 and $5,000.
>
> (Abram, 2007)

> In revising the museum's mission statement to 'bringing art and people together' the Walters [Walters Art Museum in Baltimore, Maryland] moved from being object-centered to people-centered, emphasizing enjoyment, discovery, and learning … The result has been a 100% increase in family programs, a 45% increase in attendance, and a 400% increase in the use of the museum's website … the Walters staff focuses on putting their community at the heart of all they do.
>
> (Vikan, 2011)

> The total economic contribution of museums in 2016 amounted to more than $50 billion in GDP, 726,200 jobs, and $12 billion in taxes to local, state, and federal governments.
>
> (Plaza, 2010)

> The Great Recession also had widespread impact, including on public libraries ... use climbed in the wake of economic duress, and libraries gathered resources and developed programs and services to support job seekers, the unemployed, and business owners striving to rebuild local economies.
>
> (OCLC and ALA, 2018)

See Chapter 3 for other examples of impact.

The reader will note the absence of excellent digitally oriented impact messages. It is a struggle to find them outside those already previously stated in this book. One feature of measuring impact for digital resources and collections is to accept that we are still in the early phases and excellent impact exemplars remain few, at least for now.

Communicating the results

All this effort of gathering data and measuring the impact of a digital project will lack meaning unless the findings are communicated well and promptly to the desired audiences. Share, appraise and review results and create a response to ensure that action will be a result of impact assessment. Effective communication is thus critically important to creating a call to action.

Such communication of impacts and outcomes is essential to explain the contribution of the memory institution and to state that its interactions with its community are meaningful. Communications and impact assessments are not neutral activities; they can be sensitive in various dimensions – politically, policy-wise, financially, socially, and also reflect complex community relationships. Communicating results should thus consider that different audiences may need different information, and different ways of having that information communicated to them.

The communicating of impact is about narrating a story that will resonate with the intended reader and acts as a convincing indicator of a broader trend, result, benefit or reward. The information produced must be timely, provided in as unbiased and modest a tone as feasible, while not underplaying significance. Choosing the best media outlet and format for the intended audience is a crucial factor in good communication. In order to establish a valid and authentic voice for the message to be conveyed, communication must be consistent across all audiences (Phillips, Brantley and Phillips, 2011).

Using the Strategic Perspectives and Value Lenses

In the BVI Model, measures of success and beneficial impacts can be reported in a faceted fashion using the Value Lenses across the Strategic Perspectives. All the dimensions of the impact discovered and the outcomes reported are brought together to provide a holistic viewpoint.

A full reporting of impact using the BVI Model should include the following sections.

1. Executive summary
2. The context for the digital resource
   a. The ecosystem of the digital resource
   b. The stakeholders
   c. The Value Lenses as focal points
3. The impact
   a. Social
   b. Economic
   c. Innovation
   d. Operational
4. Recommendations and next steps
5. Appendix: impact assessment method
   a. Objectives
   b. Indicators and assumptions
   c. Methods used to gather data
   d. Outputs from the impact assessment.

Using the BVI Model means that all the previous hard work in impact assessment is structured to deliver the impact report readily. This report may simply be about gathering together information and evidence already gathered and structured within the BVI Framework. Consider using the Stage 1 results at an earlier moment in the impact assessment as an interim report or for other planning purposes.

Deciding how much information to include and what to emphasise will be a matter of matching the reporting to the expected audience. It is an opportunity to consider whether the reporting is to take on an additional advocacy role. Assuming that at least some of the reporting of impact will be for decision makers to consider, then advocacy should be assumed as a natural and desirable function of the BVI Model, but advocacy only effectively happens when supported by substantial evidence.

In the digital attention economy it is worth remembering that most people within the organisation or as related stakeholders will have social media presences and profiles on which they share aspects of their lives. These may become channels to convey impact stories or to foster discussion. Many voices matter; so straightforward, convincing and evidence-driven narration of impact will encourage sharing, comment and re-use of that message.

Narration and storytelling

For digital resources based in a memory institution the narrative of impact evidence, while being organised by the Value Lenses and Strategic Perspectives, is likely to have the following main foci:

- transforming public understanding of a major issue or theme
- fostering positive social change
- developing a new audience or changing an audience attitude
- influencing practitioners' ways of working and sectoral thinking
- enabling and informing learning, teaching and educational outcomes
- influencing or informing a policy change or development
- supporting economic growth, or change in economic opportunity
- improving health and well-being
- enabling a community action to start, grow or develop.

Narrative and storytelling are essential tools in conveying these types of benefits to a community. Whether reaching outside the organisation or trying to tell a story within your walls, narrative matters. Narratives 'have the power to build the symbolic ground for cultivating and sustaining organisational culture' (Marsh et al., 2016).

Narratives have to be trusted, consistent and easy to digest and, above all, to enable the reader to process information about the impact in ways that capture the imagination. The most effective story is compelling because it mirrors or reflects 'something of the way the community lives or behaves and is about something that people know, or deals with situations or emotions for which they have strong attachment' (Canalichio, 2018).

There are several likely key foci for impact-related stories. The available evidence and the objectives of the narrative will partly define the critical point of focus. Foci divide most simply into narratives driven by:

- metrics: the story revolves around a number. For example: online usage rose by x% when digital resources were used to augment our physical exhibitions. Exhibitions attendance also increased by y% in these target groups;
- individual communities: a singular story linked to a specific broad group or community. For example: our digital resources are enabling the diaspora of a small country to reconnect with their heritage and language, as illustrated by the story of person Abc's experience;
- users: the story directly states a specific user benefit. For example: teachers at our local school have modified their teaching materials to incorporate our digital offering as an essential homework revision aid;
- relationships: the story is about changing the relationship with stakeholders. For example: our digital resources have changed our institutional relationship with LGBTQ people who would previously not have associated our mission and collections as serving their interests;
- institutional change: the story is about change in the operational aspects of the organisation. For example: we have changed our metadata practices to better suit the needs of indigenous peoples represented in our collections.

Part of a strong narrative is to explain first the 'why' of the activity, not the 'how' or 'what' of it. As Simon Sinek puts it, 'people don't buy what you do, they buy why you do it'. His golden circle of narrating value focuses on *why we do it*, followed by *how we do it* and lastly by *what do we do* (Sinek, 2011). Much narrative about digital projects and activity is obsessed with explaining how it was done, without really addressing why it was done (which will inevitably also address the 'for whom?' question). However clever the technology or however large the digital corpus, this message focus will only ever appeal to a small constituency. Explaining the purpose in clear, simple language tells the 'why' story such that the clever technology augments that mission.

Thus, a compelling narrative statement might look as follows.

Why: We exist to encourage the understanding of art in our community. Our digital vision is for everyone to be able to make, share, build and learn through our art collections.

How: Our rich content will be available digitally for existing and new audiences – placing art in every home and hand to share and make new personal experiences.

What: Millions will see our images and data by making them available as Creative Commons Zero for free use and sharing on platforms such as Wikimedia.

Different ways of presenting impact data and evidence

Using simple language will present information with clarity and make it memorable. Tools such as the Gunning Fog Formula, the SMOG Index or the Flesch-Kincaid 'reading ease' score can assist with measuring whether the language used is simple, readable and concise.

Presenting numeric content is often the purview of graphics or data visualisations. These visual cues can be powerful narrative tools, adding contrast between ideas and comparison of values much like good music augments the words of a lyric. If poorly done, they can confuse or annoy, much like a misplaced musical note; hence care should be exercised.

1. Keep the intended audience at the forefront of design intent; their understanding is the real test of a successful presentation.
2. Make sure any visualisation answers a question or makes a clear point.
3. Keep the visualisation as simple as possible and visually clear and readable.
4. Keep it familiar and relatable to the audience.
5. Choose the most appropriate charts/visualisation or language for the audience and message.

Using appropriate charts and visualisations

The most obvious, and likely to be the most commonly used, chart types are bar, line, scatter and pie charts. There are many other ways of presenting data and these four types are often not optimal for making a narrative point or presenting the data accurately. For instance, a pie chart is a poor choice for showing relationships in data. They generally fail to be clear when there are more than two or three categories. A simple bar chart may provide a better solution where a simple comparison is needed, although tape diagrams, which show ratios for how one number relates to another, might be even more explicit. Scatter charts are only really useful for showing outliers or clusters of data values and often lack clarity of purpose. Line charts are useful for showing trends or change over time or effort, but for little else.

Concentric diagrams, which look like an onion sliced sideways, can be used to reflect the relative importance of things. The central idea is the most important factor, with the values flowing outward from the centre. Europeana used this effectively to show their strategic goals reaching out to the desired impact (Figure 9.2). It is also notable that Europeana adopted the BVI Model

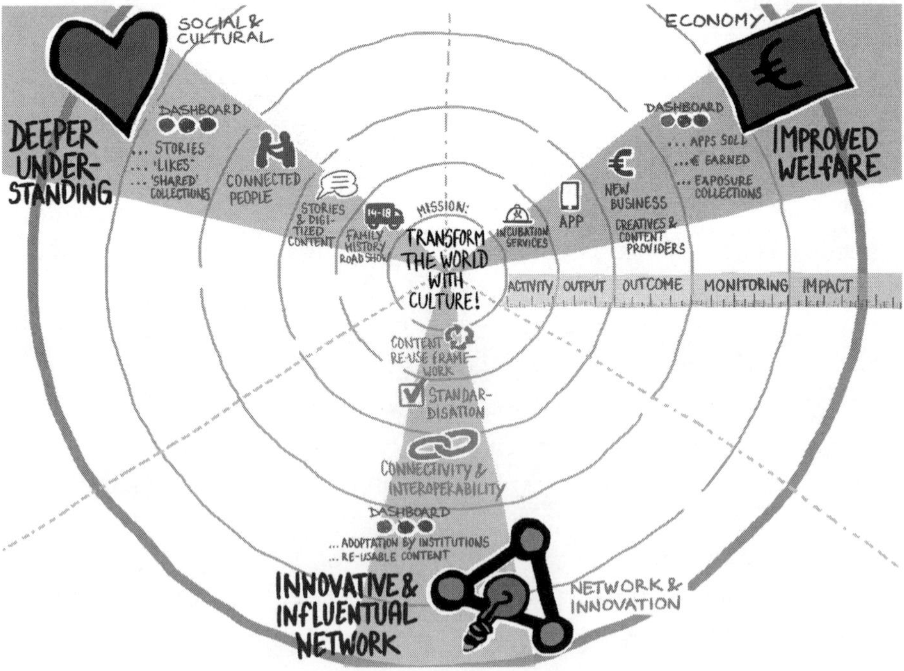

Figure 9.2 *Europeana Strategy as an impact map*

Strategic Perspectives as the basis of their core strategic impact map (they excluded operational at the time to maintain an outward focus).

Radar charts are similar in visual concept but different in effect and purpose. In radar charts, a few spokes radiate from the centre and the length of each spoke has a numeric value. The relationships and comparisons between each spoke are the reason to use this for analysing characteristics or parts of things we often see as a whole. Lines connecting spokes are added, as are shaded areas, to show change or to illustrate comparisons. Polar grids are similar to radar charts but with no limitation on the number of spokes. Both of these chart types are visually technical-looking and thus can lack resonance with audiences. They might be better used in internal reporting where decision making needs a particular viewpoint to grasp the message.

The concept of change over time will be a major mechanism to demonstrate in reporting impact, and there several ways of showing this. Spiral graphs show events spiralling outwards, from the oldest in the centre to the latest on the outside. Timelines show a time sequence, often as a snaking line, with the events shown along the line such that the eye is naturally drawn to follow along the sequence. Using a road as a visual allegory can also convey the idea of a journey over time with stages and steps along the way – it functions like a timeline but with more emotional warmth and familiarity.

Visualising comparative numbers, such as the budget and its parts, is always tricky. Tree maps, using nested rectangles, each divided into smaller ones as needed, create a hierarchy. Sankey charts, which are visually like a river flowing out or across into smaller rivers, their tributaries and streams, visualise numbers via the thickness of the line. Sankeys can show the flow of change from one state to another very well as an overview, but are weaker for showing precise numeric data.

Spatial visualisations work too, as ways of showing the reach of the impact. These could be geographic, using map visualisations, or isotype charts showing quantities of things. Maps work well to show geographic reach across a region or the world. Map charts may also be used figuratively, with landmasses representing one set of big concepts and oceans as contrasting data. Isotype charts use icons to illustrate quantities of familiar objects and can be substituted for bar and pie charts. For instance, human shapes in different colours to show numbers of people – the *New York Times* used this method to graphically illustrate the number of deaths in Iraq and the *Guardian* newspaper frequently uses this approach to its data visualisations (www.theguardian.com/data).

Analogies can also work, using physical objects that are familiar such as icebergs, staircases, roots, trees and mountains. Roots are useful for showing how a change took hold and came about; trees with spreading branches describe the spread of ideas. Both roots and trees are good analogies for knowledge and understanding impacts. Staircases work for illustrating a logic model set of steps to achieve the given outcome. Mountains show a challenge to overcome or a winning outcome that required climbing to the top. Icebergs are always used to show that the visible part of something represents a much larger underwater part that should be noted. These might work where impact indicators show a result for a representative group that is asserted to demonstrate the impact and relevance to a bigger community not measured, and thus hidden from view.

Marketing and public relations

Marketing is a process that has the intent to develop and shape the market. As Kotler would define it, marketing is the 'normative science involving the efficient creation and offering of values to stimulate desired transactions … achieving specific responses in others through the creation and offering of values' (Kotler, 1972). This focus on values links well to the BVI Model's use of Value Lenses.

A market is defined through its set of actual or potential consumers (a subset of the stakeholder groupings defined in Stage 1) who engage with a set of products or services provided by the memory institution. Consumers having a common set of needs or wants further define the market. The decisions they make in the market may reference each other, as they potentially also share information and experiences on social media or other digital spaces.

These groupings, referred to as market segments, in many ways are separate markets. The temptation to state 'we serve the public; that is our market' is always unhelpful because it is too big, diverse and diffuse to be a useful definition. Think of the market in its segments; this allows more purposeful interactions in a marketing and public relations sense. For instance, public library segments may include pre-school, early readers, school-age children, young adults, struggling readers, life-long learners, job seekers, child-driven users (e.g. parents, carers, grandparents), hobbyists, creators/makers, online-only users, library as an office, to name but a few.

No one can afford the money to market to every segment all the time; thus the prioritisation implicit in the BVI Model will have pre-selected the focal groups most engaged in the impact assessment. There are still opportunities for ongoing chain-reaction promotion through word of mouth, observed benefit or the Prestige and Existence values. The more self-referencing, self-organising and bonded the community market segment (e.g., hobbyists, or child-driven users), then the higher the opportunity for a cascade of effects. Do not under-estimate social influence and word of mouth – a good narrative of impact will spread beyond those who are the first readers. Equally, a bad experience can spread even more quickly, so care must be exercised with any messaging or marketing process. Particularly online, those things that others tell us are appreciated, liked or valued in our circle of friends and close associates will be a strong influence on what we might think worth trying, supporting or buying.

Public relations (PR) involves building long-term, positive relationships between stakeholders and the memory institution. It is about developing an identity and image that reflects the mission of the institution, then sharing a straightforward, consistent positive message with the key stakeholder communities. In some respects, PR is about validating the values of the institution and the marketing message. It goes towards developing the brand and trust in digital products.

The following playful example illustrates a shorthand for understanding the different purposes of marketing, PR, advertising and brand.

1. Marketing = 'I'm a great cook.'
2. PR = 'Trust me, he's a great cook.'
3. Advertising = 'I'm a great cook, I'm a great cook, I'm a great cook …'
4. Branding = When stakeholders say: 'Hey, I understand you're a great cook.'

The concepts overlap and interlock. Everyone involved in marketing and PR is hoping that their efforts will enhance the brand and thus bring consumers to them. Advertisers relay that brand message in the hope that repetition of the primary value offering will become widely accepted. Marketing touches every aspect of PR, advertising and branding. Each part may operate in isolation, but when used together they expand and enhance the impact message.

The results of the impact assessment are useful for expressing the values of the memory institution and, through evidence, influencing perceptions, attitudes and opinion.

However, the trend in using impact primarily as a tool of marketing cannot be recommended. Strategic, evidence-based reasons should drive pursuing impact assessment and use of the BVI Model. Being motivated to impact measurement by a purely marketing-focused goal will skew every aspect of the process and make it impossible to produce results that are truthful or trustworthy. However, if it is done well impact assessment can certainly deliver evidence worth sharing and information that may well assist in more effective marketing and promotion of the memory institution. A pivotal realisation to accept is that the most critical outcomes of impact assessment may be to guide decisions about what to stop doing now, plus where to refocus effort and resources in the future – as much as it is about what to shout about from the rooftops.

Engaging with communities

If we want our communities to engage with our memory institutions, then understanding the worthiness of that engagement and investing time and other resources to enhance it will support active engagement. Make it easy – easy to understand the benefits, easy to use the services and easy to commit to action. The core role here is to help people to answer their *actual* personal information needs, not the ones they are pre-supposed to have. Show them how the organisation helps them get to their desired destination more successfully.

To achieve this may mean marketing what the stakeholders value while continuing to do what the memory institution knows will deliver those values. For example, 44% of voters in the USA value libraries as a social space, a gathering place for community members, but do not necessarily value the managing of those physical spaces and certainly do not count the cost of it (OCLC and ALA, 2018). For them, the benefits are what matters, not the logistics of the operation. Also, while 86% of funding comes from local government sources, 59% of voters assume that it comes from elsewhere. So the library must continue to spend significant sums on the physical functions of the library but should focus their public engagement on the benefits offered, not on the unseen infrastructure. In the USA 61% of voters have either contributed or would be willing to contribute to support their local library – if only they knew that they could or needed to, or knew more about the benefits delivered to them and their community.

Communities want to hear about the benefits available to them, not the features or function. Until, that is, they have bought in; at which point people generally want to become part of the decision-making process and to help shape and direct the action, not just passively receive services.

Case study 9.1: Trove at the National Library of Australia

Trove at the National Library of Australia (NLA) is an excellent example of community engagement, and of the challenges that can also accrue. The NLA's Trove brings together freely available content to support the online discovery of the country's documentary heritage (https://trove.nla.gov.au). There are over 459 million online resources, including books, images, historical newspapers, maps, music and archives.

Trove garners around 70,000 visitors per day; its primary content is freely accessible, full-text digitised newspapers. Trove features many inclusive tools that bring users into interaction with the digital content, from personalised lists and crowdsourced text correction of newspapers to a public API. The most prolific text correctors are recognised in a hall of fame, where the top corrector has worked on over 5.4 million lines of newspaper text. At the time of writing over 300 million lines of text have been corrected by the roughly 54,000 volunteer correctors (https://trove.nla.gov.au/newspaper/hallOfFame). The open API allows anyone to re-use Trove's data in many creative ways, including re-using search results from Trove and displaying them within another website or mobile app, harvesting records for research, plus creating new tools and visualisations, such as Culture Collage (www.zenlan.com/collage). Tim Sherratt, who was Trove's manager from 2013 to 2016, maintains a fabulous 'research notebook' with many experimental uses of the Trove API and guides, such as how to make a Trove Twitter bot (http://timsherratt.org/research-notebook/).

When Trove was launched in 2009 it was immediately popular. A community grew up quite quickly around the resource and actively used the tools available. In the first six months, a user base of 1 million grew up, with ~13,000 registered users (Holley, 2010). Registration was popular as a way of establishing a community, of sharing information and for users to be recognised for their contributions in the hall of fame. It also gave these people a voice to demand new services, tools and functions from the NLA. Holley reported at the time that people wanted to work collaboratively with the Library to have as much access to as much information in one place as possible, with tools and freedom to find, get and use information. In return, the virtual community would give back to the Library '[e]nthusiasm to do stuff and help us; expert subject knowledge; time [and] dedication' (Holley, 2010). Trove delivered on those promises to a large extent and the community has indeed been an enthusiastic, dedicated and loyal collaborator with the NLA.

Any memory institution should be delighted to garner such deep and intense community engagement and collaboration. Trove is also a case of being careful what you wish for, as you may just get it! At its inception, there was minimal staff resource in the NLA to cope with the massive upsurge in users' interest, with their desire to interact with the Library and its resources. As a community of registered users and text correctors developed, their demands had to be responded to by the NLA. It was not easy, as this pulled resource allocations in several directions at once. The NLA could have gone the route of the UK's National Archives, which now thinks of itself as primarily a digital archive by instinct and design (The National Archives, 2018). Instead, the NLA made some relatively low-key attempts to show that Trove was its way to be a truly national library – but these were underfunded, especially in terms of the community engagement aspects that Trove brought to the fore.

Trove became the centre of a tussle with the Australian government over significant budget cuts that adversely affected the service. In 2016, over 20 jobs were lost at the NLA in multi-million-dollar cuts which led to an outpouring of support, especially on social media, with thousands of tweets using the #fundTrove hashtag (Belot, 2016; Jones and Verhoeven, 2016). By the end of 2016 the Australian federal government was convinced by the scale and extent of community action to refund Trove with AUS$16.4 million over four years. This example expresses the power of having a dedicated and loyal community to support the existence value of a digital resource. Trove remains at risk but has been moved, in the latest NLA annual report, to a more central strategic role at the NLA; hopefully, improved focus on impact measures will also help to provide evidence to guarantee its future (National Library of Australia, 2018).

Trove remains a perfect example of how a community can congregate around a digital resource, and of how the hosting memory institution must not take that community for granted. Genuine collaboration with the community is vital to growth and sustainability. Investing in the services and digital products that most tangibly lead to impact for these community engagements, and understanding their importance, is vital to success. Using impact measures can deliver an evidence base for reflection on future areas of development and to convince decision makers of the value and worth of the investment.

Social impact

Different groups in society will value different value propositions from their memory institutions. The impact evidence for these communities will need to be segmented and focused. When considering the impact for such groups, it may be useful to think in terms of the way that the digital resources promulgate certain beneficial impact factors. These include:

- a sense of belonging to and being part of a community or broader society;
- an enhanced sense of place and people's role within that;
- promotion of connectedness between people and stakeholder groups;
- building of social cohesion and enhancing social relationships in the community;
- an improvement in the amount or scope of community engagement;
- people taking more opportunities for learning and personal growth;
- people getting involved in democratic processes;
- a sense of self-confidence and belonging to society.

The signs of these social impact factors are visible in a variety of ways. They are shown through aesthetic enjoyment, creativity, accomplishments and feelings of confidence, hope or overall life satisfaction. They are exhibited through engagement with leisure, entertainment and recreational activities or shown by having fun. Personal growth, self-development and self-actualisation and a sense of place are likely also to be helpful indicators.

The strengths of public memory institutions are the way they can foster and empower communities by supporting citizens and communities to engage via the collections, programmes and services provided (Yarrow, 2017). Whether in person or online, they have the opportunity to provide safe spaces where a diverse and inclusive community should be in control, owning the activity and empowered to be leading the memory institutions' strategic thinking. This can happen only if memory institutions forge meaningful connections through active participation in community life – in short, building partnerships and working to eliminate barriers to equitable access to digital resources.

It should not be taken for granted that this is naturally the way that most memory institutions already work. Consider this challenging question: if a minority group in the community asked the institution to change what it was doing, what would its response be?

Would the institution be willing to give up or share some of its gatekeeping roles, to listen to outside voices that challenged its position of power and expertise? Many marginalised communities were (and still are) denied ownership and curatorship over cultural heritage collections – especially in a dominating European/North American collection context – sometimes referred to as suffering from a DWEM (Dead, White, European and Male) syndrome. The digitisation of biased collections can be open to even wider 'misappropriation and misunderstandings by outsiders' (Srinivasan et al., 2009). This concern reflects the extent of funding available for digitisation and the collections on which this funding is focused. All memory institutions, but museums especially, have the 'power to privilege particular forms of knowledge and to naturalise highly particularised sets of values' (Sandell, 2007). There are examples of digital resources and digitised collections treated as merely technical products that replicate what is currently there, without understanding that digital is neither neutral nor 'an uncontested domain … it is a site of struggle', and that the challenge is more a 'social and political one' (Pickover, 2014). If the European/North American perspective that dominates many collections are all that is digitised, and close consideration is not given to issues of decolonisation in areas such as catalogue, records and metadata, then this bias and loss of ownership will be further exacerbated.

The caveats, therefore, are about trust and unconscious bias. Sharing is the key value to be pursued, and meeting people where they are, rather than where the institution wants them to be. The use of impact measures to see the evidence from the community and to reflect the institution's willingness to adapt, change and share is a paramount desirable outcome. The trust and participation that sharing can engender in our communities are paramount factors in service to the ideal of the most information, to the most people, as freely available as is practicable.

Engaging with decision makers

Decision makers are those stakeholders who function as gatekeepers to resources or whose decisions will have a distinct effect on the operation of the institution. They may be external funding bodies, the board of directors or trustees or the executive branch (of larger institutions). In policy terms, they may be national, regional or sectoral decision makers who can affect the context for other decision making. Impact as evidence is a core component in being able to sway or nudge these decision makers towards the desired outcome.

As an institution moves to Stage 4 of the BVI Model, it is highly likely that some of these decision makers will be expecting to see or interested in hearing the results. In the case of a funder, they have provided monies for a project, activity, programme or function undertaken in response to a stated need. The persuasive request for the allocation of resources was a promise to the funder to do those activities in a certain way so as to achieve goals set at the time of funding. Impact should go beyond the simplest evaluation response stating whether the funds were appropriately spent and that all the plans have been implemented. The impact should show that behaviours have changed, that the effect of the funded activity was significant to those reached and that the activity has the potential to continue having such an effect in the future.

The value of activity acting as a model or proof of concept for others to use, adapt or embellish is often a reliable indicator of sectoral impact, as is seen in the Wellcome Library's Open Tools and Services with its Universal Viewer, interactive timeline and links to the International Image Interoperability Framework (https://wellcomelibrary.org/what-we-do/open-tools-and-services). By freely sharing their work and developments – that first served the Wellcome Library's own internal needs – with the wider community, they can demonstrate sectoral impact through the evidence of their participation and leadership in the sector. This sharing also expands the base for feedback, consultation, user testing and collaborative development. This kind of demonstrable ROI is a way to maximise the likelihood that senior decision makers will appreciate the worth and beneficial scope of an activity.

The best decision makers are evidence-driven and will always be looking for the sources of what is known as *actionable information*. Actionable information helps to guide a decision, and from it a tangible action is possible. For instance, knowing that teenagers use Instagram a lot is useful information. Actionable information is knowing that if more digital content is put on the institution's Instagram account, there will be a measurable increase in teenage interest and attendance.

Benefits and levers

Using evidence and information as a way to gain a change in management or executive decision making is a matter of understanding how to deploy them.

Most effective methods will focus on evidence of a benefit in order to promise a rewarding outcome, or will use evidence on an issue that acts as a lever to force a change in attitude or behaviour.

In the classic parlance of behaviourism and related stimulus-response theories this is known as the carrot-and-stick approach to motivation or, as the philosopher Jeremy Bentham described them, the 'alluring' and 'coercive' influences (Hart, 2001). In motivating managerial change the principle of reinforcement is being suggested, such that desired behaviours are rewarded and undesirable outcomes are punished. In the old story of a donkey, the best ways to move it is to put a carrot in front of it or to jab it with a stick from behind. The carrot represents a promised or expected reward for moving, while the stick a tangible punishment for not moving. The one encourages movement and the other forces it – both are stimulus-response behaviour modifiers.

Such a pointed tool is not suggested here to be so bluntly used, but rather as a means to understand the motivating drivers of senior managers as a factor in gaining a change – whether through support, funding or attitude. For example, an American museum's chief technology officer (CTO) went to a meeting with her chief executive (CEO) to discuss the urgent need to upgrade the membership system and spend money on updating the data held – an investment of some US$75,000. The CEO interrupted the CTO, stating that he was much more concerned with the multi-million dollar exhibition programme and did not have time to discuss such a small matter. The CTO replied: 'OK, but please be aware we are writing to dead people asking them for donations.' The CEO gave her the money immediately. The reason being that membership donations and endowments were a significant source of revenue for the museum and were thus an alluring 'carrot' motivator. The issue of dead people was an obvious coercive stick: if the museum was continuing writing to them, their family members would become angry and contact the CEO directly to complain – and probably jeopardise future donations. The CTO had found the best negative impact evidence as a lever for the benefits that she wanted to achieve on behalf of the museum.

Finding the evidence in impact results to press a case based on benefits to the decision makers will mean looking for some of the following features to emphasise.

- **Strategic fit/positioning**: does the proposal fit closely to current strategies? Does it augment and add benefits to an already approved corporate strategy?

- **Efficiency gains**: will the proposal save the organisation money or resources such that it can attain its goals more efficiently? Will these cost savings offset any investment required?
- **Support for stakeholders**: will the proposal lead to tangible benefits for those stakeholders who are a high priority to the decision maker? Such as using evidence from schools and teachers if the decision maker has an education portfolio or interest.
- **Support for staff**: will the proposal benefit how the organisation operates by supporting staff activity? An example would be making key images and videos available in the digital asset management system so that everyone can easily find and use validated, high-quality content, thus saving time and local storage costs and ensuring that only content of the highest standard is used.
- **Access**: will the digital resources improve access to information that correlates with an improved service offering? An example would be the digitising of heavily requested items so that they can be readily accessed online rather than constantly on request.
- **Opportunities for revenue**: will the proposal produce a higher income over time than it costs to implement? Are there opportunities for revenue?
- **Support for other revenue activities**: will the proposal indirectly support other income to the organisation? An example would be the existence of a top-quality digital library supporting university student recruitment or the use of digital content to promote paid membership or retail opportunities.

Alternatively, finding the levers in impact results will emphasise the personal or organisational disadvantages of not acting should include any of the following.

- **Legal accountability**: is the decision maker accountable for a proposed action that is legally required? In Europe, compliance with the General Data Protection Regulation has been a powerful motivator for behaviour change and managerial investment.
- **Loss of value**: can the proposal demonstrate evidence of the benefits lost if the activity ceases or is underfunded? Are the stakeholders who will lose out a group about whom the decision maker cares? See the Trove example in Case study 9.1.

- **Risk consequences**: do the consequences of the risk significantly outweigh the costs of reducing or mitigating the risk? By way of example, do the consequences of losing the entire digital collection outweigh the costs of a decent offsite backup solution?
- **Ownership of problem**: is the problem addressed in the proposal visibly owned or the immediate responsibility of the decision maker? It is much easier to be dismissive of problems that will be somebody else's than those which are directly attributable to oneself.
- **Accountability for legacy expenditure**: does the extent of expenditure on ICT in the organisation provide reasons for ensuring that there is a positive and clear ROI? By way of example, an organisation that invests in every publication being born digital would be considered foolish if it did not provide enough storage for the created content.
- **Criticality to the institutional mission**: if the proposed activity closely matches the institutional mission then it should be possible to measure the damage or opportunity loss to that mission if it is not carried out.

Judicious use of impact evidence through a combination of clear benefits and levers can be transformative in pressing the case for change on decision makers.

Influencing policy makers by understanding stakeholders

Relationships drive influence; evidence and pivotal stakeholder groups drive policy. Align these factors to become an effective advocate for the desired change in the world of policy making.

The process of advocacy will utilise the information on stakeholders gathered in Stage 1 (see Chapter 6). Map out the people and organisations who can affect a change in policy terms. These are the impact stakeholders, defined by their interest in the sector and in the specific area of expertise needed, plus they obviously must have the ability to effect change.

Impact stakeholders can be mapped on a stakeholder matrix (see Figure 6.4 on page 117). Mapping those persons or organisations of policy influence will enable the discovery of those that conform to the broad segments of inform, consult, engage and collaborate. Some will need to be better *informed* before they can become useful agents of change. Others will be well informed and influential but are not the ones who can initiate the change. *Consult* these, as they set the context and have crucial relationships with decision makers and those controlling policy. *Engaging* with those who hold positions of influence or the capacity to act is essential. They are often not yet informed or knowledgeable about the specifics of the area of advocacy, but may become future sources of funding or influence government policy. *Engage* equally with those who are a block to progress, as they have significant influence in an opposing direction to that desired. Do not seek just to inform these stakeholders but engage with them to persuade them to the desired action. Government departments or regional authorities often sit in this segment. The focus for *collaboration* is those most knowledgeable and active in initiating plans and policy change. These are the impact stakeholders who actively seek to press for change or adaptation and look for changes that will benefit their community. *Collaborating* will be a pivotal action to ensure that all these knowledgeable, active and influential people are working together and to similar goals.

Having completed the matrix, consider how to divide up the time and resources available according to where the impact stakeholders lie on the matrix. Should stakeholders in the collaborate and consult segments be invited to the advisory panel for the activity? The launch event may want to include those mainly in the engage segment as well. Maybe a white paper or a briefing paper would reach out to those in the inform segments. How else can they engage or become involved in the activity?

Relationships are essential to this process, and experience suggests that good advocates are exceptionally well connected. They form strong relationships based on the core values of their profession and have both credibility and trust in their community and in their advocacy relationships. They give time to others, listen and reflect. This reflective listening is part of the reason why they are present and invited to events and meetings; it allows them to understand who the impact stakeholders are who can make change possible. The ability to value and support the entire community's welfare and benefit is essential to the trust they embody – they do not act only in transactional ways for their own organisations or personal interest. Thus, when they communicate with influencers, policy makers, funders or decision makers they are not dealing with the unknown but with familiar, engaged collaborations.

Clear communication of ideas and evidence is essential for good advocacy. Having clear narratives of impact is crucial to success. The advocate also needs the skills and ability to target the most effective story of transformative impact with the greatest relevance to that specific decision maker.

In this type of communication the order of impact-related information is switched, such that the order is clearly:

1 impact on the real world and for recognisable stakeholders
2 recommendations of how to respond to this impact
3 conclusions of the actions and change needed
4 analysis, evidence and data.

This switching puts the answer to the advocacy question first, followed by arguments and ideas, with the details of actions, evidence and data following as required. This imagined scenario provides an example:

> Our water health and sanitation information app saved over 200,000 lives last year in Bangladesh. We want to extend the information available to save more lives like those of the children in villages x and y – who, like 60% of the population, must endure unsafe drinking water.
>
> Our friend, Barshi, built his own tube well and hand pump at his home using our information guide. It was a gift to his new wife, and the safe water they now have nearby supports a growing family.
>
> With your support we can also increase the language coverage beyond Bengali and English so that the indigenous people of northern and south-eastern Bangladesh can access this lifesaving information in their native languages.
>
> Our app and online information are saving lives. Can you help us to save even more?

This sort of clear messaging conforms to a simple approach of making a proposal that is personalised with proof, and following a clear set of actionable impact evidence.

Chapter 10

Impact as a call to action

BVI Model Stage 5: Review and respond

A case having been made for impact through the presentation and communication of the outcomes and results of the BVI Model, now is the moment to follow through and ensure that the purpose of the impact assessment reaps its fullest benefits.

The BVI Model Stage 5 encourages a period of reflection and response. Avoid the perception that gathering evidence of impact is something to do in response to external pressure or as a one-off event. We should embed evidence gathering in our organisations so that continuous operational improvement becomes possible, while the value and benefit of the work done become visible to our communities as partners in the process. It is important to reflect continually on what will be measured, why measurement is worthwhile, and the purposes served by systematic measurement.

As can be seen from the BVI Model (see Figure 10.1 on the next page), Stages 4 and 5 inform and interact with all the previous stages. As the impact narrative builds this will influence data gathering, impact processes implemented and the overall framework design, all iteratively and adaptively. Stage 5 allows for a holistic review of all stages. The intent is to rethink the contextual stages as these change as a result of decisions made in response to the process of carrying out an impact assessment, and to respond to the outcomes of that study. As new ideas, services, products or activities are initiated or embedded, then the context is adapted to refocus the Strategic Perspectives and Value Lenses for future assessments. As the Value Lenses change their focus, so too do the impact objectives and, thus, the various elements in the BVI Framework.

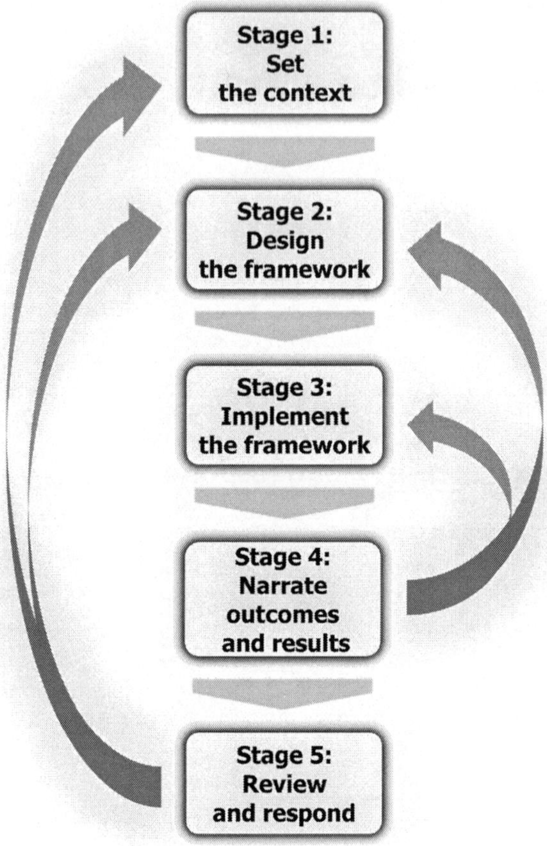

Figure 10.1 *Overview of the BVI Model stages*

The objectives of review and respond

The first task in Stage 5 is to ensure the effective communication of the outcomes of the impact measured to all the key decision makers and other relevant groups. As the results of the assessment become available, keep alert for evidence of any groups not reached with the results, and consider what actions can be done to reach them effectively.

Communicating must not remain a one-way, broadcast mechanism, but should involve engagement and active listening. Impact having been communicated, what is the response from the stakeholders? What actions or changes might stakeholders request in response to being better informed or focused on a specific issue, service or digital resource? How the institution responds to this feedback and engagement is a crucial factor in successful impact assessment. Too many institutions spend time and resources developing new initiatives rather than learning from and understanding that which has gone before. Impact assessment is part of becoming a collaborative and learning organisation that is willing to change in response to evidence.

Being responsive to the needs of a community assumes the requirement to revisit a digital product or service to improve its functions or reinvest in its redevelopment. Digitally oriented activity should not always be about adding new things to the institutional portfolio but may be about understanding how that which is already there is not achieving all the desired goals. It is quite likely that improving the platform (e.g., a move to mobile) or augmenting metadata will have a more transformative effect on use and satisfaction, but these are less exciting to those holding funds than is chasing some new initiative such as augmented reality.

When picture libraries and galleries moved from being an on-request advisory service in the 1990s to being almost entirely online image banks, it was necessary to reinvest in metadata to aid the kinds of searches that the public would do without expert knowledge of the collection. It was not helpful to maintain metadata that allowed *only* the search for Ornithorhynchus anatinus to return results for Duck-Billed Platypus, rather than allowing for more obvious searches: 'egg laying mammal', or even frivolous searches: 'funny looking Australian animal'. Reinvesting in metadata is resource-intensive, but such an investment is an essential step to allow a more folksonomy-oriented search approach to picture libraries. Many crowd-sourcing initiatives are now using a community tagging approach to improve their search responsiveness. This sort of response to improving and reinvesting in metadata was a crucial understanding for the Wellcome Library's initial impact assessment as discussed in Case study 3.1. Redevelopment of a digital resource, improving metadata or porting to a new platform are among the hardest things to get funding for (as they sound like maintenance rather than innovation), and thus using the results of impact assessment may be the evidence-based catalyst that unlocks this investment.

Stage 5 is also an excellent point at which to carry out a formal review to reflect on the level of success of the impact assessment in terms of securing the desired outcomes. When thinking about success, or even failures, it is important to consider how much of it is a function of the standard of the evidence gathered and presented, the effectiveness of the process and the modes of communication.

Reflect on issues including the following.

- What has changed? How does this affect strategic planning?
- Did the Strategic Perspectives and Value Lenses do a good job? Should the Value Lenses be modified or refocused to work better in the future?
- Would a different timeframe for measurement provide better data and results? Have there been unexpected outcomes or results, and can causal links be found to explain why they have occurred?
- Are the current methods of data gathering still worthwhile and useful?
- Revisit the SWOT analysis. Assess whether weaknesses are resolved or threats avoided. Have further strengths been added and are the opportunities more achievable now?
- What does the digital ecosystem look like now, compared to when the impact assessment started?

In summary, focus on what works to repeat those patterns, and learn lessons of what does not, to evolve future activities.

As a review and respond outcome of the impact assessment, identify a clear task list for action. Assign owners to the tasks and keep a check on progress. Ensure that task owners report back, share further experience and stay engaged with the activity so that it further informs any adjustment to the BVI Framework or helps the institution to learn from the experience. Record keeping is also a means of retaining institutional memory of the activities, decisions and outcomes, to refer back to as needed.

It is likely that internal audiences will give more attention to the impact results from the Operational and Economic Strategic Perspectives. External audiences will usually be more intrigued by the results of the Social and Innovation Perspectives. In reflecting on the Strategic Perspectives, remember that the Operational and Innovation Perspectives are inward-looking to the memory institution, while the Economic and Social Perspectives are externally measured and focused on outward benefits.

Review and respond steps ensure the use of the impact results, active reflection on them and evidence-based actions in response. Reflection on the possible institutional benefits derived from an evidence-based decision-making process will help to turn ideas into action and promote sustainable change management. Most importantly, this should be about making ever deeper connections with stakeholders to work with them in response to the evidence and insights gained. This relationship is the most likely means of gaining the most significant benefit for all.

Setting targets and performance measures

Reflecting on the impact results that accrue under the operational strategic perspective will most likely lead to a better understanding of how the organisation should set internal targets or performance measures.

In order to measure a change in anything, it is necessary to have a starting point or a baseline. Baselines are usually set in time but can also use something like service level provision (e.g., 200,000 Instagram followers with an average engagement rate per post of 3.8%). A baseline date is whatever the activity owner wishes it to be as a point of reference for change measurement. Using the outcomes of the BVI Model to set new benchmarks for service provision that are also baselines for future measurement will help to set realistic, focused performance targets.

Impact assessment should seek to better inform performance measures and targets because it focuses on the stakeholders and broader measures of the changes they experience and the effect of the memory institution on their life opportunities. Digital collections management is beset with numeric targets that are often somewhat meaningless out of context. The one insufficient advantage of digital is that it makes counting things easier, but a number alone is often not particularly informative. Quantitative targets mostly focus on the number of visitors or users and the number of items digitised or made available, but without any context or sense of the value of these numeric measures.

For instance, the Northern Ireland Assembly has set the KPIs for the National Museums of Northern Ireland (NMNI) using a metric of 'Additional number of collections-related images available online' (National Museums Northern Ireland, 2017). It is not a particularly helpful target, as there is no sense of what this number indicates in terms of performance or if the images have to be of a certain standard or relevance. It also does not take into account that digitising a 3-foot wide and 7- to 10-foot long engineering drawing of the RMS *Titanic* is going to take considerably more resource than imaging a 35mm slide collection. This KPI creates what is known as a perverse incentive to do easier but possibly less valuable work in order to achieve an arbitrary numeric target. To their credit, NMNI goes beyond these numbers to report their digital engagement and impact. As NMNI states in one of its reports, the organisation aspires '[to connect] with a broader range of audiences and [to promote] digital equality in our society through interventions that help remove traditional barriers to visiting museums', and to promote social responsibility so as to 'help improve employability and encourage economic activity [and] social inclusion' (National Museums Northern Ireland, 2017).

With this in mind, it is essential when reviewing impact to consider which aspects worked well or could be changed, paying particular attention to the effectiveness of the indicators, objectives and criteria used in the BVI Framework. The impact results across all of the Strategic Perspectives will help to inform this understanding. The indicators formed for Operational and Economic perspectives are the ones most likely to be useful. These can inform targets or KPIs if they prove to be effective measures.

How to build change-management strategic processes

Two outcomes from measuring impact in a strategic context are the need to manage change and the need to be innovative in approach. Reflect on the change indicated within the organisation in terms of the impact results and the process of carrying out the assessment. The people within the organisation may have changed because of an increase in skills or knowledge, or there may have been changes in the way they interact with the community. These may lead to organisational change as new activities become embedded as business-as-normal, some are reduced in priority, while others are identified as desirable but still needing to develop.

If the organisation measures impact well and communicates the findings effectively, then impact should ideally and logically lead to change. In the digital sphere, the emphasis of change management should be people and resources, as most technical problems are fixable with the right team, explicit requirements, time and money. Strategic change management requires the co-ordination of a structured period of transition from one situation to a new, desirable situation to achieve lasting change within an organisation. It relies on the application of knowledge, tools and resources to deal with change and defining and adopting corporate strategies, structures, procedures and technologies. Technology is relatively easy to change, as it is accessible to logic; the work behaviour of people less so. Change management is about convincing people that the change proposed is needed and the benefits of change will outweigh the disadvantages or temporary costs to them. Impact evidence will help with making a convincing case for change.

The evidence provided by impact (probably found in the Operational Strategic Perspective) should also be used to assess opportunities for staff development, training and professional growth. The evidence might identify a lack of skills in certain areas that training or future recruitment could rectify. The evidence of impact may equally celebrate the skills already available, reinforce the organisational culture and guide staff development.

Thinking of innovation

Investigation and reflection on the impact results for the Innovation Strategic Perspective will inform and help to refocus any innovation that is ongoing or planned. Innovation is a process through which value (intellectual, cultural, social or economic) is extracted from knowledge via the generation, development and implementation of ideas. The intended result of innovation is to produce new or improved ways of thinking, capabilities, services/products, strategies or processes. The BVI Model is intended to support memory institutions to become more innovative, learning organisations.

Innovators should be tasked to develop a new capability first, and to introduce new technology only if needed. As stated previously, digital tends to perpetual development, beta testing, upgrades and sometimes non-delivery. Software development is not always innovation and should be managed according to the needs of the organisation. Digital sits within innovation but is not the entirety of it. Taking impact results as pointing only to technical needs and ignoring the other dimensions of innovation would be to unnecessarily limit its scope.

Technology must not drive content or curatorial decisions. Content, context and user needs should inform all technology decisions. An excellent example of user experience and needs-driven technology innovation is at the UK's Tate, in its use of virtual reality (VR) to explore Modigliani's last Parisian studio (Tate, 2017). It is clear that this was designed not because Tate wanted to use VR but because this was an optimal way to tell the narrative and explain the artist's life using the actual studio space as a template.

To make innovation become a healthy activity for the organisation, establish a sandbox environment. Sandboxes enable genuine experimentation with ideas while not losing sight of day-to-day 'business as usual' deliverables. The sandbox concept can provide near-term opportunities for innovators and help consultation with the community before committing to long-term investments. A sandbox environment should support best practices for digital solutions and technical content production by allowing for iterative, low-risk development and testing. Note that a sandbox may be a formal technical area with tools, etc. It can also be a metaphorical space where the team can play with low consequences and can destroy and rebuild successive, imperfect attempts at creating something.

Responding to community needs

Impact results for the Social Strategic Perspective will be most useful for reflecting on community needs. The Economic and Innovation Perspectives will also factor in consideration to a lesser degree.

Memory institutions must continue to engage and take affirmative action with community stakeholders. Continuous reflection and engagement are vital because the collection narrative told is very often a singular one, normalised as if it were neutral through decisions embedded in cataloguing, metadata, digitisation, databases and interfaces (Gibson, 2019).

Such action and engagement should include working with community stakeholders:

- to identify the core areas of benefit and loss revealed by the impact results;
- to address proactively both the positive and negative impacts discovered, such that the community can be consulted and engaged in planning future actions;
- to consider the changes needed in the relationship between the institution and its community to foster trust, engagement and active collaboration;
- to plan future interventions together and identify what actions might best resolve any negative impacts discovered;
- to enable stakeholders to have a voice as both champions and agents of change for the institution.

Agency for community stakeholders will be challenging to achieve in a digital ecosystem. Infrastructure costs often dwarf other budgets and drive decisions without much consultation (either internally or externally). Thus, it takes effort and commitment to achieve. Community agency must be championed at all echelons of the institution. Those in active contact with community stakeholders need support, and responsive change must be a reality, not a vague promise. Community activity should seek to provide opportunities for self-expression and personal development, and to actively steer the work of the institution. This could be through facilitating community-led exhibitions, curation and programming.

Community action groups/panels can be an effective way to diversify the voices that steer the work of the memory institution, drawing together those who want to help shape the direction of plans and activities. These should be made up of people of diverse ages, backgrounds and interests. They could meet very regularly, possibly even monthly, with institution representatives at a time and place that best suits the community stakeholders (including in the evening or at the weekend). The purpose is to engage them actively in strategy, impact matters, digital resource development and planning.

Bringing the threads together

Impact as a call to action

The purpose of measuring impact is to accumulate enough data to create a critical mass of actionable evidence. In turn, this is intended to generate a chain reaction of actions that spread throughout the stakeholders. Even if the institution initiates the impact assessment, its results can be carried forward by the user community or other broadly engaged stakeholders. As Bell and Morse state, 'the circle needs to become a spiral of action' (Bell and Morse, 2008).

The transition from thought to action is always fraught with unforeseen obstacles. This is normal. Use the BVI Model and the Framework as a means of retaining focus on objectives and tasks as the inevitable obstacles are traversed. Keep the task record alive and active with regular discussion and sharing of experience with the stakeholders. Use SMART objectives to remain focused on what is achievable. Measure success against meaningful indicators.

Avoid the superficial bright lights of technologies that appear to offer user involvement. Social media is no panacea. I share the worries of Holgaard and Valtysson that superficial engagement through Facebook 'likes' is 'effortless participation' which can quickly dissipate. Their call to action concentrates on embracing people's knowledge and creativity as the key to user engagement and serious involvement in 'doable activities' (Holgaard and Valtysson, 2014).

Participation by the public is critical to becoming an activist institution that responds to impact with action. When it is done well, the institution integrates this mode of participatory engagement into its soul, with the result that it resonates far more profoundly than superficial consumption. Especially in the face of our attention economy, it is crucial to have a common understanding of the core values of the institution and to deliver these hand in hand with your community.

Adapting impact for evidence-based decision making

Pfeffer and Sutton popularised the phrase 'evidence-based decision-making'. They wanted to move away from a common managerial practice of 'doing–knowing' where decision making is done without knowing enough and then either later justified or only learning once the consequences have materialised (Pfeffer and Sutton, 2008). They claimed that managers tend to substitute for the best evidence 'obsolete knowledge, personal experience, specialist skills, hype, dogma, and mindless mimicry of top performers' (Pfeffer and Sutton, 2006).

Previously, I have playfully engaged with these concepts as the 'Digital Death Spiral' (Tanner, 2013). The assumptions and substitutions include the following.

- Digitisation = funding.
- Digital is everything today.
- Who knows how much it will cost, but digital is bound to be wonderful.
- Planning is so 20th Century, let's be Agile!
- Because our competition/Google/my peers are doing it …
- Because if we build it, they will come!

We can see many similar issues played out at massive scale in the BBC's ill-fated Digital Media Initiative (DMI), which failed to deliver after spending £125.9 million (National Audit Office, 2014). The plan of DMI was for a single, overarching, one-size-fits-all digital solution for video archiving and digital production across the entire BBC. It was always an ambitious plan, with 184 BBC staff and contractors working on it at its peak. DMI's failure had many causes, but many of the decision-making failures are reflected in the Digital Death Spiral, and particular among them was a distinct lack of evidence-based management.

At the heart of evidence-based approaches for improved organisational performance is the commitment of leaders to apply the best evidence to support decision making. Leaders set aside conventional wisdom in favour of a relentless commitment to gathering the most useful and actionable facts and data to make more-informed decisions. Evidence-based management is a humbling experience for leaders when it positions them to admit what they do not know and to work with their team to find the means of gathering that information. Evidence-based management is naturally a team-oriented and inclusive practice, as there is little room for the know-it-all or for an exclusively top-down leadership style. Good managers act on the best information available while questioning what they know.

Measuring impact fits into this management approach by being a frequent source of actionable evidence and a continuous challenge to revisit and review the status quo. Using the five stages of the BVI Model allows for a structured approach that continually narrows the perspectives to the core values to be investigated. The fact of measuring impact puts questions of efficacy on the agenda every time a strategic or technical change is proposed. The deep thinking involved in setting impact objectives and indicators will make people in the institution more disciplined in their thinking.

By bringing innovation and engagement more centrally to the strategic focus it then also becomes possible to treat the organisation as an organic, growing work in progress that is seeking to improve continuously, much like a garden. Being able to encourage trial activities, piloting in the sandbox and enabling experimentation in close collaboration with the stakeholder communities will develop the internal knowledge base and skills.

Reward the learning gained from experience; record it, even in failed ideas. Appreciate that negative impacts can happen and are an opportunity to do better. In these ways, the knowledge base increases and the organisation can benefit from evidence-based management, with a more enlightened staff and a clearer vision of strategic direction.

I believe that memory institutions need to become learning organisations in their management practice. When guided by actionable evidence, especially in relation to engaging communities and large-scale technology decisions, memory institutions will manage their affairs more effectively. Impact measures and the discipline that comes from applying the five stages of the BVI Model will help leaders to continuously seek new knowledge and insight while updating their assumptions, understanding and skills.

Beware of comfortable metrics

Evidence-based management is not about piling up random, meaningless data in the hope that the sheer volume of numeric data will produce the desired answer. Metrics for metrics' sake is a particular problem that can occur if the evidence or impact agenda is applied without clarity of purpose. Uncritical emulation and casual benchmarking are similar problems, with cherry-picking of data. In such cases, decision makers rely on the metrics of perceived high performers in their sector. They make decisions that emulate perceived peers without understanding the contexts or strategic differences that may have driven the top performers. This is the classic comparison of oranges and apples.

There is also a tendency for managers to choose comfortable metrics. These are easily achievable, because who wants to miss a target? However, they also will not stretch the organisation to grow or develop. Comfortable metrics do not seek to know anything that might challenge the status quo. Change is a threat (probably because it has been in the past) and, as such, it becomes hard to innovate or to take any risks. Digital innovation can be very challenging for a deeply embedded culture where there is a conservatism born out of fear of failure, criticism or mistakes. In such circumstances the perfect often becomes the enemy of the good, stifling the development of new ways of working. Fear of not reaching a performance metric that is artificially set, with no intent to learn from the data gathered, will keep such a negative culture alive and kicking.

The usage of any metric should be the result of the hard graft put in to understand, with clarity, the nature of the measure, how to collect it and the useful data it will provide. The BVI Model affords a deep understanding of the context, ecosystem and strategic intent that should provide clarity for which metrics are worthwhile pursuing. Any performance metric that does not produce an actionable response is usually pointless.

Celebrate success and develop collective excellence

Strong strategic leadership founded on evidence-based management with robust feedback loops is very desirable. All public-facing activities benefit from advanced, data-strong evaluations of their digital visitors and from evidence-led decision making to inform strategic decisions and prioritisation. Collaborating with community stakeholders in decision making and fully involving them in the organisation shares agency and leads to a better understanding of the most impactful changes. Celebrate together the successes and appreciate the collective excellence of all involved to learn, develop and foster a sense of ownership in the future direction of the organisation.

At present, many memory institutions are innovating and developing new initiatives without enough information about the success of these activities or the demand for them. It is tending to make what I term 'accidental management' occur more frequently. This term mirrors the popular concept of 'accidental parenting'. In accidental management, mini-decisions are made to solve an immediate problem (often technical in nature) without reflection on longer-term consequences or without reference to the mission and values of the institution. Through abdication, these mini-decisions become embedded in organisational culture as 'how we do things here'. Such mini-decisions are often unrecorded and cumulative, and thus hard to challenge. Because no one formally owns responsibility for them, they are hard to review and change.

This tendency to drip-feed mini-decisions below the radar usually goes hand in hand with the way that most organisations also tend to adopt change in an all-or-nothing fashion. If the top leadership are behind the idea, it goes ahead; if not, it withers away. This tendency hampers the opportunity to learn. Intellectually ambitious people will find a way, either by stealth or using the chance that accidental management affords, to start their activities. The outcome they hope for is that, as it becomes more visible, it will be embedded as 'that's how we do things here' or will be successful enough to be adopted as the way forward. However, this approach tends to substitute specialist skills for evidence. As an alternative to collaborating with others who might challenge their specialised knowledge, the expert defaults to decisions that capitalise on their strengths in experience and skill. To a hammer, everything looks like a nail. However, when specialisms of the 'trust me, I'm a doctor' variety replace evidence, they lead to unchallengeable assumptions that can be very costly, especially in technological terms. Bringing these projects out of hiding, into a clear space for experimentation, sharing and collaboration, will disarm these disadvantages and allow more open appreciation of innovation and success.

Leaders who apply impact measures and practise evidence-based management openly challenge and regularly interrogate the strategic direction of the institution. These approaches will strengthen, not weaken, the management strategies. Leaders can delegate decisions more confidently, since everyone is working to the same goals. Review the strategy with an evidence-based approach, not biased by hidden assumptions or perverse incentives. The outcomes of a well done impact assessment may be unsettling for some leaders, as the results may undermine their perceived power and prestige. Broadening the base of influence and decision making to be inclusive of the whole organisation and bringing in the opinions of external stakeholders can be hard to accept. Facts, evidence and impact data are great levellers of hierarchy. If the factual data available is relevant to a decision, then all data is equal, wherever it originates in the team. Thus, leadership's subjective opinion has lesser force. By replacing intuition with data as the paramount model of decision making, this changes the power dynamic that would have previously privileged seniority, authority, reputation and other power-based factors.

Successful digital collections and content, with the services and products that they generate, are rarely the work of lone champions or geniuses. However, this is how we often tell these stories. It is vital to respect and celebrate the roles of everyone in the teams and communities that develop ideas and bring them to fruition. To make any digital initiative work requires the co-ordinated actions and commitment of many people. If they feel ownership, sharing success and recognising their accomplishments will generate increased commitment.

Concluding thoughts

What memory institutions do matters to the publics that they serve. Whether the impact is measured or not, they will still make a difference to those who use them or benefit from their existence. As these quotes below remind us, museums, libraries, archives and other memory institutions make meaningful differences to people's lives.

Barbara Kingslayer, author: 'I'm of a fearsome mind to throw my arms around every living librarian who crosses my path, on behalf of the souls they never knew they saved.' (Kingslayer, 2014)

Jill Scott, singer, poet and actress: 'I thought, "if my mother hadn't taken me to libraries, art museums and dance recitals, I could end up in a lot of trouble and I wouldn't be where I am today. I just want to offer my kids something. I'm going to take care of my hood and you take care of yours!"' (Taylor, 2010)

Ganesh Paudel, a Nepalese journalist on Wikipedia: 'If a very small user base for a language can find their content in any online or Internet site, then they are very happy and that helps to develop their culture and their many things and it helps them to introduce themselves to the rest of the world.' (Cited in Fox, 2013)

Stephen McGann, Explore Your Archive ambassador: 'When my requested parish register arrived, it took me a full minute to get over the impact. An enormous leather-bound book from a different age … Yet the kind assistant had simply placed the book at my desk and left a 17 year-old in sole custody of it! It was my citizen's right to view this treasure – a part of our national heritage that I could hold in my own shaking hands … [archives] tell us more about ourselves than we could ever imagine.' (McGann and Cowdrey, 2017)

Sister Wendy Beckett, art historian: 'A country that has few museums is both materially poor and spiritually poor. Poverty, whether spiritual or economic, leaves us enslaved … Here, we can move out of our personal anxieties and disappointments into the vast and stable world of human creativity.' (Beckett, 2000)

At the same time, memory institutions are competing in an attention economy against a range of other content providers. The attention economy demands recognition that our living environment is information and content rich, so much so that it consumes the attention of its inhabitants. Content consumers must choose how they spend their time, creating a *de facto* marketplace based on digital content and use. This attention-based environment especially challenges memory institutions, because their commitments, concerns and values do not always align with the concerns of the marketplace. Nor should they.

Memory institutions must engage with and challenge the attention economy or they will defer their value to other content providers who will inexorably syphon off the attention and engagement of the public. In some ways, the digital domain also offers the chance for smaller organisations to play on an equal footing with the largest players, as the digital public is agnostic on the host of the resources. People are motivated more by the value of the content than the provider. Growth in the digital domain has also led to additional mandates, which remain mainly underfunded. Everyone in the sector exists in a very competitive environment. Funding and investment are predicated on defined goals set by various gatekeepers to money, such as the government, funding bodies, trustees or commercial interests. If memory institutions cannot demonstrate to these gatekeepers the value of the work they do, then funding will not flow.

The BVI Model is a way to implement impact assessment and demonstrate that value, especially for digital resources. It reflects the broader process of impact assessment and strategic planning. The principles from the BVI Model can be applied in different settings or at a less advanced level than specified in this book. The BVI Model challenges an organisation to be more evidence-based and to investigate the underlying assumptions driving institutional values and strategies. In short, the key questions remain.

- What to assess?
- Why assess that?
- How to use the intended results?
- What is it worth to know this information?

The BVI Model is a means to structure strategic contexts, decide what to measure and add purpose, direction and a disciplined approach to the often vague concept of impact.

The structured outcomes from use of the BVI Model should advocate for a digital resource through the four Strategic Perspectives. The summary narrative is, thus, as follows.

1 Rich digital content is available for existing and new audiences – placing content in every home and hand to share and make new personal experiences. This resource has changed our stakeholders' behaviour in ways that link to benefits in education, social life, community cohesion, a sense of place and improved welfare. (Social impact)
2 Because of these changes we are also delivering substantial economic benefits to our stakeholders that demonstrate the worth and value of our endeavours in clear monetary terms. (Economic impact)
3 Innovation in the building of the digital resource and its functionality means that we are gaining a strategic advantage in a vital area of activity for the future sustainability of services and engagement. (Innovation impact)
4 This digital resource enables our organisation to be more effective and efficient in delivering change and resultant benefits to stakeholders, both internally and externally. (Operational impact)

Providing a strong narrative backed with clear evidence of the change achieved will ensure that decision makers can make better-informed decisions and are more likely to follow the recommendations made. Each organisation can become better at learning from its activities and thus better at planning the future to make the most significant impact and benefit for its stakeholders.

I believe that memory institutions will play a pivotal role in the digital future of society. They can play this impactful role even in the midst of the fury of technological change and the clamour of the attention economy by keeping the Value Lenses focused on their core values and mission. An attitude of inquisitive pro-activeness, learning from and using data to generate better-informed decisions, will improve strategic planning and sustainability. Memory institutions must be fully embedded in their societies and in an ongoing public dialogue to expose the shared values and opportunities for a better future together.

This book began by reminding us that 'life writes its own stories'. The impact of a memory institution on people's lives will happen whether we note it or not. Just as newspapers gather life stories otherwise untold, so too should we meditate on the changes in the lives and life opportunities that are touched every day in experiences fostered via a library, museum, archive or other memory institution. We collect, curate, catalogue and create a record of all human life – let us also record and celebrate our contribution.

References

Abram, S. (2007) *The Value of Our Libraries: impact, recognition and influencing funders,* Arkansas Libraries, http://stephenslighthouse.com/files/ArkansasLA_Value.pdf.

Ahlberg, J. and Rosen, H. (2019) *Digidaily | Digitalisering av svensk dagspress, Digitization of Swedish Daily Press Blog,* https://digidaily.blogg.kb.se/.

Atkins, D. E., Brown, J. S. and Hammond, A. L. (2007) *A Review of the Open Educational Resources (OER) Movement: achievements, challenges and new opportunities,* Open Educational Resources.

Badenoch, D., Reid, C., Burton, P., Gibb, F. and Oppenheim, C. (1994) The Value of Information. In Feeney, M. and Grieves, M. (eds) *The Value and Impact of Information,* Bowker Saur, 9–77.

Bakhshi, H., Freeman, A. and Hitchen, G. (2009) *Measuring Intrinsic Value – How to Stop Worrying and Love Economics,* Mission Models Money, https://mpra.ub.uni-muenchen.de/14902/1/MPRA_paper_14902.pdf.

Beckett, W. (2000) *Sister Wendy's American Collection,* HarperCollinsPublishers.

Bell, S. and Morse, S. (2008) *Sustainability Indicators: measuring the immeasurable?* 2nd edn, Earthscan, doi: 10.1016/S0743-0167(99)00036-4.

Belot, H. (2016) Budget Cuts Will Have a 'Grave Impact' on the National Library, Staff Told, *Sydney Morning Herald,* 22 February, 1–3, www.smh.com.au/national/budget-cuts-will-have-a-grave-impact-on-the-national-library-staff-told-20160222-gn0co2.html.

Bergold, J. and Thomas, S. (2012) Participatory Research Methods: a methodological approach in motion, *Forum: Qualitative Sozialforschung/Forum: Qualitative Social Research,* **13** (1, Art. 30), 31.

Bogh, M. (2017) Interview with Mikkel Bogh, Statens Museum for Kunst, Denmark, 6 July 2017.

Borg, M., Karlsson, B., Kim, H. S. and McCormack, B. (2012) Opening up for Many Voices in Knowledge Construction. A case illustration of co-operative inquiry — a research project on 'Crisis Resolution and Home Treatment', *Forum Qualitative Social Research*, **13** (1), article 1.

Brennan, S. and Kreiss, D. (2014) *Digitization and Digitalization*, Culture Digitally, http://culturedigitally.org/2014/09/digitalization-and-digitization/.

Broadcasting Audience Research Board (2019) *UK TV Audience Figures*, www.barb.co.uk/.

Brophy, P. (2006) Projects into Services: the UK experience, *Ariadne*, **46**, www.ariadne.ac.uk/issue46/brophy/.

Buckland, M. K. (1991) Information as Thing, *Journal of the American Society for Information Science*, 42(5), 351–60.

Campbell, D. T. (1979) Assessing the Impact of Planned Social Change, *Evaluation and Program Planning*, **2** (1), 67–90, doi: 10.1016/0149-7189(79)90048-X.

Canalichio, P. (2018) *Expand, Grow, Thrive : 5 proven steps to turn good brands into global brands through the LASSO method*, Emerald Publishing Limited.

Carson, S. (2006) *MIT OpenCourseWare 2005 Program Evaluation Findings*, Massachusetts Institute of Technology.

Chaplin, S. (2014) E-mail message to Simon Tanner, 10 October.

Colbron, K., Chowcat, I., Kay, D. and Stephens, O. (2019) *Making Your Digital Collections Easier to Discover*, JISC Guide, www.jisc.ac.uk/full-guide/making-your-digital-collections-easier-to-discover.

Colson, F. and Hall, W. (1992) Educational Systems: pictorial information systems and the teaching imperative. In Thaller, M. (ed.), *Images and Manuscripts in Historical Computing*, Scripta Mercaturae Verlag, 73–86.

Consumer Barometer – Second Screens (2017) www.consumerbarometer.com/en/graph-builder/?question=M8&filter=country:united_kingdom.

Consumer Barometer – Trending Data (2017) www.consumerbarometer.com/en/trending/?.

Crookston, M., Oliver, G., Tikao, A., Diamond, P., Liew, C. L. and Douglas, S.-L. (2016) *Kōrero Kitea: Ngā hua o te whakamamatitanga (The impacts of digitised te reo archival collections)*, InterPARES Trust.

Davenport, T. H. and Beck, J. C. (2001) The Attention Economy, *Ubiquity*, ACM, (May), doi: 10.1145/375348.376626.

Dempsey, L. (2000) Scientific, Industrial, and Cultural Heritage: a shared approach: a research framework for digital libraries, museums and archives, *Ariadne*, (22), www.ariadne.ac.uk/issue22/dempsey/.

Department for Business, Information and Skills (2015) *Better Regulation Framework Manual: practical guidance for UK government officials*, www.gov.uk/government/uploads/system/uploads/attachment_data/file/468831/bis-13-1038-Better-regulation-framework-manual.pdf.

Digital Science (2016) *Publication Patterns in Research Underpinning Impact in REF2014*, https://dera.ioe.ac.uk/26933/1/2016_refimpact.pdf.

du Rausas, M. P., Manyika, J., Hazan, E., Bughin, J., Chui, M. and Said, R. (2011) *Internet Matters: the net's sweeping impact on growth, jobs, and prosperity*, www.mckinsey.com/~/media/McKinsey/Industries/ High Tech/Our Insights/Internet matters/MGI_internet_matters_exec_summary.ashx.

Dunning, A. (2012) *Deliverable 4.1: European newspaper survey report*, www.europeana-newspapers.eu/wp-content/ uploads/2015/05/ENP-Deliverable_4.1_final.pdf.

Durose, C., Beebeejaun, Y., Rees, J., Richardson, J. and Richardson, L. (2012) *Towards Co-Production in Research with Communities*, Connected Communities, doi: 10.1002/ana.23654.

Economic Development Research Group (2015) *2015 Economic Impact Study of the Museum of Fine Arts, Boston*, Economic Development Research Group.

Ellwood, S. and Greenwood, M. (2016) Accounting for Heritage Assets: does measuring economic value kill the cat? *Critical Perspectives on Accounting*, Elsevier Ltd, 38, 1–13, doi: 10.1016/j.cpa.2015.05.009.

Erichsen, N. (2017) Interview with Nicholaj Erichsen, Statens Museum for Kunst, Denmark 6 July.

Eschner, K. (2016) *The Story of the Real Canary in the Coal Mine*, Smithsonian.com, www.smithsonianmag.com/smart-news/story-real-canary-coal-mine-180961570/.

European Commission (n.d.) *Key Documents – Impact Assessment – European Commission*, http://ec.europa.eu/smart-regulation/impact/key_docs/key_docs_en.htm.

Europeana Foundation (2014a) *Europeana Strategy 2015–2020, Impact*, http://ec.europa.eu/dgs/connect/en/content/public-services-digital-service-infrastructures-connecting-europe-facility.

Europeana Foundation (2014b) *Europeana Strategy 2015–2020: 'We transform the world with culture'*, http://pro.europeana.eu/files/Europeana_Professional/Publications/ Europeana Strategy 2020.pdf.

Fallon, J. (2017a) *Developing the Impact Toolkit: supporting impact assessment in the cultural heritage sector 2017*, Europeana Foundation.

Fallon, J. (2017b) *Impact Assessment Task Force, Europeana Professional*, https://pro.europeana.eu/project/impact-assessment.

Fallon, J. (2017c) *Impact Insights: testing the impact toolkit on Europeana to develop a better understanding of our impact 2017*, https://pro.europeana.eu/post/impact-insights-2017.

Fallon, J. (2019) *Making the Case for Impact at SMK*, Europeana Pro, https://pro.europeana.eu/post/making-the-case-for-impact-at-smk.

Finnis, J., Chan, S. and Clements, R. (2011) *Let's Get Real: how to evaluate online success?*, Report from Culture24 Action Research Project, 1–40.

First Followers (2009) *The Book from Sinai*, Vision, http://subscribe.vision.org/first-followers/bid/35878/The-Book-from-Sinai.

Fox, D. (2013) *The Impact of Wikipedia: Ganesh Paudel*, https://blog.wikimedia.org/2013/02/05/the-impact-of-wikipedia-ganesh-paudel/.

Fox, H. (n.d.) *Beyond the Bottom Line: evaluating art museums with the Balanced Scorecard*, http://citeseerx.ist.psu.edu/viewdoc/download?doi=10.1.1.615.5506&rep=rep1&type=pdf.

Freedman, L. (2013) *Strategy: a history*, Oxford University Press.

Frey, B. S. (2003) *Arts and Economics: analysis and cultural policy*, Springer-Verlag, doi: 10.1007/978-3-540-24695-4.

Frey, B. S. and Pommerehne, W. (1990) *Muses and Markets: explorations in the economics of the arts*, Blackwell.

Garcés, J. (2007) *Codex Sinaiticus: transcript of audio. Juan Garcés, curator of the British Library's Codex Sinaiticus Project, gives his personal thoughts on the project and on the manuscript itself in April 2007, The British Library*, www.bl.uk/onlinegallery/sacredtexts/podjuangarces.html.

Giannetti, F. (2018) A Twitter Case Study for Assessing Digital Sound, *Journal of the Association for Information Science and Technology*, doi: 10.1002/asi.23990.

Gibson, L. (2019) *Decolonising South African Museums in a Digital Age: re-*

imagining the Iziko Museums' Natal Nguni catalogue and collection, King's College London.

Giupponi, C. (2002) *From the DPSIR Reporting Framework to a System for a Dynamic and Integrated Decision-making Process*, www.researchgate.net/publication/229047372.

Goodhart, C. A. E. (1984), *Monetary Theory and Practice: the UK experience*, Macmillan Education UK, 91–121, doi: 10.1007/978-1-349-17295-5_4.

Gooding, P. (2017) *Historic Newspapers in the Digital Age : 'search all about it!'*, Routledge.

Green, A. (2014) Alexander Green, research interview with Simon Tanner on the Wellcome Library Codebreakers impact assessment, September.

Green, A. and Andersen, A. (2017) Museums and the Web: finding value beyond the dashboard, http://mw2016.museumsandtheweb.com/paper/finding-value-beyond-the-dashboard/.

Griffiths, J.-M. and King, D. W. (1994) Libraries: the undiscovered national resource. In Feeney, M. and Grieves, M. (eds), *The Value and Impact of Information*, Bowker Saur, 79–116.

Gross, B. M. (1964) *The Managing of Organizations: the administrative struggle, volume 2*, Free Press of Glencoe.

Harley, D. H. (2006) *Use and Users and Digital Resources: a focus on undergraduate education in the humanities and social sciences*, https://eric.ed.gov/?id=ED503076.

Hart, H. L. A. (2001) *Essays on Bentham: studies in jurisprudence and political theory*, Clarendon Press.

Hartley, J. and Benington, J. (2000) Co-research: a new methodology for new times, *European Journal of Work and Organizational Psychology*, **9** (4), 463–76, doi: 10.1080/13594320050203085.

Henshaw, C. and Kiley, R. (2013) The Wellcome Library, *Ariadne*, **71**, www.ariadne.ac.uk/issue/71/henshaw-kiley/.

Hjørland, B. (2000) Documents, Memory Institutions and Information Science, *Journal of Documentation*, **56** (1), 27–41, doi: 10.1108/EUM0000000007107.

Holgaard, N. and Valtysson, B. (2014) Perspectives on Participation in Social Media. In Sanderhoff, M. (ed.), *Sharing Is Caring: openness and sharing in the cultural heritage sector*, Statens Museum for Kunst, 221–31.

Holley, R. (2010) Trove: innovation in access to information in Australia, *Ariadne*, **64**, 1–9, www.ariadne.ac.uk/issue64/holley/.

Huberman, B. a. (2013) Social Computing and the Attention Economy, *Journal of Statistical Physics*, **151** (1–2), 329–339, doi: 10.1007/s10955-012-0596-5.

Hügel, S. (2012) *Evaluating the Sustainability of AHRC-funded UK Arts and Humanities Projects with Digital Outputs*, University College London.

Hughes, L. M. (ed.) (2012) *Evaluating and Measuring the Value, Use and Impact of Digital Collections*, Facet Publishing.

IIIF Consortium (n.d.) *IIIF Frequently Asked Questions (FAQs) — IIIF | International Image Interoperability Framework*, http://iiif.io/community/faq/#what-is-iiif.

Imperial War Museum (2007) *Imperial War Museum Equality Strategy 2007–2010*, www.iwm.org.uk/sites/default/files/public-document/EqualityStrategyInternet-2011-01-20.pdf.

International Association for Impact Assessment (2009) *What Is Impact Assessment?*, www.iaia.org/uploads/pdf/What_is_IA_web.pdf.

Irwin, B. (2017) The Cost of Doing Nothing. In Irwin, B. and Silk, K. (eds) *Creating a Culture of Evaluation: taking your library from talk to action*, OLA Press, 3–40.

Irwin, B. and Silk, K. (eds) (2017) *Creating a Culture of Evaluation: taking your library from talk to action*, OLA Press.

Jensen, C. (2017) Interview with Christina Jensen, Statens Museum for Kunst, Denmark, 6 July.

Jones, M. and Verhoeven, D. (2016) Treasure Trove: why defunding Trove leaves Australia poorer, *The Conversation*, 26 February, 1–4, https://theconversation.com/treasure-trove-why-defunding-trove-leaves-australia-poorer-55217.

Kaplan, R. S. and Norton, D. P. (1996) *The Balanced Scorecard: translating strategy into action*, Harvard Business Review Press.

Kapsalis, E. (2016) *The Impact of Open Access on Galleries, Libraries, Museums, and Archives*, http://siarchives.si.edu/sites/default/files/pdfs/2016_03_10_OpenCollections_Public.pdf.

Kennedy, R. F. (1968) *Robert F. Kennedy Remarks at the University of Kansas, March 18, 1968*, Robert F. Kennedy Speeches – John F. Kennedy Presidential Library and Museum, www.jfklibrary.org/Research/Research-Aids/Ready-Reference/RFK-Speeches/Remarks-of-Robert-F-Kennedy-at-the-University-of-Kansas-March-18-1968.aspx.

Kenney, A. R. (1997) The Cornell Digital to Microfilm Conversion Project:

final report to NEH, *RLG News*, **1** (2), 1–3, http://worldcat.org/arcviewer/1/OCC/2007/08/08/0000070511/viewer/file941.html.

Kenny, E. (2017) *History: the Europeana we recognise today launched in 2008 but has much deeper roots*, Europeana Pro, https://pro.europeana.eu/our-mission/history.

King's College London and Digital Science (2015) *The Nature, Scale and Beneficiaries of Research Impact: an initial analysis of Research Excellence Framework (REF) 2014 impact case studies*, www.kcl.ac.uk/policy-institute/assets/ref-impact.pdf.

Kingslayer, B. (2014) How Mr Dewey Decimal Saved My Life. In Patchett, A. and Moyers, B. (eds), *The Public Library: a photographic essay*, Chronicle Books, Princeton Architectural Press, 78.

Knowles, S. (2018) *Narrative by Numbers: how to tell powerful and purposeful stories with data*, Routledge.

Kotler, P. (1972) A Generic Concept of Marketing, *Journal of Marketing*, **36** (2), 46–54.

Kristensen, P. (2004) The DPSIR framework, http://wwz.ifremer.fr/dce/content/download/69291/913220/file/DPSIR.pdf.

Kritzeck, M. (2018) Correspondence with the Mandy Kritzeck, Digital Media Producer/Project Manager at the Corning Museum of Glass.

Library of Congress (2017) *Update on the Twitter Archive at the Library of Congress*, https://blogs.loc.gov/loc/files/2017/12/2017dec_twitter_white-paper.pdf.

Library of Congress (n.d.) *Chronicling America: historic American newspapers*, http://chroniclingamerica.loc.gov/search/titles/.

Los Angeles Times (1987) James Has a Notion Where Blame Belongs, *Los Angeles Times*, 28 August, http://articles.latimes.com/1987-08-28/sports/sp-2763_1_blame-belongs.

Malde, S. and Finnis, J. (2016) *Let's Get Real 4: report from the fourth Culture24 Action Research Project*, https://weareculture24.org.uk/our-research-reports/.

Mao, Y. (2016) *The Sustainability of Digitised Collections in Memory Institutions*, University College London.

Marchionni, P. (2009) Why Are Users So Useful? User engagement and the experience of the JISC digitisation programme, *Ariadne*, **61**, www.ariadne.ac.uk/issue61/marchionni/.

Markless, S. and Streatfield, D. (2006) *Evaluating the Impact of Your Library: a practical model*, Facet Publishing.

Maron, N. L., Smith, K. K. and Loy, M. (2009) *Sustaining Digital Resources: an on-the-ground view of projects today*, Ithaka Case Studies in Sustainability, : https://sca.jiscinvolve.org/wp/files/2009/07/sca_ithaka_sustainingdigitalresources_report.pdf.

Marsh, D. E., Punzalan, R. L., Leopold, R., Butler, B. and Petrozzi, M. (2016) Stories of Impact: the role of narrative in understanding the value and impact of digital collections, *Archival Science*, Springer Netherlands, **16** (4), 327–72, doi: 10.1007/s10502-015-9253-5.

Matthews, J. (2013) Adding Value: getting to the heart of the matter, *Performance Measurement and Metrics*, **14** (3), 162–174, doi: 10.1108/PMM-08-2013-0024.

Matthews, J. R. (2008) *Scorecards for Results: a guide for developing a library balanced scorecard*, Libraries Unlimited.

McGann, J. (2010) *Online Humanities Scholarship: the shape of things to come*, Connexions, http://cnx.org/content/col11199/1.1.

McGann, S. and Cowdrey, L. (2017) *Why Do You Love to #explorearchives*, The National Archives Blog, https://blog.nationalarchives.gov.uk/blog/love-explorearchives/.

McGlone, P. (2015) America's 'National Library' Is Lacking in Leadership, Yet Another Report Finds, *Washington Post*, 31 March, www.washingtonpost.com/entertainment/museums/americas-national-library-is-behind-the-digital-curve-a-new-report-finds/2015/03/31/fad54c3a-d3fd-11e4-a62f-ee745911a4ff_story.html.

McKernan, L. (2017) Correspondence with Luke McKernan, 14 July 2017.

Meeker, M. (2015) Internet Trends 2015 *Code Conference*.

Meeker, M. (2018) Internet Trends 2018 *Code 2018*. doi: 10.1016/j.ajoms.2015.09.005.

Meyer, E. T. and Eccles, K. (2016) *The Impacts of Digital Collections*, Oxford Internet Institute.

Meyer, E. T., Eccles, K., Thelwall, M. and Madsen, C. (2009) *Usage and Impact Study of JISC-funded Phase 1 Digitisation Projects and the Toolkit for the Impact of Digitised Scholarly Resources (TIDSR)*, 1–179, www.jisc.ac.uk/guides/toolkit-for-the-impact-of-digitised-scholarly-resources.

Miller, D. (2008) The Uses of Value, *Geoforum*, **39** (3), doi: 10.1016/j.geoforum.2006.03.009.

Mindell, J., Biddulph, J., Taylor, L., Lock, K., Boaz, A., Joffe, M. and Curtis, S. (2010) Improving the Use of Evidence in Health Impact Assessment,

Bulletin of the World Health Organization, **88** (7), 543–50, doi: 10.2471/blt.09.068510.

Moore, J. F. (2013) *Shared Purpose: a thousand business ecosystems, a worldwide connected community, and the future*, CreateSpace Independent Publishing.

Museum of Fine Arts Boston (2014) *The Economic and Community Impacts of the Museum of Fine Arts, Boston*, www.mfa.org/about/economic-impact-report.

Mussell, J. (2013) *Parsing Passing Events*, jimmussell.com. A blog about the Victorians, the media and the digital humanities, http://jimmussell.com/2013/03/13/parsing-passing-events/.

Nasiruddin, M. (2014) Libraries for Socially Disadvantaged People in Bangladesh: a new approach for changing lives from sex workers to human resources, *Global Advanced Research Journal of Library, Information and Archival Studies (GARJLIAS)*, **2** (1), 8–13.

Nasiruddin, M. (2017) Digital School Libraries in Bangladesh: a role model for changing lives of the extreme poor children, *International Journal of Library and Information Science*, **9** (4), 25–36, doi: 10.5897/ijlis2016.0747.

Nasiruddin, M. and Nahar, L. (2013) Brothel-based Community Digital Libraries: changing lives of the Sex workers in Bangladesh. In Ganguly S. and P K Bhattacharya, P.K., *International Conference on Digital Libraries* (ICDL), The Energy and Resources Institute, 1165–6.

National Audit Office (2014) *BBC Digital Media Initiative, Independent Report Commissioned by the BBC Trust from the National Audit Office*, www.nao.org.uk/wp-content/uploads/2015/01/BBC-Digital-Media-Initiative.pdf.

National Library of Australia (2018) *National Library of Australia Annual Report 2017–18*, doi: 10.1136/vetrecjbvasection.

National Library of Australia (n.d.) *Australian Newspaper Digitisation Program*, www.nla.gov.au/content/newspaper-digitisation-program.

National Museums Liverpool (2013) *The Power of Museums: economic impact and social responsibility at National Museums Liverpool*, www.liverpoolmuseums.org.uk/about/corporate/reports/index.aspx.

National Museums Northern Ireland (2017) *National Musuems Northern Ireland Annual Report and Accounts 2016–17*.

Neisser, U. (2014) *Cognitive Psychology: classic edition*, Psychology Press.

Nelson, T. (1974) *Computer Lib: and dream machines*, Self-published.

Nielsen (2019) *US TV Audience Figures*, www.nielsen.com/us/en.html.

Noel, W. (2012) *Revealing the Lost Codex of Archimedes*, TEDxSummit, www.ted.com/talks/william_noel_revealing_the_lost_codex_of_archimedes.

O'Brien, D. (2013) *Cultural Policy: management, value and modernity in the creative industries*, doi: 10.4324/9780203583951.

OCLC and ALA (2018) *From Awareness to Funding: voter perceptions and support of public libraries in 2018*, OCLC, doi: 10.25333/C3M92X.

Office for National Statistics (2010) *[Archived content] Measuring the Economic Impact of an Intervention or Investment, 2010 – ONS*, http://webarchive.nationalarchives.gov.uk/20160129145340/http://www.ons.gov.uk/ons/rel/regional-analysis/measuring-the-economic-impact-of-an-intervention-or-investment/measuring-the-economic-impact-of-an-intervention-or-investment/index.html.

Ong, W. J. (1982) *Orality and Literacy: the technologizing of the word*, Routledge, doi: 10.1111/j.1460-2466.1980.tb01787.x.

Osterwalder, A., Pigneur, Y., Smith, A. and Clark, T. (2010) *Business Model Generation: a handbook for visionaries, game changers, and challengers*, John Wiley & Sons, https://strategyzer.com/.

Ottawa Public Library (2016) *Check Out the Benefits: the economic benefits of the Ottawa Public Library*.

Owen, H. (2008) *Open Space Technology: a user's guide*, Berrett-Koehler Publishers.

Palliative Care Outcome Scale (n.d.) https://pos-pal.org/.

Pearce, D. and Özedemiroglu, E. (2002) *Economic Valuation with Stated Preference Techniques. A summary guide*, Department for Transport, Local Government and the Regions, doi: 10.1016/S0921-8009(04)00058-8.

Pfeffer, J. and Sutton, R. I. (2006) Evidence-based Management, *Harvard Business Review*, January, https://hbr.org/2006/01/evidence-based-management.

Pfeffer, J. and Sutton, R. I. (2008) *Hard Facts, Dangerous Half-truths, and Total Nonsense: profiting from evidence-based management*, Harvard Business School Press.

Phillips, J. J., Brantley, W. and Phillips, P. P. (2011) *Project Management ROI: a step-by-step guide for measuring the impact and ROI for projects*, John Wiley & Sons.

Pickover, M. (2014) Patrimony, Power and Politics: selecting, constructing and preserving digital heritage content in South Africa and Africa. In Mackiewicz, E., *IFLA WLIC 2014 – Libraries, Citizens, Societies: Confluence for Knowledge*, IFLA, 16–22, http://library.ifla.org/1023/1/138-pickover-en.pdf.

Plaza, B. (2010) Valuing Museums as Economic Engines: willingness to pay or discounting of cash-flows?, *Journal of Cultural Heritage*, **11** (2), 155–162, doi: 10.1016/j.culher.2009.06.001.

Poort, J., van der Noll, R. Ponds, R., Rougoor, W. and Weda, J. (2013) *The Value of Europeana*, SEO Economic Research, https://pro.europeana.eu/post/europeana-strategy-2020-value-assessment-seo.

Poundstone, W. (2011) *Priceless: the hidden psychology of value*, Oneworld.

Powell, S. (2014) *Embracing Digital Culture for Collections*, Museums Aotearoa, https://blog.museumsaotearoa.org.nz/2014/08/11/embracing-digital-culture-for-collections-by-sarah-powell/.

Quint, B. (2002) *OCLC* , Olive Software Ally to Digitize Library Newspaper Archives, *Information Today*, http://newsbreaks.infotoday.com/NewsBreaks/OCLC-Olive-Software-Ally-to-Digitize-Library-Newspaper-Archives-17172.asp.

Ranganathan, S. R. (1931) *The Five Laws of Library Science*, Madras Library Association.

Reeves, M. (2002) *Measuring the Economic and Social Impact of the Arts: a review*, www.artscouncil.org.uk/news/publicationsindex.html.

Rimmer, J., Warwick, C., Blandford, A., Gow, J. and Buchanan, G. (2008) An Examination of the Physical and the Digital Qualities of Humanities Research, *Information Processing and Management*, **44** (3), 1374–92, doi: 10.1063/1.2756072.

Robehmed, N. and Berg, M. (2018) Highest-paid YouTube Stars 2018: Markiplier, Jake Paul, PewDiePie and More, *Forbes*, 3 December, www.forbes.com/sites/natalierobehmed/2018/12/03/highest-paid-youtube-stars-2018-markiplier-jake-paul-pewdiepie-and-more/.

Robinson, H. (2012) Remembering Things Differently: museums, libraries and archives as memory institutions and the implications for convergence, *Museum Management and Curatorship*, **27** (4), 413–29, doi: 10.1080/09647775.2012.720188.

Ross, C. (2014) *Radical Trust Works: an investigation of digital visitor generated content and visitor engagement in museum spaces*, http://discovery.ucl.ac.uk/1458024/1/CRoss_PhD_Final_RadicalTrustWorks_2014_COMPLETE.pdf.

Rusbridge, C. (2006) Excuse Me ... Some Digital Preservation Fallacies, *Ariadne*, **46**, 1–6, www.ariadne.ac.uk/issue46/rusbridge/.

Sandell, R. (2007) *Museums, Prejudice and the Reframing of Difference*, Routledge.

Sanderhoff, M. (2014) This Belongs to You: on openness and sharing at Statens Museum for Kunst. In Sanderhoff, M. (ed.), *Sharing Is Caring: openness and sharing in the cultural heritage sector*, Statens Museum for Kunst, 20–133.

Sanderhoff, M. (2017) Interview with Merete Sanderhoff, Statens Museum for Kunst, Denmark, 3 July.

Selwood, S. (2010) *Making a Difference : the cultural impact of museums. An essay for NMDC*, www.nationalmuseums.org.uk/media/documents/publications/cultural_impact_final.pdf.

Shafer, J. (2010) On the Trail of the Question, Who First Said (or Wrote) that Journalism Is the 'First Rough Draft of History'?, *Slate*, www.slate.com/articles/news_and_politics/press_box/2010/08/who_said_it_first.html.

Shear, M. D. (2015) Library of Congress Chief Retires under Fire, *New York Times*, 10 June, www.nytimes.com/2015/06/11/us/library-of-congress-chief-james-hadley-billington-leaving-after-nearly-3-decades.html.

Simon, H. A. (1971) Designing Organisations for an Information-rich World. In Greenberger, M., *Computers, Communications, and the Public Interest*, The Johns Hopkins Press, 37, doi: citeulike-article-id:986786.

Sinek, S. (2011) *Start with Why: how great leaders inspire everyone to take action*, Portfolio/Penguin.

Smith, J. H. (2018) Finally: a new website for SMK, *Medium*, August, https://medium.com/smk-open/finally-a-new-website-for-smk-c1d3c863779e.

Smith, L. and Campbell, G. (2018) The Tautology of 'Intangible Values' and the Misrecognition of Intangible Cultural Heritage, *Heritage & Society*, **10** (1), 1–19, doi: https://doi.org/10.1080/2159032X.2017.1423225.

Smith, R. (2007) *Being Human: historical knowledge and the creation of human nature*, Columbia University Press.

Smith, S. and Panaser, S. (2015) *Implementing Resource Discovery Techniques at the Museum of Domestic Design and Architecture, Middlesex University – Social Media and the Balanced Value Impact Model*, Jisc 'Spotlight on the Digital' project, http://eprints.mdx.ac.uk/18555/1/case_study_resource_discovery_moda.pdf.

SMK (2017) *Who Are We? – Statens Museum for Kunst*, www.smk.dk/en/article/organization/.

SMK (2018) *SMK for All. SMK-Strategi 2018–2021*, https://smk.dk/wp-content/uploads/2018/06/Bilag_2_-_SMK_Strategi_2018-2021.pdf.

Srinivasan, R., Enote, J., Becvar, K. M. and Boast, R. (2009) Critical and Reflective Uses of New Media Technologies in Tribal Museums, *Museum Management and Curatorship*, **24** (2), 161–81, doi: 10.1080/09647770902857901.

Stanziola, J. (2008) Developing a Model to Articulate the Impact of Museums and Galleries: another dead duck in cultural policy research?, *Cultural Trends*, **17** (4), 317–21, doi: 10.1080/09548960802615455.

Steg, L. (2005) Car Use: lust and must. Instrumental, symbolic and affective motives for car use, *Transportation Research Part A: policy and practice*, **39** (2–3 special issue), 147–62, doi: 10.1016/j.tra.2004.07.001.

Stravinsky, I. and Craft, R. (1959) *Conversations with Igor Stravinsky*, Doubleday.

Streatfield, D. and Markless, S. (2012) *Evaluating the Impact of Your Library*, 2nd edn, Facet Publishing.

Stroeker, N. and Vogels, R. (2014) *Survey Report on Digitisation in European Cultural Heritage Institutions 2014*, www.enumerate.eu/fileadmin/ENUMERATE/documents/ENUMERATE-Digitisation-Survey-2014.pdf.

Sweeny, K., Fridman, M. and Rasmussen, B. (2017) *Estimating the Value and Impact of Nectar Virtual Laboratories*, https://nectar.org.au/wp-content/uploads/2016/06/Estimating-the-value-and-impact-of-Nectar-Virtual-Laboratories-2017.pdf.

Tanner, S. (2004) *Reproduction Charging Models and Rights Policy for Digital Images in American Art Museums*, A Mellon Foundation funded study, King's College London, https://kclpure.kcl.ac.uk/portal/files/104647946/Reproduction_charging_models_TANNER_Published_2004_GREEN_VoR.pdf.

Tanner, S. (2006) Managing Containers, Content and Context in Digital Preservation: towards a 2020 vision. In Chapman, S. and Stovall, S. A. (eds), *Archiving 2006: final program and proceedings, May 23–26, 2006, Ottawa, Canada*, Society for Imaging Science and AMP; Technology, 19–23.

Tanner, S. (2011a) Inspiring Research, Inspiring Scholarship: the value and benefits of digitized resources for learning, teaching, research and enjoyment. In Zwaard, K. and Metcalfe, W. (eds), *Archiving 2011 –*

Preservation Strategies and Imaging Technologies for Cultural Heritage Institutions and Memory Organizations – Final Program and Proceedings, IS&T, 77–82, www.scopus.com/inward/record.url?eid=2-s2.0-84860644438& partnerID=40&md5=d02b3d8167408d617477e7b1179fee88.

Tanner, S. (2011b) The Value and Impact of Digitized Resources for Learning, Teaching, Research and Enjoyment. In Hughes, L. M. (ed.), *Evaluating and Measuring the Value, Use and Impact of Digital Collections*, Facet Publishing, 103–20.

Tanner, S. (2012) *Measuring the Impact of Digital Resources, The Balanced Value Impact Model*, King's College London, https://kclpure.kcl.ac.uk/portal/files/5675881/BalancedValueImpactModel_SimonTanner_October2012.pdf.

Tanner, S. (2013) Avoiding the Digital Death Spiral – Surviving and Thriving through Understanding the Value and Impact of Digital Culture. In Oliver, M. (ed.), *National Digital Forum 2013 Conference, Wellington, New Zealand*, National Digital Forum, www.youtube.com/watch?v=kDyBCmPomFQ.

Tanner, S. (2016a) *Europeana – Core Service Platform MILESTONE MS26: recommendation report on business model, impact and performance indicators*, http://pro.europeana.eu/files/Europeana_Professional/Projects/Project_list/Europeana_DSI/Milestones/europeana-dsi-ms26-recommendation-report-on-business-model-impact-and-performance-indicators-2016.pdf.

Tanner, S. (2016b) Open GLAM: the rewards (and some risks) of digital sharing for the public good. In Wallace, A. and Deazley, R. (eds), *Display at Your Own Risk: an experimental exhibition of digital cultural heritage, 2016*, http://displayatyourownrisk.org/wp-content/uploads/2016/04/Display-At-Your-Own-Risk-Publication.pdf.

Tanner, S. (2016c) Using Impact as a Strategic Tool for Developing the Digital Library via the Balanced Value Impact Model, *Library Leadership & Management*, **30** (4).

Tanner, S. and Bearman, G. (2009) Digitising the Dead Sea Scrolls. In LeFurgy, W. (ed.), *Archiving 2009: preservation strategies and imaging technologies for cultural heritage institutions and memory organisations: final program and proceedings, Society for Imaging Science and AMP, Technology (IS&T's Archiving Conference, 6)*, 119–23.

Tanner, S. and Deegan, M. (2010) *Inspiring Research, Inspiring Scholarship: the value and benefits of digitised resources for learning, teaching, research and enjoyment*, JISC, www.webarchive.org.uk/wayback/archive/20140614060402/http://www.jisc.ac.uk/whatwedo/programmes/digitisation/reports/digitisationbenefits.aspx.

Tate (2017) *Modigliani VR: The Ochre Atelier, behind the scenes*, www.tate.org.uk/whats-on/tate-modern/exhibition/modigliani/modigliani-vr-ochre-atelier.

Taylor, D. B. (2010) *Jill Scott Gives Back to North Philadelphia Youth*, Essence, www.essence.com/news/jill-scott-blues-babe-foundation-charity/.

Tenopir, C. (2013) Building Evidence of the Values and Impact of Library and Information Services: methods, metrics and ROI, *Evidence Based Library and Information Practice*, **8** (2), 270–4.

Tessler, A. (2013) *Economic Valuation of the British Library*, www.oxfordeconomics.com/my-oxford/projects/245662.

The British Library (2004) *BL Economic Impact Assessment Value and Results 2004*.

The British Library (n.d.) *Increasing Our Value*, https://web.archive.org/web/20170511140032/http://www.bl.uk/aboutus/stratpolprog/increasingvalue/.

The National Archives (2018) *Annual Report and Accounts of The National Archives 2017–18*, www.nationalarchives.gov.uk/documents/annualreport-11-12.pdf.

The Wellcome Library (2019a) *Codebreakers: makers of modern genetics*, https://wellcomelibrary.org/collections/digital-collections/makers-of-modern-genetics/.

The Wellcome Library (2019b) *What We Do: digitisation at the Wellcome Library*, https://wellcomelibrary.org/what-we-do/digitisation/.

Theory of Change Community (n.d.) www.theoryofchange.org/.

TIDSR: Toolkit for the Impact of Digitised Scholarly Resources, Internet Archive, https://web.archive.org/web/20180309024133/http://microsites.oii.ox.ac.uk/tidsr/.

Torkington, N. (2011) *Where It All Went Wrong* (November), http://nathan.torkington.com/blog/2011/11/23/libraries-where-it-all-went-wrong/.

Town, S. J. and Kyrillidou, M. (2013) Developing a Values Scorecard, *Performance Measurement and Metrics*, **14** (1), 7–16, doi: 10.1108/14678041311316095.

Travers, T. (2006) *Museums and Art Galleries in Britain. Economic, social and creative impacts.* National Museum Directors' Conference and Museums,

Libraries and Archives Council.

Tuck, F. and Dickinson, S. (2015) *The Economic Impact of Museums in England for Arts Council England*, TBR.

Tudur, D. (2018) *How the Impact Playbook is Empowering Libraries – a User Perspective*, Europeana Pro, https://pro.europeana.eu/post/how-the-impact-playbook-is-empowering-libraries-a-user-perspective.

Tudur, D. and Evans, J. (2018) *Exploring Our Impact at the National Library of Wales*, Europeana Pro, https://pro.europeana.eu/post/exploring-our-impact-at-the-national-library-of-wales.

UK Research and Innovation (2019) *Guidance on Submissions REF 2019/01*, www.ref.ac.uk/publications/guidance-on-submissions-201901/.

US Aid (n.d.) *USAID Impact | The Official Blog of the U.S. Agency for International Development*, http://pdf.usaid.gov/pdf_docs/PNADW119.pdf

US General Services Administration (n.d.) *Office of Information and Regulatory Affairs*,www.reginfo.gov/public/jsp/Utilities/index.jsp.

Vanclay, F. (2003) International Principles for Social Impact Assessment, *Impact Assessment and Project Appraisal*, **21** (1), 5–12.

Vanclay, F. (2004) The Triple Bottom Line and Impact Assessment: how do TBL, EIA, SIA, SEA and EMS relate to each other? *Journal of Environmental Assessment Policy and Management*, **6** (03), 265–88, doi: 10.1142/S1464333204001729.

Vancouver Island Regional Library Authority (2016) *Assessing the Economic Impact of Vancouver Island Regional Library on Our Member Communities*, http://virl.bc.ca/wp-content/uploads/2018/08/ROI-Report-PRINT.pdf.

Verwayen, H., Fallon, J., Schellenberg, J. and Kyrou, P. (2017) *Impact Playbook: for museums, libraries, archives and galleries*, https://pro.europeana.eu/what-we-do/impact.

Verwayen, H., Wilms, J. and Fallon, J. (2016) *Workers Underground. an impact assessment case study – Europeana 1914–1918*, http://pro.europeana.eu/files/Europeana_Professional/Publications/workers-underground-an-impact-assessment-case-study-europeana-1914-1918.pdf.

Vikan, G. (2011) Demonstrating Public Value. In Mack, D., Rogers, N. and Seidl-Fox, S. (eds) *Libraries and Museums in an Era of Participatory Culture*, IMLS, p. 14, www.imls.gov/sites/default/files/publications/documents/sgsreport2012_0.pdf.

Vittle, K., Haswell-Walls, F. and Dixon, T. (2016) *Evaluation of the Casgliad y Werin Cymruu / People's Collection Wales Digital Heritage Programme.*

Impact Report, ERS Research and Consultancy.

W. K. Kellogg Foundation (2004) *W. K. Kellogg Foundation Logic Model Development Guide: using logic models to bring together planning, evaluation, and action,* www.wkkf.org/resource-directory/resource/2006/02/wk-kellogg-foundation-logic-model-development-guide.

Wallace, A. and Deazley, R. (2016) *Display at Your Own Risk,* https://displayatyourownrisk.org/publications/.

Warwick, C., Terras, M., Huntington, P. and Pappa, N. (2008) If You Build It Will They Come? The LAIRAH study: quantifying the use of online resources in the arts and humanities through statistical analysis of user log data, *Literary and Linguistic Computing,* **23** (1), 85–102, doi: 10.1093/llc/fqm045.

Wavell, C., Baxter, G., Johnson, I. and Williams, D. (2002) *Impact Evaluation of Museums, Archives and Libraries: available evidence project,* Resource: The Council for Museums, Archives and Libraries, www3.rgu.ac.uk/file/dorothy-williams-impact-evaluation-of-museums-archives-and-libraries-available-evidence-project.

Weil, S. E. (2002) *Making Museums Matter,* Smithsonian Institution Press.

Welsh, A. (2015) *Why Do We Write?* Academic Book of the Future Blog, http://academicbookfuture.org/2015/10/02/why-do-we-write/.

Wilson, L. A. (2003) If We Build It, Will They Come? Library users in a digital world. In Lee, S. H. (ed.), *Improved Access to Information: portals, content selection, and digital information,* Haworth Information Press, 19–28.

Wood, E., Zivcakova, L., Gentile, P., Archer, K., De Pasquale, D. and Nosko, A. (2012) Examining the Impact of Off-task Multi-tasking with Technology on Real-time Classroom Learning, *Computers & Education,* **58** (1), 365–74, doi: 10.1016/j.compedu.2011.08.029.

Woodley, P. M. (2006) *Culture Management Through the Balanced Scorecard: a case study,* Cranfield University.

Yarrow, A. (2017) Designing and Communicating Social Impact. In Irwin, B. and Silk, K. (eds), *Creating a Culture of Evaluation: taking your library from talk to action,* OLA Press, 83–100.

Zimmer, M. (2015) The Twitter Archive at the Library of Congress: challenges for information practice and information policy, *First Monday,* **20** (7), http://firstmonday.org/ojs/index.php/fm/article/view/5619/4653.

Zorich, D. M. (2012) Transitioning to a Digital World: art history, its research centers, and digital scholarship, *Journal of Digital Humanities,*

1 (2), http://journalofdigitalhumanities.org/1-2/transitioning-to-a-digital-world-by-diane-zorich/.

Index